PIGMENT

CURRENT TRENDS IN THE PERFORMING ARTS IN FLANDERS

EDITED BY
MICHEL UYTTERHOEVEN

WITH ESSAYS BY
MANU CLAEYS
JORIS JANSSENS
VEERLE KEUPPENS
RUDI LAERMANS
MICHEL UYTTERHOEVEN

DESIGNED BY
PAUL BOUDENS

LUDION / VLAAMS THEATER INSTITUUT

(IM)MOVABLES

NOMADS

PROLOGUE

PIGMENT is published simultaneously in Dutch and English, not least because the Vlaams Theater Instituut/Flemish Theatre Institute (VTi) has embraced the international promotion of performing artists from Flanders as one of its core tasks. In this publication we have concentrated on a generation of artists, organizations and phenomena that emerged in the course of the 1990s and in that sense are clearly distinguishable from the 'Flemish wave' of the 1980s. They do not deny artistic affinities with, or legacies from, that – now almost mythical – flood of talent of twenty years ago, but this book is first and foremost interested in charting and documenting their specific interpretation, in rendering the shades and nuances of their journey, the more so because we firmly believe that this new generation has the wherewithal to excite notice on the international stages as well.

In its colourfulness PIGMENT mirrors the enormous diversity of what is new on the Flemish performing arts scene. It likes to see itself as an adventurous travel guide in the land of writers and actors, circus artists and performers' collectives, music theatre productions and projects involving amateur players, multimedia art forms and postgraduate dance courses. It escorts the reader to run-down swimming pools, newly built and restored cultural buildings, fairy-tale brothels and gastronomic roundabouts, to labyrinths, waterfronts, streets, squares and filling-stations. Not the sort of theatre one could have 'expected and foreseen' (as Jan Fabre would say), but a kaleidoscope of unfamiliar and untried possibilities between the sensual fingers of a number of highly trained and inspired young artists.

In that respect this book is a continuation of the *Critical Theatre Lexicon*, which our predecessors at the Institute worked on with such commitment. The *Critical Theatre Lexicon* invariably hinged on one prominent figure – historical or contemporary – from the world of theatre in Flanders. We, however, ensure the preservation of the memory of the Flemish theatre scene through the website www.podiumarchief.be, where we give the theatre community the opportunity to help develop interactively and take responsibility for archiving and opening up the history of our performing arts.

Even more importantly, this book is VTi's sequel and response to *Alles is rustig. Het verhaal van de kunstencentra* [All is quiet. The story of the arts centres] (1999). What was particularly striking about that story was the almost romantic sense of loss of the original ideals of the arts centres, which went hand in hand with their professionalization, petrifaction, commercialization and recognition. 'It pains me to have to say that we have allowed recuperation to happen again', wrote Marianne van Kerkhoven in the book. The title of the brochure that was added to the book, 'The lost honour of the arts centres', was also telling.

PIGMENT goes proactively in search of those artists, who through their creative practice today begin to provide an answer to those listless feelings of loss and nostalgia.

Starting from their own experience as spectators, a core editorial team of VTi staff went in search of innovative phenomena in the Flemish theatre of recent years and, thus, after many hours of animated discussion, we arrived at a short-list of twenty-five subjects.

A number of traits immediately became apparent: the colourfulness already referred to, the tendency to jump over the partitions between genres (which inevitably suggests concepts such as crossover, hybridism and *métissage*), the almost obvious way many projects look beyond Flanders' borders, the polyphony of the senses (theatre is more than sitting, looking, listening, it is also walking, smelling, tasting, building and joining in). And what was striking above all are the reflections and attitudes in connection with stones and walls, not only that magical 'fourth wall', which has given the theatre its specific character since the Renaissance, but also the place of the theatre building in the city, the choice of centre or periphery, or the more radical options of not settling in one place but opting for a more nomadic and atopical existence in the 'global village'.

These considerations and observations eventually gave PIGMENT its four-part structure: 'Nom donné par l'auteur' (with thanks to Jérôme Bel), 'Hybrids', '(Im)movables' and 'Nomads'. It is not canon law, but a temporary and fluid arrangement, one possibility out of many.

For the twenty-five subjects we then sought twenty-five writers, experienced dramaturges or seasoned performing arts critics, but also young journalists or writers who had never written about theatre before. They were given the opportunity to meet and track their subjects for a whole season. Their brief was to unscramble the DNA code of an artistic practice in a short article and whether or not in consultation with their subject. The result is a colourful mix of texts and images, as spicy, madcap and variable as the theatre landscape itself.

The book is interlarded with five more in-depth essays. Manu Claeys provides a round-up of the participation debate launched by former Minister for Culture Bert Anciaux in his famous speech at the Vooruit arts centre in Ghent in September 2000. Rudi Laermans considers the extent to which the artists and organizations that emerged in the 1990s owe a debt to their predecessors, but also why they are different from them. Joris Janssens discusses hybrid dramaturgical forms of presentation (labyrinths, trails, etc.) and looks at why stage artists want to address our different senses. Veerle Keuppens argues for building open theatres in the city and for involving all the different parties in the planning of them. At the end of this book, I myself try to embed the generation of the Nineties in the recent history of theatre, to spin a few more threads and to tie up some loose ends.

Finally, we devoted thought and energy to incorporating a great deal of useful information into PIGMENT: a brief summary for each subject discussed, a selective bibliography for those who want more, more in-depth information, and accurate, easy-reference contact details – all drawn from the documentation and archives the Flemish Theatre Institute has been storing and making accessible on library shelves and in databanks for two decades.

A sincere word of thanks to our publisher Ludion and in particular to Jan Denolf. Ludion has made a name for itself, also internationally, with impressive visual art and architecture publications. For the first time Ludion is publishing two books on performing arts this winter, namely PIGMENT and *Tussen De Dronkaerd en Het Kouwe Kind* [Between 'The Drunkard' and 'The Cold Child'], which is about 150 years of Nationael Tooneel, KNS and Toneelhuis in Antwerp.

A word of praise, too, for designer Paul Boudens, who has made a name for himself with his work for Antwerp's fashion world. He has given PIGMENT a 'look' that does justice to the chameleonic state of the contemporary performing arts and to the work of a new generation of photographers, who kindly made their work available for this publication.

We are also very grateful to the thirty guest writers and to the translators, whose creativity has given colour and spice to this book. And also, of course, to the Ministry of the Flemish Government which provided the financing necessary to make this ambitious publication possible.

The whole of the Flemish Theatre Institute team has worked on PIGMENT with commitment, perseverance and an eye for detail. They, too, can be proud of the result.

Finally, of course, we must express our gratitude to the twenty-five artists and organizations this book is about. What we were aiming to capture was the vision, the quality and the enjoyment redolent of their work. Their cooperation on this publication was refreshing and makes one long for an encore.

MICHEL UYTTERHOEVEN
Director, Flemish Theatre Institute

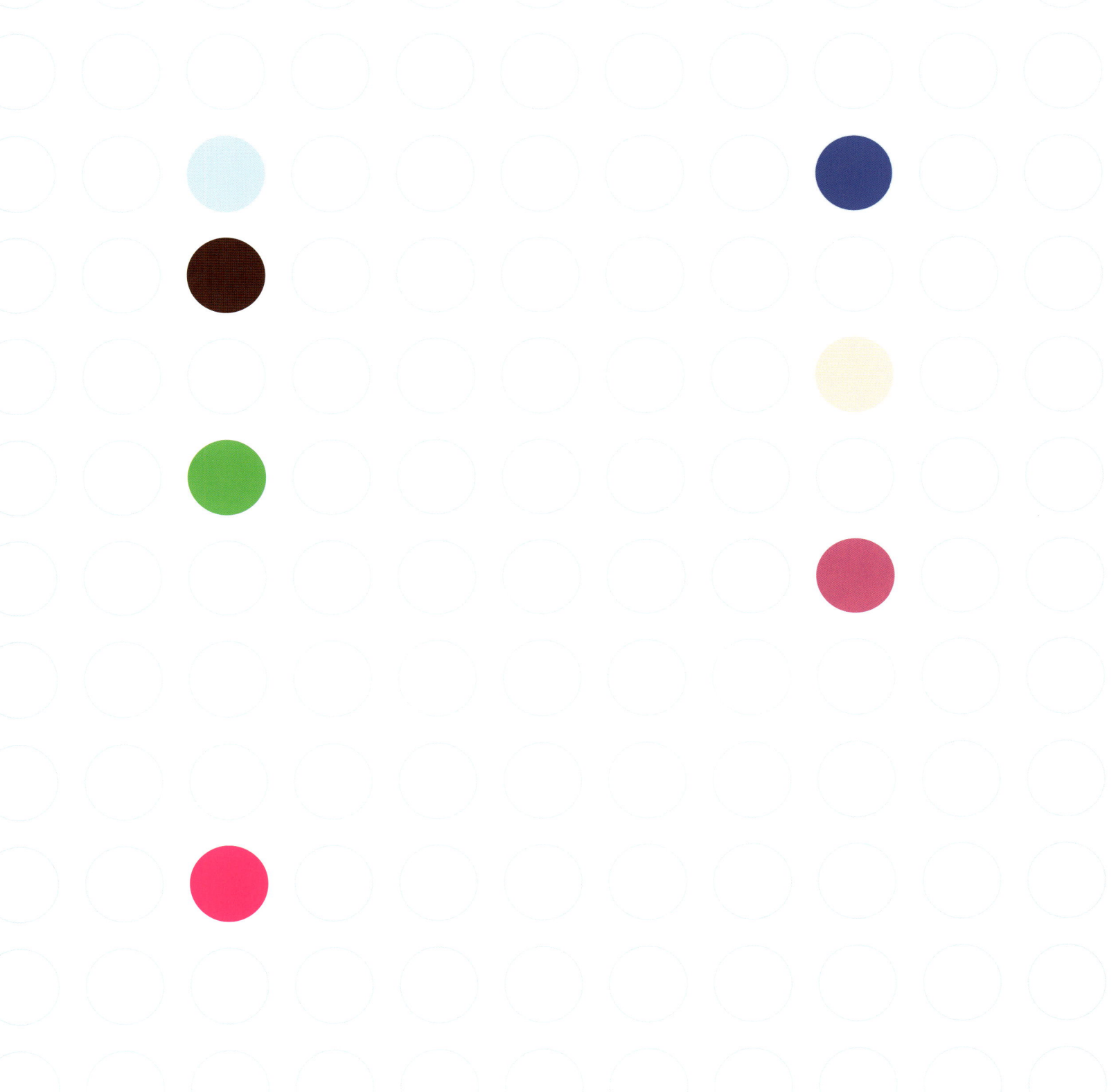

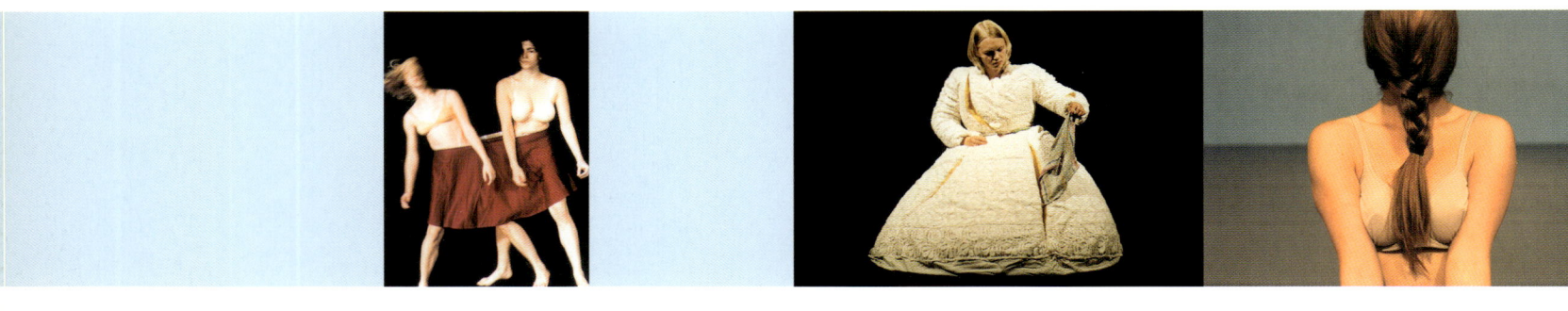

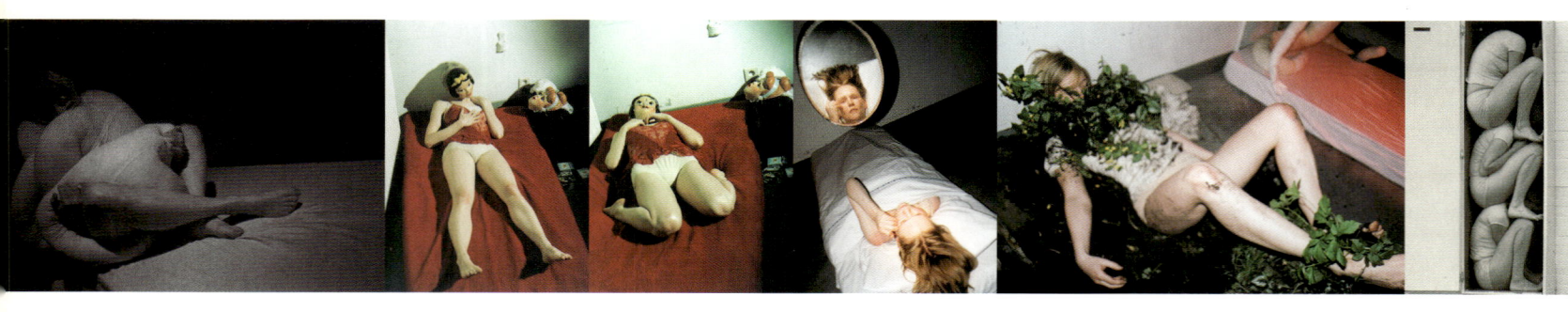

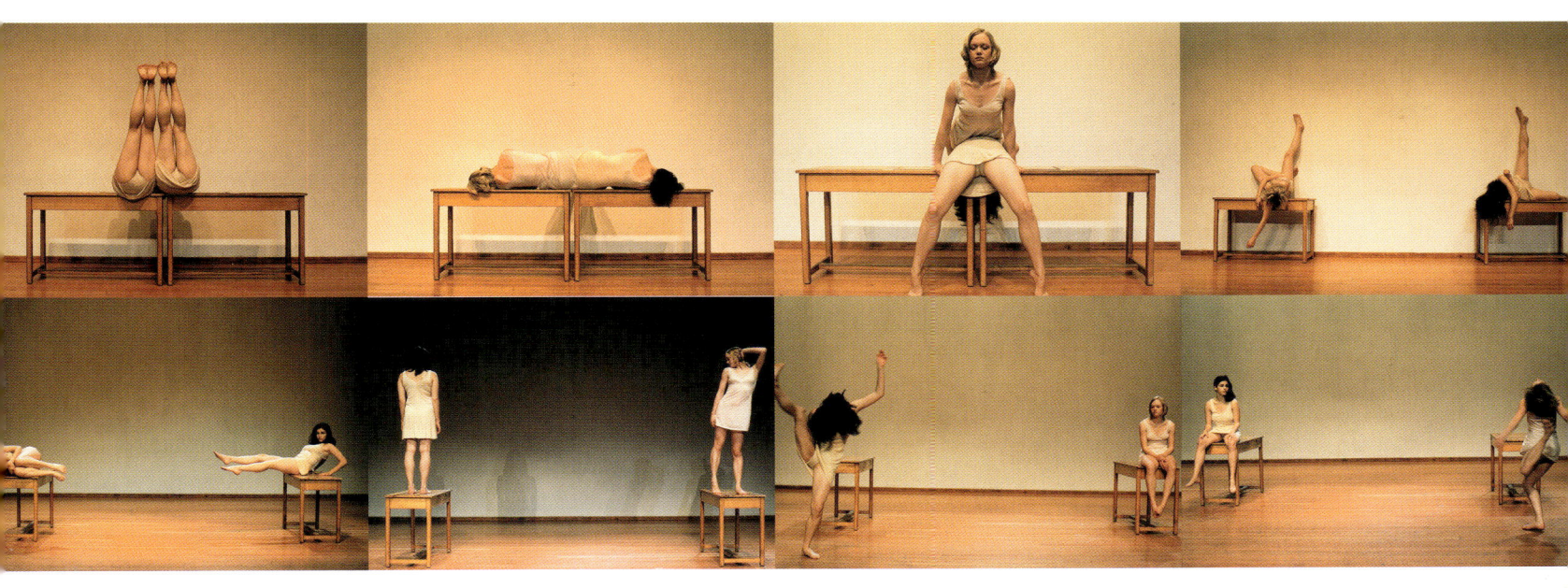

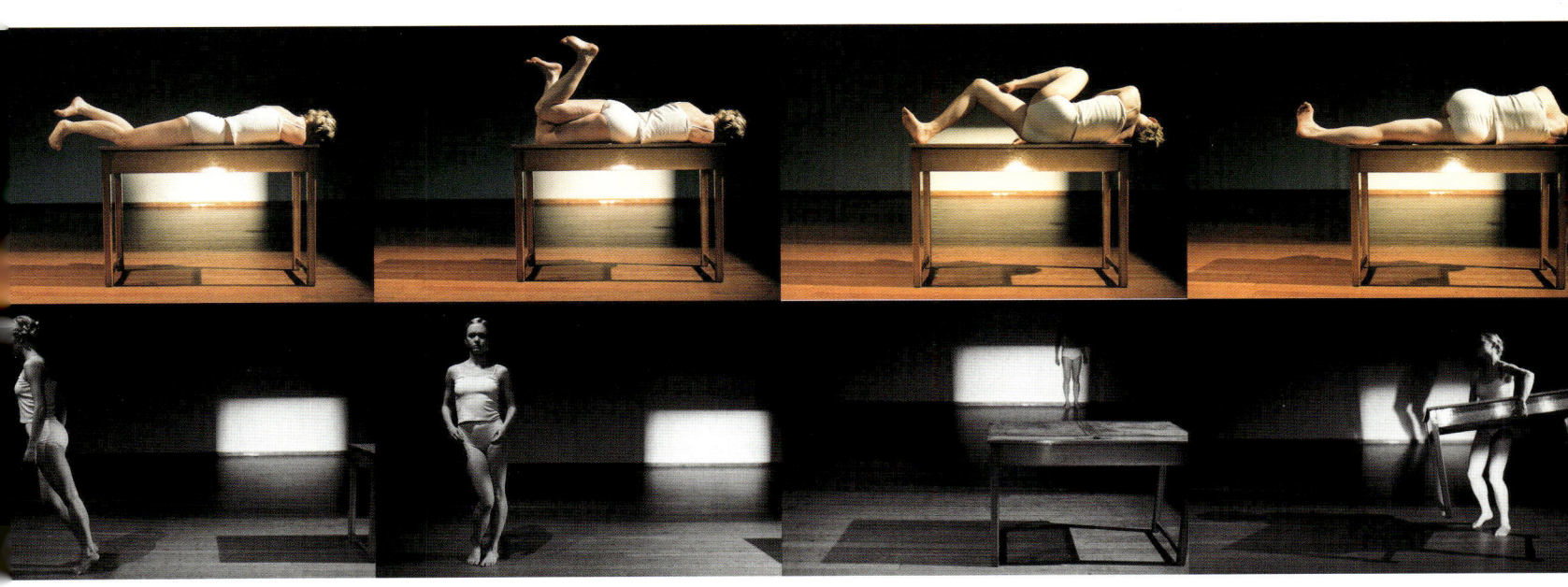

THE SECRET WORLD OF CHARLOTTE VANDEN EYNDE

Immediately striking is the ambiguous play on words, the – basically untranslatable – 'joke' in titles like *Benenbreken* [Breaking legs], *Zij Ogen* [They look/Them eyes], *Vrouwenvouwen* [Folding women/Female folds] and *Lijfstof* [Body material]. Only on closer examination do we see that they are more than simple distortions of well-known expressions or words. *Vrouwenvouwen*, for example, is alliteration first and foremost. Yet the combination of two words that differ only by one letter while meaning something totally different is a noteworthy discovery, and one that calls up latent similarities in meaning and absurd associations. A whole world of meaning might be concealed in the difference of just one letter, yet the word defies interpretation. Charlotte Vanden Eynde makes theatre images in precisely the same way. Her collages of simple objects, words and above all bodies immediately suggest many meanings, but afterwards we are invariably left without a conclusive, never mind exhaustive, explanation of these images. They affect us, but we never know precisely what it is that affects us. The only thing that is certain is that they unmistakably stem from a woman's exploratory relationship with her own body. The body as something that is not taken for granted, the body as a source of concern. *Vrouwenvouwen* opens, for example, with a woman, Vanden Eynde herself, enveloped in a long, oversized lace dress filled with plastic foam. This doll-like figure looks impassively at the audience and ferrets around in her sleeve for a pair of scissors with which she proceeds to make precise cuts in the dress. From the protruding foam she pulls out banal household objects such as a dishcloth, a comb, a dummy, children's toys, but also a tress of hair. And so it goes on until three women lift her out of the dress and leave her on the stage stark naked... These images are often isolated. They are followed fairly abruptly by another, without an explicit link. In the performance *Stand* that logic is taken to the extreme: the middle part of it consists of an impassive demonstration of different ways of stacking three female dancers in three cupboards.

This 'obscurity' in her work says something about the special place Charlotte Vanden Eynde occupies in con-

temporary dance. From her very first production, *Benenbreken*, she was bracketed together with other choreographers who seize upon dance as a way of dealing with (the meanings of) the body. Dance not as part of a tradition (ballet, modern dance, etc.) but as a special form of conceptual art. *Benenbreken*, however, immediately makes it clear that Vanden Eynde does not want to examine the political or social meanings of the body (on stage) from a preconceived concept, as is all too often the case, but that she starts from the things themselves, from seemingly ordinary things rather than physical extremes. Lying on a table she shows the audience her legs in all sorts of positions, while repeating as often as three times, in a toneless voice, such observations as 'Straight legs are better than bandy legs', 'White legs are not sexy', 'Legs can break' and 'Toes are funny'.

The genesis of the work sheds light on what is at issue here. As a student at PARTS she noted to her dismay that the self-image she had developed during her youth and her earlier studies at the Lier dancing academy bore little resemblance to the impression, or rather the lack of it, she made on the PARTS teachers. Consequently, *Benenbreken* was first and foremost a way of showing what she had to offer. The work tackled the question of how we appear to, and communicate with, others. This inevitably happens, certainly as a dancer, through the body. But we only see half of our own body, and then mainly the bottom half. It always seems to be at a distance, somewhere on the edge of our consciousness. It has no face. The face is – certainly for someone with a preliminary classical training like Vanden Eynde – more like a mask which smirks at us from the mirror. So the body that is shown here is the body as it studies itself from above. From this radical and subjective standpoint Vanden Eynde can suddenly show what is going on inside her. 'Toes are funny' alludes to the bare fact that the body is unknowable, even though it is also the socle of all self-awareness. The sentence recalls a statement by the poet Paul van Ostaijen: 'My body is a light and a darkness to itself. My feet are other shapes and I make them play.' However, she also shows the disquiet that prompts endless self-study of the body. It is not only

vulnerable and finite: 'Legs can break.' It never shows it-self as it 'really' is: others always seem to look on crit-ically. Thus observation of one's body arouses a longing for something different. But in the search for what others see, there are only clichés, 'Straight legs are more beautiful than bandy legs', like a false guide.

Charlotte Vanden Eynde continues her exploration of this imaginary world of the body in subsequent works, including when she works with Ugo Dehaes in *Lijfstof*. Similar themes are treated. Bodies appear like dolls. Dolls are stand-ins for a real presence. The face, the most expressive part of the body, but also the part we can never see directly (and so which can also betray us), disappears behind masks, for example, in *Ligging* [Position] as if behind a protective 'persona'. In that pro-duction Vanden Eynde and Constance Neunschwander show the spectator almost obscenely intimate images: it is as if we are surprising girls at the 'wrong' moment. But because of the mask, a Disney Snow White, those images are hurled back to the spectator. What seems ob-vious, is only semblance. You can't 'grasp' the reality be-hind it, even though you are there with your nose pressed up against it. This is even more apparent in an-other, bizarre scene in which the two female dancers ro-tate in a flowerbed.

Vanden Eynde's refusal to allow herself to be pinned down to a clear meaning has been very much apparent in her work from the outset. *Stand*, her latest perform-ance, is an important, though ironic statement in this re-gard. She sits motionless alongside her 'work', a series of actions by three female dancers. She only brings on the props, once keeping time vocally. First the women writhe, entwining in all kinds of combinations, to and fro like machines, then they wriggle their way like hunks of flesh into cupboards, before performing a mockery of the French cancan with one leg tied to their body and ending like cephalopodal creatures when they perform a headstand with skirts over their head. From the stand-point of the almighty male image-maker she shows an imaginary world which can only be a woman's, indeed, only hers. And which always just manages to be out of the reach of the spectator.

PIETER T'JONCK

CHARLOTTE VANDEN EYNDE

Charlotte Vanden Eynde's choreographies are closer to performance than to dance. For example, *Lijfstof* [Body material] is a series of tableaux vivants, which might equally be presented in a gallery or museum. Vanden Eynde's work is akin to that of choreographers like Meg Stuart, Jérôme Bel, Boris Charmatz, Tom Plischke and Vincent Dunoyer, who investigate the basics of dance, theatre and other art forms.

Vanden Eynde trained as a dancer at the Hoger Instituut voor Dans in Lier and at PARTS in Brussels. With *Benenbreken* [Breaking legs], *Zij Ogen* [They look / Them eyes] and *Vrouwenvouwen* [Folding women / Female folds] she succeeded in creating powerful productions even before she had finished her training. In 1999 she graduated and set up the non-profit Kwaad Bloed, together with Ugo Dehaes (also a former PARTS student and dancer in Meg Stuart's *Highway 101* and *appetite*). With Dehaes she presented the duet *Lijfstof* in 2000.

Benenbreken, the solo Charlotte Vanden Eynde made during her final year at PARTS, is a sculptural choreography for legs, feet and toes. It at once set the tone for the rest of her work, in which the emphasis is on plastic rather than dancing values, on examining the body, the questioning of the norms of beauty, of the intimate, the vulnerable and non-virtuoso.

Zij Ogen, a duet with Sharon Zuckerman, is about how the female body is seen and eroticized, and about the woman's reaction to being looked at. The streamlined yet graceful choreography reproduces as it were the doubling of one body in two (very different) female dancers.

Charlotte Vanden Eynde's graduation piece at PARTS was *Vrouwenvouwen*, a choreography for four dancers. It is a study of the concept of 'woman', which is being folded in all directions like an origami paper. In this piece Vanden Eynde shows her passion for objects and materials for the first time. Even the bodies start to look like objects, when they form a tangle of hair and limbs.

In *Lijfstof* Vanden Eynde takes her fascination with objects, bodies and observation a step further. A thing becomes an extension of the body, the body a thing. This results in surprising, but also sobering images.

In 2001 Vanden Eynde created two installation performances: *Ligging* [Position], a continuous improvisation on five mattresses, whereby images relating to intimacy are created and examined, and *Stand*, a loop performance whereby Vanden Eynde has three female dancers perform their acts, while she looks on.

On three occasions Vanden Eynde has worked with dramatist Jan Decorte for Het Toneelhuis. In 2001 she played the part of Ophélie in *Amlett*, for which she also choreographed two intimate and delicate dances (a duet with Decorte about love and death and a solo which symbolizes her death by drowning). In 2002 she made a choreography for ten young actors for Decorte's *Cirque Danton* and in 2003 she created two graceful dance pieces for *Cannibali!*.

In 2002 she also appeared in *Most Recent*, a dance production by Marc Vanrunxt, and she made her debut as a film actress in *Meisje* [Girl] by Dorothée van den Berghe. In 2003 she appeared in *Van den Heiligen Drien* [The holy threesome], a short film by Karen Vanderborght; she is presently attending a part-time course of video and film at the KASK in Antwerp. Her show *MAP ME* premièred in October 2003.   CVP

PASCALE PLATEL

GOOD LUCK WITH THE PROPHECIES!

We had arranged to meet to prepare this piece in the famous Mokabon, the historical coffee-house in Ghent where an assortment of artists, obscure poets, people on the dole, spiritually retired, weirdoes and moustached Turks have been rubbing shoulders for ages.
More than twenty years ago, long before Pascale and her brother Alain were born 'artistically', we would hang out there on a regular basis, Pascale a young photography student at St-Lucas (St Luke's art school), I myself busy with Radeis. Our memories of that time are of long discussions ranging from the animated to the wearisome, sometimes taking up large chunks of the day until our stomachs had become brown acid bags of accumulated caffeine and our windpipes hoarse from a chain of Tigra cigarettes.

19 May 2003, 9.15 am. The Mokabon was exactly as we had remembered it; time had stood still. Still the same waitresses, an almost-identical clientele and the same old (and aged) *habitués* as before leafing through a quality newspaper or *Türkiye* (depending on their origin) or slating everything that is wrong with this wicked world. At the table next to us sat a highly confused and seemingly schizophrenic boy with a large ear in our direction. On leaving the establishment, he wished us good luck with 'the prophecies'. A title can be the make or break of a fine work of art. We were well on our way!

My 'writing assignment' should not be too dull, so it was agreed to give the theatre a wide berth. A reference book on Chinese astrology was produced, after which I received a detailed explanation delivered with Pascalian enthusiasm about my being a Monkey. Pascale's obsession with astrology dates from when she was thirty, after she had paid a visit (on the recommendation of Jan Vroman) to an alcoholic fortune-teller in Brussels who instead of a crystal ball had a glass eye. Pascale has judged people horoscopically ever since. And, as is usually the case in astrology, she's invariably spot-on...

Our friendship dates from 1984, the year the Nieuwpoorttheater opened. And the trio (young and from Ghent) that appeared from nowhere made its debut with something to *Stabat Mater*. As well as a certain Alain Platel and Johan Grimonprez, the tall girl from the Mokabon was also in it. Her contribution to the act was the ill-mannered consumption of a rather nice cake lavishly covered with a generous layer of *crème fraîche*. Her equally tall brother, Alain, executed a sort of choreographic ritual with his extraordinarily long arms as if trying to measure the stage. With well-founded artistic blah, a few self-appointed connoisseurs (now they are much younger and more numerous) deemed that such a lack of talent had no place there, and certainly not at the opening festival of the Nieuwpoorttheater. Bingo!

There can be no disputing Pascale's sublime sense of virtuoso theatrical foolishness in the much-reviled and applauded, provocative productions of Alain Platel's dance group. When Les Ballets C de la B was founded and Alain created *Bonjour Madame* (this time with professional dancers), Pascale decided to start writing. Her first scripts appeared in 1993. Victoria presented *Slijmjurkje* [Clever-clogs] as a monologue during Antwerpen 93 and commissioned the radio play *Ik ga naar huis* [I'm going home]. So much for the early history. But, dear reader, let us now take a look at how life has treated Pascale Plate since then.

It is simple: that's when it all started, believe it or not. Her 'market value' was assessed, as it should be, by several artistic entrepreneurs and... *Slets Go*. The Flemish theatre was said to have acquired a new phenomenon, a winner even. Pascale surrounded herself with several artistic friends and deliberately kept away the dramaturgical know-it-alls, because *'they really get on my nerves'*. Dante's maxim, 'Go on your way and leave people to prattle', is applicable here.

Pascale Platel, who exactly is that? What sort of person is she? How has she become what she is? Answers to these questions are quite complicated in their simplicity. In her work she was trained by men, in life and in love by women, that's how it is. And she cherishes a number of idols of both sexes whom we are not going to mention by name here.

What she does on stage is nothing more than give a visual account of her view of muddling through life on a day-to-day basis. Life as a colourful patchwork to which she adds her own piece of crochet. No deep psychological, autobiographical probing, but a record of an abundance of frivolous chimaeras and fantasies, inspired mainly by memories of a family life where she '*was wrapped in a warm nest hole*'. The Platel family was an entertaining clan, a mini-stage where stories, anecdotes and robust linguistic quips were centrifuged in the vivid, zinged-up Ghent dialect. Various colourful aunts contributed stories and a festive atmosphere and these sparkling female conversations, this womb-like 'society', became the humus of her artistic manoeuvres.

Platel behaves in much the same way on stage and at a street café on the Vrijdagmarkt. The line between 'acting' and 'being' is wafer-thin. There is little difference between the surprising flights of fancy on stage and the protracted spiritual confabs over a glass of wine with friends. The fundamental, aberrant, lopsided thinking in her writing and her acting style, but also the way she frolics through life, are at the root of her talent.

Talking about her work cannot be separated from the way she looks at life, the way she absorbs what is going on around her, the way she embraces with great love the trivialities and garbage of life, the way she shows her obsessive interest in camouflaged, dirty goings-on between the folds of the sheets, the way she flirts serenely with perversity, the way she excavates for the banalities of life, her firm belief in superstition.
Living and working is *vivre* and *savoir vivre*. '*Kissing is important, very important... First kiss and then work, if the kissing is good, then work, but first kiss, and kiss well, and only then work.*'

Unlike her fellow writers, she never asks herself in advance what her script will be about. She has no storyline in her head. Every work begins with the title; only when that is in place and it is good, does the first line appear and thus she advances slowly but surely. In so doing she wonders what paragraph she can add, and only when it is written, does she know what it is about.
The scripts she writes in this way, you have to 'see'. And above all, nothing must be in accordance with the rules of the art. '*It is like it is with a drawing: you can spit on it to improve it if you want, or splash coffee or something else over it. But I fear I shall never get that far, for I am a mother and a woman...*'

Anyway, she does what she feels and as she plays around with language she takes young and old with her into the catacomb of her twisting thoughts. '*Above all it should be exciting because otherwise they concentrate too much on my appearance; on stage I want to forget what I look like. I want to keep everything close to me, small and nice, as in life; preferably alone or perhaps a tête-à-tête, a trio is another possibility, not four but three, four is too many, three is good but only just. Above all, no fussing about with lots of extras, unless they are made of cardboard.*'

And then there is also the ritual she enacts both on and off stage: during the show a little candle burns in the box in the auditorium next to her statue of St Anthony. The medallions hanging from her knickers include one of St Christopher to avoid getting lost on stage, 'because if you lose your way...' And, whatever you do, never wash clothes, they must feel the same as they did at rehearsal. Only if these superstitions are carefully followed does she feel that all will be well.

And another thing. Anyone who thinks that Pascale Platel's theatre is noncommittal should think again: everything that happens in and around the erogenous zone of life, banishes the chills from the heart. If that isn't consciousness-raising theatre!

P.S. Have no illusions: just because there is a gnome laughing in your front garden, it doesn't mean there cannot be a war tomorrow.

DIRK PAUWELS

Pascale Platel uses her absurd imagination to string together a number of situations which travel down side-roads and take roundabout routes. The moment she steps onto the stage she doesn't hesitate a second about the truthfulness of her own inimitable story. She addresses both children and adults.

Besmeurde witte laarsjes [Mud-stained white boots] about 'shoeshopaholics'; *Gezegend zij* [Blessed be] about Jesus and Aunt Elisabeth; *Ola Pola Potloodgat* about lonely elephants and children for sale in a shop; *Connaissez-vous votre géographie?* about Martian women cycling at full speed; *De Koning van de Paprikachips* [The king of paprika crisps] about a slipper with macho airs, etc.

If by now Pascale Platel has a lengthy list of stories and plays to her name, the list of nominations and prizes she has snapped up is equally impressive. In 1999 she won the Flemish Government's Signaalprijs for *De Koning van de Paprikachips*; in 2000 *Connaissez-vous votre géographie?* was nominated for the Flemish–Dutch 1000Watt prize; with *Ola Pola Potloodgat* Platel won two major Flemish–Dutch prizes in 2002: the 1000Watt prize and the Theaterfestival prize; in 2003 *Gezegend zij* was nominated for 1000Watt. But her list of awards also includes the Dutch Gouden Tomaat [Golden Tomato] for *Via Viola*, voted the worst play of 2001!

In the mid-1980s Platel joined the contemporary dance formation Les Ballets C de la B led by her brother, Alain Platel, as a dancer-actor. In 1993 she moved to textual theatre for the lead role in *Kom terug* [Come back] by Eric De Volder. In 1995 Nieuwpoort-theater gave her her first commission as a writer. The result was *Een namiddag in mei* [An afternoon in May], directed by Eric De Volder, who has since continued to support Platel's development. More plays and stories were written at the request of Victoria and Nieuw-poorttheater.

In 1997 she enjoyed success at the BRONKS Festival with a crazy story about Red Riding Hood's confrontation with a Power Ranger. BRONKS became her operating base, and it was there that she made her first full-length production for children, *De Koning van de Paprikachips*. Platel also forged a link with Speel-teater / De Kopergietery. In 2000 she wrote a monologue for the company for 'Spa Bruis' (a mini-festival for small projects). Other monologues followed. She also wrote a libretto for Muziektheater Transparant.

When Pascale Platel sits down to write, she starts from a general departure point, and from there she begins to glean. She collects notebooks full of flashes of wit and photographs and she surrounds herself with books of Edward Hopper's art, novels by Truman Capote, CDs, etc. She will never gear her story to children; she simply takes them with her into her own world.

As an actor-narrator, most of her experience has been with monologues. But with *Ola Pola Potloodgat*, in co-operation with dancer Randi de Vlieghe, and *Besmeurde witte laarsjes*, a project for which Michaël Pas was invited, Pascale Platel proved that she can also manage a duet.   CVP

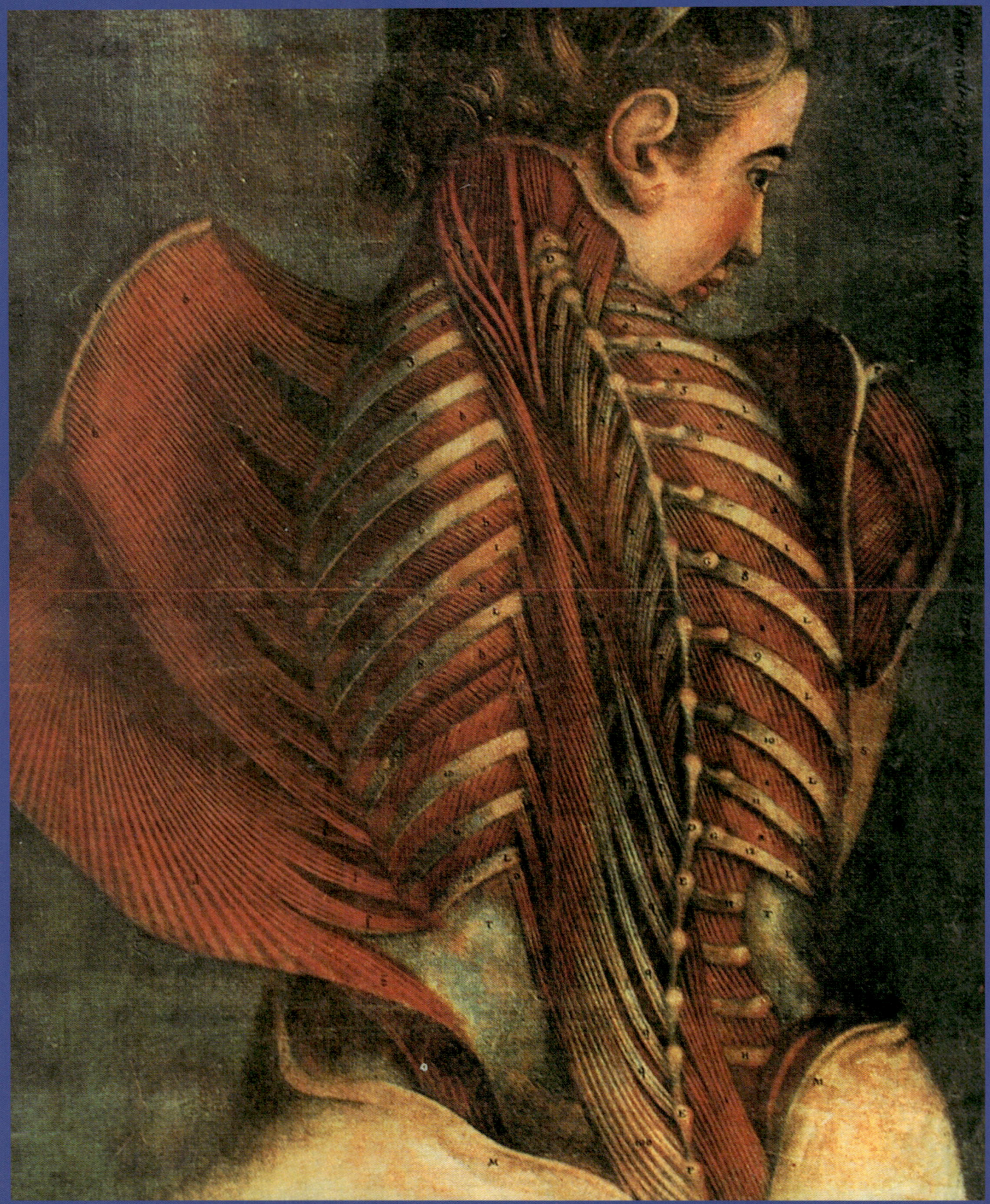

PIETER DE BUYSSER

1. BY WAY OF OPENING: THE FOOL GIVES A WARNING

It was a day like many others, at a time and in a place as in a story. Exactly at noon of that day a fool with a lamp walked across the market square, fixed his gaze on the mocking bystanders and shouted:
'Dead! We have killed Him! Where will we find solace, we murderers of all murderers? The holiest and mightiest that the world has ever possessed, has bled to death under our knives. Who will wipe away that blood? Does the magnitude of this deed not exceed our powers? Should we not become gods ourselves to at least seem worthy of it?'

Not that that holy He could cease to be because of this deed, no, it was only His familiar appearance that had been taken up with capital letter and all into the hole above which He had been water-walking all that time, the gap which pushes its way through all stories like a hole through ice. It is the red apple that vanished from the Tree of Knowledge, it is the hole behind the image (and the word) of the apple which is not an apple, it is the hole of the apple-red switch before and after Hiroshima.

2. BY WAY OF CONTINUATION: KANT'S SERVANT EATS AND REFLECTS

Lampe was startled when the fool smashed his lamp to smithereens on the cobblestones. He was just sitting and enjoying a piece of black pudding with mustard on the sun-drenched terrace of an inn – a welcome break after making purchases for his master at the market. Lampe recognized the problem the fool had raised at the top of his voice, but he himself saw things in a different light. He remembered the opening lines of a text by his master and how his eyebrows hunched up like his back when he read them: 'Enlightenment is choosing to cast aside man's self-imposed immaturity. Immaturity is the incapacity to avail oneself of one's reason without the guidance of another.' Not the holy He but Reason has now appeared above the hole and its guiding hand leads man, who sees it as his duty not to be guided by stories inspired by another, but to act autonomously in accordance with his own reason. That, however, is not taking into account the innkeeper, thought Lampe, who is a foreigner, draws beer as the best and gives him food: black pudding for the belly, words and sentences for the mouth, a lavatory to relieve himself, inflaming emotions for the heart, a parasol against the fierce sun, and more of those necessities of life which enable us to see, feel, think, do and speak. But sometimes the foreigner can make it eerily quiet. When he is pushed into a corner by local discourse, he bangs his hand on the counter and makes the guests stammer. No, thought Lampe, maturity is an impossible objective in a story whose words still stumble over Dachau, the black smoking hole in History that stupidly thought it was called Progress and on the way to the Highest Good and to that end cleverly tried to eliminate what stood in its way.

Yet Lampe was fascinated by the study his master had made of Reason, Nature, God and the Law that governs every acting and judging person. That Law is the stone in which God's ten commandments are chiselled: 'Thou shalt have to.' And there is no getting away from it, however mature you may be. After all, in these times, as Lampe knows, Reason has been 'touched': its tongue is on fire because of an ardour within, which drives it out and makes it speak. It has to render account to and at the same time is aware of the other who hands him the pungent mustard-pot and forbids him to belch after polishing off a piece of black pudding. Man is dependent on the Law of the other, which will forbid sooner than order: 'Thou shalt not'. No, you may not leave your golden sandals behind on the edge of Etna, jump into the emptiness of the crater and melt there into the unchained fire god. That absolute pleasure is forbidden, it frees you from reality and so also from human existence. You may not go into the crater, even if you have a crater gurgling sensually deep inside yourself.

That crater is the same hole, Lampe saw, as that of the mustard-pot on the table. In its existence, the pot has to take account of the emptiness around which its material is shaped. At the same time its material provides the emptiness with a *raison d'être*, it shapes but cannot possess the emptiness within it. It circles round it, like speech circles round things in reality, and like desire surrounds the empty place in the Tree of Knowledge. That is why the enraptured lips burn when they speak: they long all too intensely for that volcanic thing around which they circle, but can only reach for it and glow through the scorching heat they feel within but which is beyond their reach. So they may taste the mustard that briefly occupies the emptiness of the pot, but only in small quantities.

For Lampe one thing is clear: the mouth has no choice but to fall in love with its own immaturity, and to recognize the other's space. That is why the mouth of touched reason does not speak for the sake of it, but feels obliged to speak: it does not stretch out a helping hand to the reality around it, but a hand in greeting. 'Hello, mustard-pot,' Lampe greets things. 'Hello, parasol.' – 'Hello, little sunshine of mine.'

3. BY WAY OF APPENDIX:
HERE ON THE STAGE FOR ALL TO SEE,
IS THE QUACK CACKLING AWAY CHEERFULLY

— I write scripts. Imagine I am a young boy, about eight years old. One day he takes a piece of paper and he wants to write down the all of all on that white sheet. O-o-o-o. He writes: god. That has to be the all of all, he thinks. But now the boy has a problem: he would love to write and write — just as lovers want to go on and on making love — but now he has written it all… He decides to erase the word. And to keep on writing it.

— Lampe says to me: 'May there be light.' After all, now there is no light, only lamps that you have to ignite. In my imagination Lampe has written a new trilogy in the margins and on the drafts of his master's work. In so doing he wants to draw attention to the diminutive, to what escapes from the framework that you want to impose on reality. You may never obscure the view of infinity, the fact that our norms have no ultimate ground, and that we must constantly question our behaviour and judgement. That is the command of Law to me: I must realize that I have no ground to stand on. If I stand somewhere, then I pull the ground from under my feet. I am intrigued, yes, I am in love with that groundlessness and that tumbling. That is a personal experience, of which I am diffident, about which I can hardly speak, but it is what sets me ablaze. That hole, that is my trick. I am a playwright. I produce fiction, I invent 'tricks'. At the same time there is something erotic about that trick — I constantly want to touch it. Like a burning lover I have a more than intimate relationship with that hole.

— With my scripts I want to make theatre, because I want to examine the friction between the Word and the Flesh. The Word can become Flesh on stage, but that incarnation is doomed to fail. The theatre is the pawnshop between facts and fiction. The factuality of the floor boards suddenly becomes the seaside resort of Koksijde-Bad. And the fiction of 'I was washed ashore here' changes in the fact that the actor still has the same skin as five minutes ago in the dressing-room. There is always something irreducible in the corporality of the actor. He has to embody, but at the same time his own body stands in the way of a complete embodiment of the Word. A cough interrupts the eloquence of the script, the public can get spit on its face. Once the Word is spoken, it hangs like a piece of flesh, a firm nipple.

— In my work I want to go where the lizards sleep. Where is that? They lie in a very warm spot, one you can never reach. They cannot stand light. There is only the stone under which they lie, a hot stone you bump your feet against. And that stone is an unruly force in the world of theatre.

MAARTEN DE POURCQ

* 'Kritiek van de Geraakte Rede'.

Where is God?

God is everywhere. Why is god
on earth: to serve me
and so to be able to forget Me.

Did I die to be able to pierce god?
Yes, to be able to pierce God
I first washed myself from head to toe
and finally allowed myself to be pierced
by constantly pushing Him away.

Does it matter if I really existed?

I don't know. More than ever
she is the most beautiful there will ever be:
After all she is everywhere. Dearest,
what has become of us. Or would You
like me to return as it Is.

HANS FAVEREY, excerpt from *Hinderlijke goden* [Irksome gods]

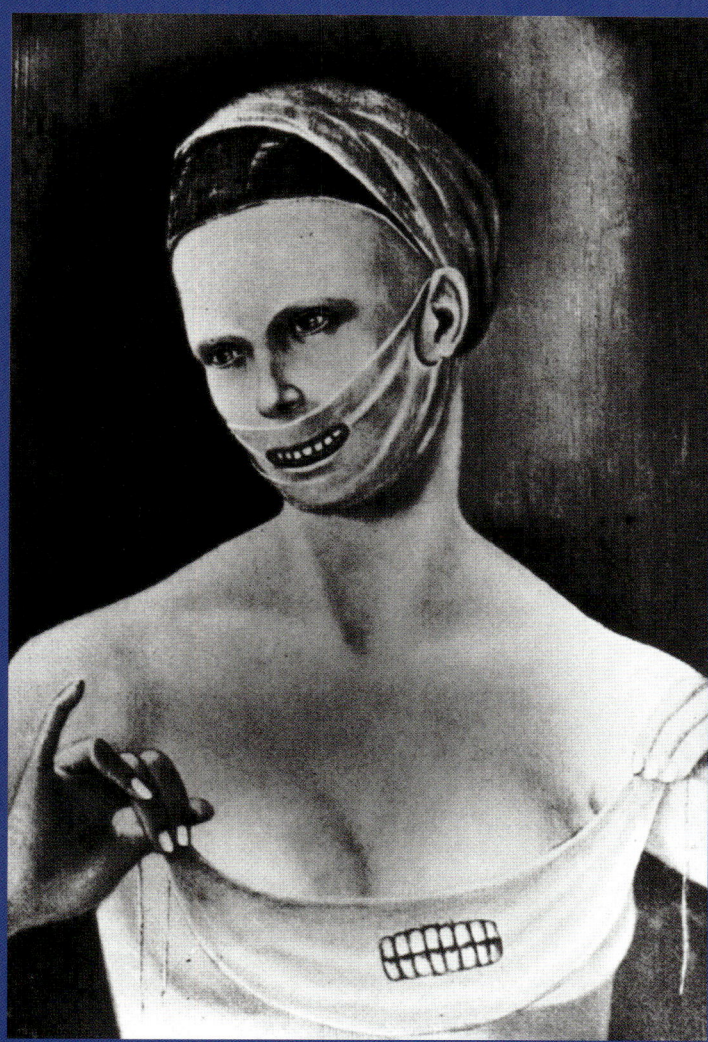

Pieter De Buysser has made productions and written scripts. 'I write and blithely look for an open theatre, a theatre without foundations. A theatre as a machine of possibilities. I dream of a utopian theatre which I hope will provide some scope for experimentation that is above suspicion.'

For a while Pieter De Buysser attended theatre courses at the Antwerp conservatoire. He then went on to study philosophy, first in Antwerp (UFSIA University) and later in Paris (*Licence* and *Maîtrise* at the Collège International de Philosophie, 1996–98). In the meantime he wrote nine theatre scripts and five essays about the theatre world. He also wrote and produced two films. In 1998 he was awarded the Emile Zola prize for his essay 'Tijdpraktijken, een aangeklede rede' [Time practices, a dressed-up reason].

Lampe is the non-profit organization that brings Pieter De Buysser, Valentine Kempynck and Benjamin Verdonck together. Pieter De Buysser makes the most intensive use of this structure, both for his film experiments (under the slogan 'Lampe Schijnt' [Lampe shines]) and for his theatre work. *Kritiek van de Geraakte Rede* [Critique of touched reason] is the trilogy on which he founds his theatre research.

In *Het Litteken Lip* [The scarred lip] (2001), the first play he directed himself, Adriaan Van den Hoof and Wouter Hendrickx performed to great public acclaim a series of grotesque fables, linked by means of an account of the travels of Immanuel Kant's domestic servant. The work as a whole was described, not without a touch of humour, as a 'metaphysical thriller'.

For *Lotus Drive* (2002) Pieter De Buysser drew inspiration from the section about the lotus eaters in Homer's *Odyssey*. Those who swallow the leaves of a lotus flower, lose their memory for ever. *Lotus Drive* is about the catastrophic and at the same time life-affirming energy released when an individual is freed of memory and history. Riina Saastamoinen, Lise Solar, Raven Ruëll and Jean-Baptiste Lefebvre shaped the play's poetical 'pidgin' language. Pieter De Buysser completed the third part of the trilogy, *Aangesproken, de as en de boter* [Broken into – the ashes and the butter] (2003), with Sien Eggers and Tine Embrechts. The textual material consisted of a package of love declarations addressed to unknown persons, farewell letters, scribbled notes, prayers, shopping lists, etc., which tell us much about the female authors: 'In their eagerness and cheerful serenity they chatter their way into the most incomprehensible banalities.'   DM

HET MUZIEK LOD

THE HEROES OF
ERIC DE VOLDER AND DICK VAN DER HARST

The stage is scantily lit. A female character carrying an old-fashioned shopping bag appears. She is dressed very plainly and has a scarf tied round her head. A younger character becomes involved in the play as a 'missy, missy'. She circles the stage relentlessly: the beginning of a 'story', which is told falteringly or (half) sung, sometimes detached in the third person, sometimes in the first person. They break into song, together, alone, address one another, embrace. To judge by the tonality, what unfolds before our eyes seems to be a tragedy. These are laments. These actresses are giving vent to their grief. You are a witness to a language that you don't know but that speaks to you.

*and after eating
d'I have to say it?
d'you want to hear't?
Death is wandering round there
all those who went on sitting at the table
and I recognized'em
I certainly did
including Quasimotherwoman
and the so-called daughterchild – a girl
and I'm sorry to have to say't
they're going to die
beginning with themselves
because listen!
I don't want to know! shouts the second one
that's the sign, to be sure,
that there's a row and arguing again
not a good sign
that after eating something else must be digested:
couple of old feuds*

In *Achter 't eten* [After eating] De Volder sought inspiration in a bundle of letters written in the 1970s by two women seeking mutual comfort. During the rehearsal process, the plot was 'transformed' into a mother and a daughter who find each other, but cannot help one another in an almost genetic spiral of incest in a minor provincial town. After *Diep in het bos* [Deep in the forest] (1999), *Vadria* (2000) and *Zwarte vogels in de bomen* [Black birds in the trees] (2002), *Achter 't eten* is the fourth coproduction resulting from the collaboration between director-writer Eric De Volder and composer Dick van der Harst. In terms of resources, it is reduced to the bare minimum. It is shaped purely with speech and song, scanty lighting and three props on the stage.

'... THEY SPEAK SO STRANGE ...'

At the start of rehearsals, odd notes and a file containing text and pictures lay on the director's table; there was no finished 'script'. In his plays characters do not speak normally; they stammer, falter, eat the words, which they then present in a form that is in keeping with their character.

[De Volder:] 'I have always written the plays myself, and the linguistic idiom has gradually developed. That was influenced partly by the sources I used, for example with *Achiel De Baere*, whose diary is littered with mistakes, and partly through the language and sound improvisations of the actors on the stage. In developing a series of characters they often start to 'dictate' a language that has its own colour. Once I have that material, I set to work. The form of the text follows the pace of the rehearsals. Every fragment of a sentence is shaped on the basis of what the actors have experienced during the process, with my adaptation of course.'

'... HOW IS IT THAT I ACCEPT THAT SOMEONE ON STAGE BURSTS INTO SONG AND I DON'T FIND IT RIDICULOUS?...'

You know that you have seen too much opera, that nineteenth-century superb artefact with its set of conventions that are scarcely questioned, and you know that you didn t believe a word of it. You don't like musicals, so what do you like? As a music freak, you seek refuge in the wide and complex field that is called music theatre. You want to see and hear new forms. Not cardboard stars and cardboard aesthetics.

[Van der Harst:] 'With Het muziek Lod the starting point lies partly with the composer, who together with the director works out a project. It is still the case that we – together with Jan Kuijken and Kris Defoort, Het muziek Lod's other two composers-in-residence – choose the director to realize the idea we have. As our collaboration has continued, that is the way it has remained: if I see something in a suggestion made by Eric or vice versa, then we go ahead together. In other cases we both have solutions for putting our ideas into practice.'

In their collaboration De Volder and Van der Harst look for the point at which the actors actually start to give voice to the script and embody it. They have more than one fascination in common: a fascination with the popular, the forgotten, and with the grandeur of what is small. While as a writer and 'acting coach' De Volder seeks inspiration in photographs, newspaper cuttings, diaries and correspondence, Van der Harst likes to dip into the caverns of music history to emerge with, for example, Breton recitative songs as the music form for *Diep in het bos*.

De Volder and Van der Harst do not necessarily choose well-trained voices, but first and foremost look for expressiveness. How far does an actor or actress go in the improvisations to find his or her character? How far does their 'faith' in the power of the music they are singing go? It is always difficult to switch mid-sentence from parlando to singing and from there to sound improvisation, often at highly emotionally charged moments, when rational language falls short.

Van der Harst was responsible for writing the songs for *Achter 't eten*. 'This production is small by comparison with the previous coproductions, and moreover unaccompanied. This time we have a dialogue between two women and nine songs that tell a story. The women also become the respective characters when they start to sing. These characters have a name: the one who begins to sing is also the one who experiences it as herself, or it is the "I" that sings a song about the situation.'

Dick van der Harst, one of whose ambitions is to write and stage a mass, describes what he expects of music theatre:

'It is a strange fact that in the theatre quality norms and standards have been developed for all the other aspects, whereas the music often sounds like a film score, or worse: like wallpaper music. You may expect a director who is precise with script and direction down to the zerozerozero one after the full stop, to use the music with the same precision. What I insist on in my form of music theatre is that the music, even though it plays a subsidiary role, should actually be able to work *concertante*. In our cooperation I come into the story with a musical story and look for the right balance. Eric allows the power of the music to work for itself instead of using it as support, and in this way the musical element becomes a parallel leitmotiv, which gives you an extra basis for your story.'

'HOW CAN A FLANDERS THAT NO LONGER EXISTS APPEAL TO ME? CAN THE PROVINCIAL BE UNIVERSAL?'

In *Diep in het bos* you saw seven actresses, with over-accentuated make-up, evolve in a group across the stage. They sang songs which seemed to come from nowhere and told of a terrible secret (the Dutroux child murders). Precisely because it was not literally named, you recognized what it was about. Psychologists would call this 'the collective memory'.

As the setting or situation De Volder often opts for a provincial village somewhere in a pre-1980s Flanders. The themes he plays with, examines, or 'evokes' say something about a small-town world in transition, about the anti-hero who could have been a hero, about life's little joys and great sorrows. They are always situations of grief and suffering which, whoever finds himself in it, cannot or does not want to comprehend because that suffering is too great. As the performance moves forward, the narration of something becomes subordinate to the mourning for it or the coming to terms with it. A performance becomes a cleansing ritual, which temporarily allays the suffering, or so it seems.

[De Volder:] 'Most of the plays are set between the period following the Second World War and now. If you open the newspaper and turn to the so-called "short news items", the family dramas, child murders, then a theme like that of *Achter 't eten* is as plausible now as it was in the 1970s when the letters, which served as the source, were exchanged.... I regard my (common) characters as potential heroes in the classical sense. It is not fatalistic: they find themselves in a difficult situation, but they are given a chance. Almost naïvely I want to give them that status and with that belief in possibilities I create tension. In *Achter 't eten* they themselves name the things which potentially they could do, they question things, reach out to each other, but don't succeed...'

The performance is nearing its end. The lights go out. Will you applaud loudly? Will you laugh away your fear? Like the procession which came to life during the show, a whole succession of associations files past you. And echoes of a song, snatches of language, opinions about the world news, opinions about the small print in tabloids. Pain, the unspeakable. And you know whom you saw there; their size is of no importance. These are heroes.

HENDRIK TRATSAERT

The quotes are taken from interviews with Eric De Volder, Ghent, 7 June, and Dick van der Harst, Ostend, 9 August 2003.

HET MUZIEK LOD

The Ghent music theatre company Het muziek Lod began life in 1989 organizing weekly lunchtime theatre performances in a Ghent brasserie. Until 1993 Het muziek Lod also organized an annual Narrative Festival focusing on the relationship between word and music. Not long after that, Het muziek Lod decided to concentrate on producing contemporary music theatre, in the broadest sense of the word, whereby music, theatre and often also dance are treated in a similar way and juxtaposed.

Rather than opting for one regular company, artistic director Hans Bruneel prefers to work with a number of music-makers and music theatre-makers: Dick van der Harst, Kris Defoort and Jan Kuijken, three composers-in-residence, each of whom has the scope within Het muziek Lod to map out his own path and to create his own musical language. With changing but often recurring partners (Karine Ponties, Guy Cassiers, Eric De Volder, et al.), they work on the most diverse productions.

In the case of *The Woman who Walked into Doors*, Kris Defoort's first opera, a classical orchestra and a jazz ensemble, an actress, a soprano and a video screen together shape a female alcoholic who is battered and marginalized.
Another example is *Diep in het bos* [Deep in the forest], an a cappella music theatre production in which seven women give vent to their emotions about the Dutroux affair. Van der Harst's music was inspired by Breton songs.
Capture d'un Caillot and *Taroupe* are two intimate dance productions. In each case Jan Kuijken enters into dialogue with two dancers.

After more than ten years of exploration and discovery, Het muziek Lod has carved a unique place for itself on the Flemish and international music and music theatre scene. Undaunted by the new, the old, the different or the unfamiliar, the composers are building a highly individual oeuvre which cannot be categorized and in which social commitment plays an increasingly important role. Music is juxtaposed with dance, theatre, text and video. As well as the mix of disciplines, there is also a mix of genres within the music.
In 2002 Het muziek Lod's 'impressive track-record' won it the Océ performing arts prize.   YB

DO

OR

DARE

OLYMPIQUE DRAMATIQUE

The name of the group is a joke. It sounds intentionally hard and dialectic when uttered in Franco-Flemish, with a rolling *r* – 'olleimpik / drammatik' – the mere sounds covering the feel of it, as in *'pas avec nous, hein, godverdoeme'* ('not with us, damn it'). I have rarely heard the name spoken in proper French *à la Parisienne* (except once, that is, at deSingel) and it would not in any case be to the group's credit, if you ask me. A posh pronunciation with protracted '-que' would immediately give it a sort of salon-like ring and that is precisely what you should not expect from O.D. They are not salon artists. Nor are they beach bums, right? Each of the members is officially 'a master of dramatic arts', but it seems to me that they would not wish to flaunt this rather stuffy title, hence, I suspect, the gentle irony in 'drammatik'. Dramatic art, phew, what would they want with that? Here theatre is made with hammer and chisel, with mortar and clay, with spade and trowel. Rather than masters, they are mere apprentices. They nick from everyone (with their eyes or otherwise) and then make their own construction: often unpolished, rough even, sometimes wobbly, but with an extremely solid base that can certainly withstand a blow. And not just a blow from outside, but also a blow from inside. In particular the blows they give themselves during rehearsals and shows. Their acting often reminds you of ten- to twelve-year-old boys playing cowboys and Indians: *'Baaaaang, you're dead.'* – *'No, I'm not dead.'* – *'Yes, I hit you right in the heart.'* – *'OK then, I'll be dead for a minute... But now I'm joining in again.'* A watertight logic in fact because on stage and in the forest of our youth nobody really dies. At most they end up with a torn pair of trousers and a grazed knee. Which leads us to the indestructible acting pleasure you encounter in O.D.'s productions. You don't need to be an actor to want to jump up on stage and join in; it doesn't matter that you don't know the script, O.D. will take care of you. It's something you rarely come across in the theatre: the urge to join in, the hope that the play is not yet over, that it is just the interval. All too rarely.

Even more rarely do you come across groups that still want to act the story. Often you find only vague atmospheric creations which, according to the makers, are designed to hit you right in one or other intestine, but, alas, all too often those productions lack substance, a story. Their own story prevails a priori on the writer's story. Not so with O.D. Though the story is told according to their rules and norms, at least they tell it with respect for the original author. Again an exception, alas.

But we haven't said anything yet about the first part of the group's name: 'Olympique'. Are they referring to the Olympic ideas? To Baron de Coubertin's motto 'taking part is more important than winning'? Not entirely, I think. It seems to me that taking part is important to the O.D.s, but winning the occasional sprint or steep mountain climb should certainly be possible too. (Of course they would love to have won the darned theatre festival with *De krippel* [The cripple].)

So why then 'Olympique'? In their own world they are gods, aren't they? A little club of gods who have built their own Olympus and fight tooth and nail any demi-gods who challenge their trade with all kinds of theories unsuited to the 'do or dare' theatre world of O.D. 'Do or dare', indeed, because I suspect that they only do what they want and not what others want and I suspect that they blindly dare to make choices that are distasteful to others.

The O.D.s also appear elsewhere, often far from their Olympus. For example, they turn up in comedy series on entertainment channels. An O.D.er does what he likes and practises his craft wherever he can and not only where he is deemed to do so. They don't build walls for royals only, they also build walls for ordinary people, and that is to their credit. Gods who come down from on high. As far as I'm concerned, they are not concerned with art either. Who can still be engaged in art these days? Art has not existed since Duchamp placed a urinal in a museum. What calls itself art or is called art by others is usually nothing more and nothing less than calling art into question, or worse: a happy find. Art that exalts itself, that celebrates itself. Not without good reason do the O.D.s perform *Drie kleuren wit* [Three colours of white], which is highly accessible and says a great deal about art. O.D. does what theatre has to do: it holds up a mirror to nature (or something like that).

If this piece sounds rather idolatrous, then there is only one reason: O.D. has delivered the finest theatre of recent years and though in some establishments promises have sometimes been made late in the evening with regard to a cooperation with the undersigned, nothing has come of it yet. Let this be my last application!

Yours respectfully,
STANY CRETS

OLYMPIQUE DRAMATIQUE

Olympique Dramatique's artistic core consists of four young actors who first met while studying at the Studio Herman Teirlinck in Antwerp. Tom Dewispelaere, Ben Segers, Stijn Van Opstal and Geert van Rampelberg graduated in 1998 and joined forces in a bid to make narrative theatre that would move people. Their productions are invariably laced with a great deal of humour.

At the invitation of the Limelight arts centre (Kortrijk), during the 1998–99 season Olympique Dramatique created *Neen, serieus* [No, seriously], a promising adaptation of *Hamlet*, inspired by Tom Stoppard's *Rosencrantz and Guildenstern are Dead*. Rosencrantz and Guildenstern, minor characters in Shakespeare, take centre stage in the play and as anti-heroes they turn the tragedy of Hamlet into comedy. The next season the four were nominated for the Signaalprijs with their production of *Het aanzoek*, based on Chekhov's one-acter *The Proposal*. Youth theatre BRONKS asked them to adapt the script for children, and Olympique Dramatique discovered that Chekhov's text contains a considerable degree of slapstick. They also added humour inspired by such comedians as Charlie Chaplin, Buster Keaton and Harold Lloyd.

The company made its real breakthrough with *De Krippel* (2001–02). For this production, based on *The Cripple of Inishmaan* by Martin McDonagh, the young enthusiasts devised a language of their own to match McDonagh's vivid dialect in translation. It is a mix of Flemish dialects, English, German and French. The suppleness with which the actors use this concocted language, the compelling humour, the obvious and contagious acting pleasure and the cleverness of the production earned them a place on the short-list of the Theaterfestival 2002. A project grant from the Flemish Community enabled the company to invite a number of guest actors to star in *De Krippel*. Together with the core team, they decide about the set, direction, lighting, etc. In this respect Olympique Dramatique joins the tradition of Flanders' many actors' collectives.

Apart from their cooperation in Olympique Dramatique, the four actors have taken part in youth theatre productions by BRONKS and HETPALEIS. Tom Dewispelaere is one of the core actors of Het Toneelhuis. Geert van Rampelberg works with Lampe and KVS / de bottelarij, Stijn Van Opstal is earning his stripes with De Werf, Theater Stap and De Queeste, and Ben Segers can be seen with Walpurgis and in several television comedy series.   IT

L A S H E D - U P

One ordinary afternoon I am sitting with my father and my brother at the table. 'Work going well?' asks my father. 'Not too badly,' I say. We talk about this and that, about people in the street, about the neighbours. An outsider wouldn't have a clue what we were talking about, I guess; it would all be a mystery to him. It is also very banal. Exceedingly dull. Or seemingly so. Because the essential is never spoken. It is concealed. We could pay each other very nice compliments, but we could also cause each other a great deal of pain. Saying what rankles. It could be something cruel, but perhaps also very warm and confidential. Or shabby and wicked. In any case, it would be intense and life would go on without loss or injury. So why don't I do it? What is the difference between confiding your nastiest thoughts and not speaking them?

Are those thoughts not also a part of the reality we live in? And where could they fit in our progressive, open and supposedly free-thinking society? That I am revolted by the idea that my mother and I are sitting at the table wearing a bloody tampon? That we actually like farting and are amazed by the stink we as people can create? That I wonder how my brother or father watch pornography? The list is endless. They are all desires, ideas and situations that are familiar to us, but that are nevertheless filtered out of (our representation of) everyday human traffic. They show a person's embarrassment, nakedness and vulnerability. They make it awkward for us. They are recognizable, but we would prefer not to know about them and not to show them.

The theatre collective De Zweep [The lash] avidly gropes its way out of this barrel of the unspoken. In smartly trimmed dialogues, the group's core – Herwig Illegems, Bart Meuleman and Mark Verstraete – show the hidden excesses of our everyday reality. In the first three plays, collected under the title *De smerige trilogie* [The dirty trilogy], they looked for situations we would instantly recognize. It was no accident that they chose the sitting-room culture with characters whose name or history you didn't know. This abstraction narrowed the distance between the Other and yourself. They wanted the identification process to be as great as possible. On a deeper level they develop a fragmentary sketch of the way people relate to each other, without giving any indication of where they themselves are coming from or what dictates their passions and longings. Arguments, slanging-matches, abuse, puke, group sex and torture – not the most cheering portrayal of mankind. They provide hyper-realistic portraits; not social sketches but a reality stripped of all its frills. The images bombard your retina, you can't escape them, they creep like dirt into your clothes. You would expect to feel miserable after so much brutality and harshness, but no, the result is hilariously funny! Moreover, you discover that this pitch-black reality actually contains a great deal of warmth and tenderness. No opinions are expressed. De Zweep shows that when you put all your trust in each other, you can also accept the cruellest things. De Zweep stages that human beauty we so rarely dare to experience. And the result is very moving.

In their most recent play *Show* the company blurs the border between the character and the actor. They enter the stage as themselves, in the charming company of trainee Kyoko Scholiers. The dining-table becomes the work-bench around which a performance is developed. According to Bart Meuleman, they wanted to 'have the reality of the stage come as close as possible to the fiction of the stage'. This resulted in a sort of 'intermediate reality' between theatre and reality. They retain their house style, which is radical and fragmented, but in this production the story-line is clearer. Kyoko, also in real life a student at the performing arts school Studio Herman Teirlinck, arrives for an internship. Together with Bart, Herwig and Mark she makes a production that is called 'Show'. The company shows what it plans to do with Kyoko. You expect the worst of the three men and that is what you get. They call her a cunt, French-kiss her long and extensively – the microphones transmit the lewd sounds into the auditorium – but they also put their complete trust in her and they defend themselves before her. Despite the fact that they are on a stage here, which in itself is a cheerless sort of place, a place lacking in atmosphere, a blank place, they manage to fill it with great intimacy by means of a table, four chairs and a cardboard box. We are allowed a glimpse of their laboratory. Kyoko is evaluated and approved of. She is also allowed to have her say about them. Eventually they start arguing, leave the stage and make way for a video projection. Kyoko has the upper hand, she wears the trousers, is made pregnant by Mark and Bart in a hilarious scene in a damp cellar, before going off with Herwig who in the meantime has undergone a sex change. The group has cleverly inserted references to reality TV formats (such as 'Idol') in the video.

The production is strong stuff and you can only take it in small doses but the members of De Zweep would not want it any other way. It would not be physically feasible either. Their working style completely rules out hierarchy. Meuleman: 'De Zweep is a communal voice we have found. Everyone is equal, there is no director, everyone is dramaturge.' In the past they have invited people to take part in their creative process, but everything is done in the strictest confidence. 'We embrace the newcomer and then we lock the door again. Because what we do in that room is pick our noses round a table. Memories of what has been, fantasies about things we love, about danger, about the worst thing that could happen to us – all this is thrown on the table. It is not a leisurely chat, a time for reflection. We brainstorm vehemently, and at the end of the day you are totally round the bend.' Every production is a real marathon session. After that they go back to square one. And each time the question remains whether there will be another production, or even whether the members of De Zweep will ever again appear on stage under that name.

AN MERTENS

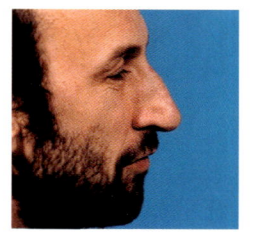 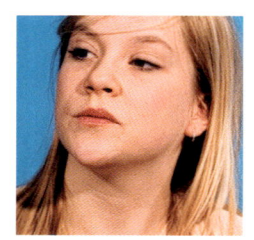 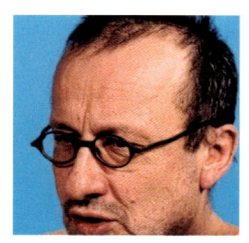 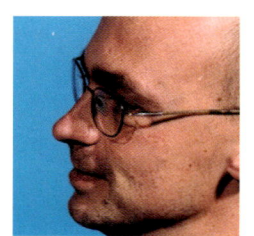

BART MEULEMAN

Since the early 1990s Bart Meuleman (1965) has been carving out a career as actor, dramaturge, writer and publisher. *De smerige trilogie* [The dirty trilogy] (1999–2001), the notable piece by De Zweep about the beauty of shabbiness, is the most recent lap of this journey. Mark Verstraete's and Herwig Ilegems' fascination for human ugliness is given plenty of scope in their cooperation with writer Bart Meuleman. *'We take childish pleasure in doing dirty things.'* The trio began a collective artistic process. Highly personal material was written and then, after much discussion, tried out during rehearsals. This collective and yet personal study of fear, shame and humiliation is carried out patiently and thoroughly and shown to the public without cynicism or show. Meuleman applied the same process to *Mille Feuilles*, commissioned by Theater Antigone (2001), another hyperrealistic product of social criticism, and to De Zweep's most recent production (*verkoopt Show*, 2003).

In 1998 Bart Meuleman argued for a greater degree of intellectual involvement on the part of actors in the theatre. It led him to call for the resignation of the dramaturge to make way for a permanent dramaturgy. For Meuleman a performance must speak for itself, each member of the audience should be able to make the production himself. Thus De Zweep never produce promotional texts or explanatory programme notes which they find not only irritating but also deadly boring.

In spite of that, Bart Meuleman had worked as a dramaturge after studying film at the RITS and theatre at Leuven University – first with Het Gevolg (then still involved in youth theatre), later on with Theater Zuidpool. In those early years he regularly appeared on stage himself with kindred spirits such as Dito'Dito, Tg. Stan, Tristero and Het Bordes.

At the same time he revealed himself as a writer, producing theatre scripts for Het Gevolg (*Dr Zero op een ziggurat*, 1990), for Tristero (*Hyperventilatie*, 1994) and Dito'Dito (*Voetstuk/Piédestal*, 1998). As a publicist, Meuleman is interested above all in art, politics, economics and television. He has written a number of articles for *Etcetera, AS/Andere Sinema* and *De Witte Raaf*. He set up the *Blinddoek, levend tijdschrift* project, with live interviews in the Stuc (1996). That same year his first collection of poetry entitled *Kleine criminaliteit* [Petty crime] appeared. In 2002 he was writer-in-residence for the literary magazine *Yang* and the children's book *Mijnheertje Kokhals* appeared, which he had produced together with Paul Verrept. Querido is to publish a new poetry collection, *Hulp*, in 2004.

Together with Paul Verrept, he founded Bebuquin, publishers of stage plays in 1994. With the financial support of a number of arts centres, companies and the Flemish Theatre Institute, Bebuquin has published some fifteen works in the space of just over three years. The writer's linguistic flair is the number-one criterion in the selection of the scripts.

Meuleman's career can best be described as a consistent balancing act between intuition and reflection, qualities that will no doubt also be displayed in the project to be mounted in cooperation with Theater Antigone in the spring of 2004 (*Entertaining Mr. Sloane*).   NW

MOHAMED 'BEN' BENAOUISSE

AGADIR...
le plus grand COUSCOUS du monde!

CLUB BRUGGE K.V.

Olympialaan 74, 8200 Brugge
☎ (050) 38 71 55 / 38 72 09

Olympiastadion, zaterdag 8 augustus 1987 te 20u

12e TORNOOI "DE BRUGGE METTEN" - 1ste dag - 2e match

CLUB BRUGGE KV heet U allen hartelijk welkom !!

SCHEIDSRECHTERS : HH. PIRAUX, MATTHYS en LAMBRECHT

SAMENSTELLING VAN DE PLOEGEN

CLUB BRUGGE KV	NAT. PLOEG MAROKKO
1. VANDE WALLE Philippe	12. AZMI
2. TEW Mamadou	3. NAJID
3. VAN DER ELST Franky	5. JILAL
5. VAN WIJK Dennis	8. MOURAD
7. VAN DER ELST Leo	4. HCINA
8. QUERTER Alex	16. BENABICHA
9. CREVE Peter	6. DOLNY
10. DE GRYSE Marc	10. BARK
11. ROSENTHAL Rony	7. ABDERRAHIN
12. BEYENS Luc	11. KIDDI
16. GOYVAERTS Jean	9. CHAOUCH

Wisselspelers:

4. BROOS Hugo	1. HAFARYA
13. JENSEN Birger	2. BIDAR
14. VEREYCKEN Stefan	14. LACHHABI
17. BRYLLE Kenneth	19. HASSAN
15. HINDERYCKX Kurt	18. EL GHORF
6. AUDOOR Yves	17. MEZYANE

DRUKKERIJ
BRUNET

1
1ère LEÇON
ALPHABET ARABE

L'alphabet arabe se compose de 28 lettres qui sont:

ث sa	ت ta	ب ba	ا a
د dâl	خ khâ	ح h'a	ج djim
س sîne	ز zaîne	ر raye	ذ ja
ط thâ	ض dhâ	ص çâd	ش chîne
ف fâ	غ ghaîne	ع a'îne	ظ za
م mîm	ل lam	ك kaf	ف qâf
ى yâ	و wâou	ھ hâ	ن noûne

A ces lettres il faut ajouter le hamza(ء) qui est signe ayant la valeur de a'

Lam (ل) peut s'accoupler avec alif (ا) et prend la forme (لا) ou (لا) cet ensemble s'appelle lâm-alif et se prononce lâ

CAFFÈ MACCHIATO

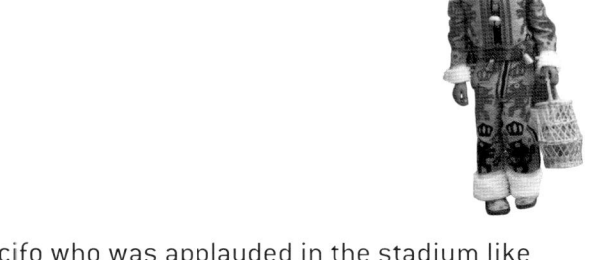

I first saw him on the dance floor. He moves in structures you never forget. He said he had learnt to dance like that as a way of rebelling against a mapped-out future. He did not want to disappear down a mine shaft every day or behind a factory gate, like his father. He opened up his own future by delving into the past.

The last time that I looked at him, we drank *caffè macchiato* in Ghent. We drew lines on an imaginary map. From South to North. From Morocco to Belgium. From dark to white. From mocca to milk-coloured. And back. We thought we would discover a point somewhere in Spain, which would explain much of our communality. A historic turning-point. A place where mosques were burned so that cathedrals could be built on the scorched earth. One day we would reconstruct the historic path our culture had trodden. We would develop a joint memory. We knew what it was to lose: losing one's way, losing a diary, losing a parent, losing oneself. That is why we knew the power of reconstruction that arises from necessity. We talked of the paths people follow, places people leave, circles people turn in. We analysed the choreography of life's course.

Mohamed Ben Benaouisse is a Moroccan Belgian. I always thought that umbrella term sounded like a hollow collective noun. Too geographical, too little Ben. I believe a person's identity is determined by his memory.

The mineral Benaouisse brings to the surface when he delves into his memory, consists of a thousand and one things:

– The story of his father who arrived in France from Morocco with a lorry.
– The house where he was born in Wallonia.
– Father with false teeth who claimed he had once sold a motorbike to the future King Hassan II of Morocco.
– Father slaughtering a sheep in the garden in La Louvière.
– Father who supported La Louvière football team.
– Little Ben playing football with the words 'Jean'store Jery' on his T-shirt.

– Enzo Scifo who was applauded in the stadium like a god.
– Saint Michel without filter tip.
– Father and Mohamed who went together to watch the Club Brugge–Morocco match on Saturday, 8 August 1987.
– Mother who carried a dead child in her belly.
– Father who liked playing cards.
– Michael Jackson.
– Polyphony and requiems.
– Memories of the beach.
– Eating mussels.
– Hospital bed CNP 971.
– Father's wish to be buried in Belgium.
– Snippets of text from books by Georges Perec.
– Father's dead body being flown back to Morocco in an aeroplane .

Bric-à-brac.
'My mother liked flea markets.'
Two months after my father's death, his material presence had been erased.
'My mother didn't want my father's things lying round the house.'
He says that thanks to his mother he has learned to clean. 'She liked cleanliness.'
He says that he sometimes finds himself in knick-knacks and old photograph albums, even those belonging to people he doesn't know.
Ben Benaouisse is a thousand and one things. He is a dancer, writer, actor and visual artist. Above all he is a master at dealing with memories. The stage sets that he moves in consist of memories. He is constantly drawing up inventories. In juridical terms the word 'inventory' means: the list of items in a file submitted to the judge. His judge is the public.

He gave me a copy of the wonderful booklet published to mark the exhibition *Ben Benaouisse – Invasif II*. It contains a lovely photograph of his father behind a glass door. The glass is interwoven with thin wire to form a lattice of small squares. It looks like a blank crossword puzzle. *'Papa derrière la porte'*, Benaouisse wrote on it.

I can just remember the same picture of my father. One day when no words were possible, he stood behind a very similar glass, like a crossword puzzle. It was the day he rang his own front doorbell for the first time in his life, to tell his children that their mother was dead. With his images, Ben Benaouisse also draws up the inventory of his public.

Not only his *Invasif*, but all his productions with objects, scripts, photographs, music, sounds and movements, trigger invasions by memories. But never in a hostile way. He first bares himself so as to become a metaphor for everyone else. He reviews and revises ordinary things. I don't know anyone who can describe the sacred dimension of football like Benaouisse. The drawings with which Ben indicates his surroundings remind me of the choreographic movements I once saw sketched in notebooks belonging to Anne Teresa De Keersmaeker. Benaouisse's dancing, his whole oeuvre, is a mysterious way of occupying a place. Everyone goes through life in some way looking for a path in the world. And you have to have come from somewhere to know where you are going. Sometimes that has precious little to do with geography.

ANNA LUYTEN

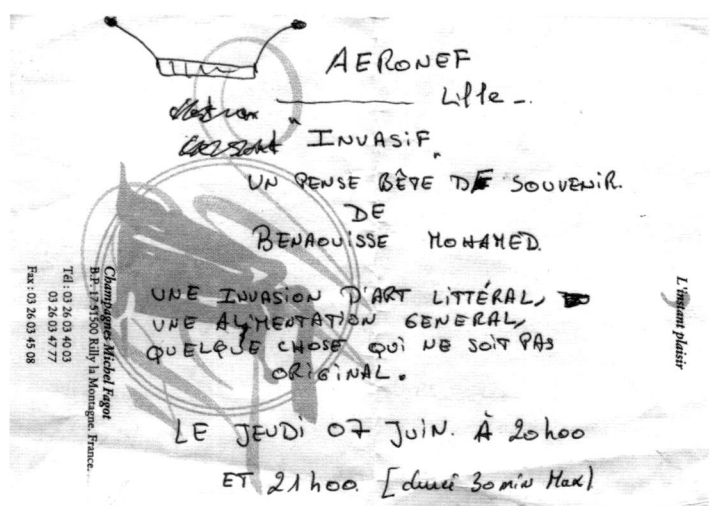

MOHAMED 'BEN' BENAOUISSE

In 1993 the Ghent production house Victoria went in search of thirty young dancers for the production *Ja Wacht!* [Yes, wait!], a creation for Antwerp Cultural Capital of Europe 1993. At the request of the Koning Boudewijnstichting/Fondation Roi Baudouin, one of the coproducers, auditions followed in both Flanders and Wallonia. 'I dance hip-hop and funky, I sing a little and I rap too': Mohamed Benaouisse, a French-speaking Belgian of Moroccan origin, was selected at the audition in Liège. *Ja wacht!* is also the production in which Benaouisse met his dance partner Helmut Van den Meersschaut.

In 1994 Benaouisse found himself back at Victoria, when he took part in the dance competition *De Beste Belgische Danssolo* [The best Belgian dance solo], an idea of Alain Platel. He finished second. From then on, Mohamed called himself 'Ben'. When he was asked to take part in *Moeder en Kind* [Mother and child] (1995) by Alain Platel and Arne Sierens, he settled permanently in Ghent, and became an actor as well as a dancer.

Together with Helmut Van den Meersschaut and Noël Van Kelst, Benaouisse set up the dance collective Latrinité. They produced their first show, *Dansé Donsé Dan Dan*, for the second Victoria Festival (1995). This energetic production was a cross between theatre and dance. The next two Latrinité productions, *Auri Sacra Fames* (1997) and *Limbus Patrum* (2000), were also both theatre and dance productions.

Productions, projects and workshops, training courses, short films made at home and abroad opened up new horizons and created artistic opportunities. After his spell with Victoria and his experience with Latrinité, Benaouisse wanted to tell his own story.

In *Invasif I* (L'Aeronef, Lille, 2001) Benaouisse examined what theatricality can mean in the context of an exhibition. As his starting point he took memories and the objects attached to them — both typically Arab and typically Belgian issues, both personal and collective ideas, both subjective and objective documentation.

Benaouisse used the material from *Invasif I* as a point of departure for a series of new exhibitions and a theatre production. With *Het is Lam* [It is lamb] (2002) he brought the elements of *Invasif I* into the black box of the theatre and made a musical score of objects and memories: *les accessoires font de la danse, les acteurs sont des souvenirs. Invasif II* (Caermersklooster, Ghent, 2002) and *Invasif III* (De Brakke Grond, Amsterdam, 2002) are exhibitions with performances at fixed points in time. In that way Benaouisse juxtaposes the conventions of the performing arts — where productions are of a specific length — with the individual freedom to come and go of the exhibition-goer. LA

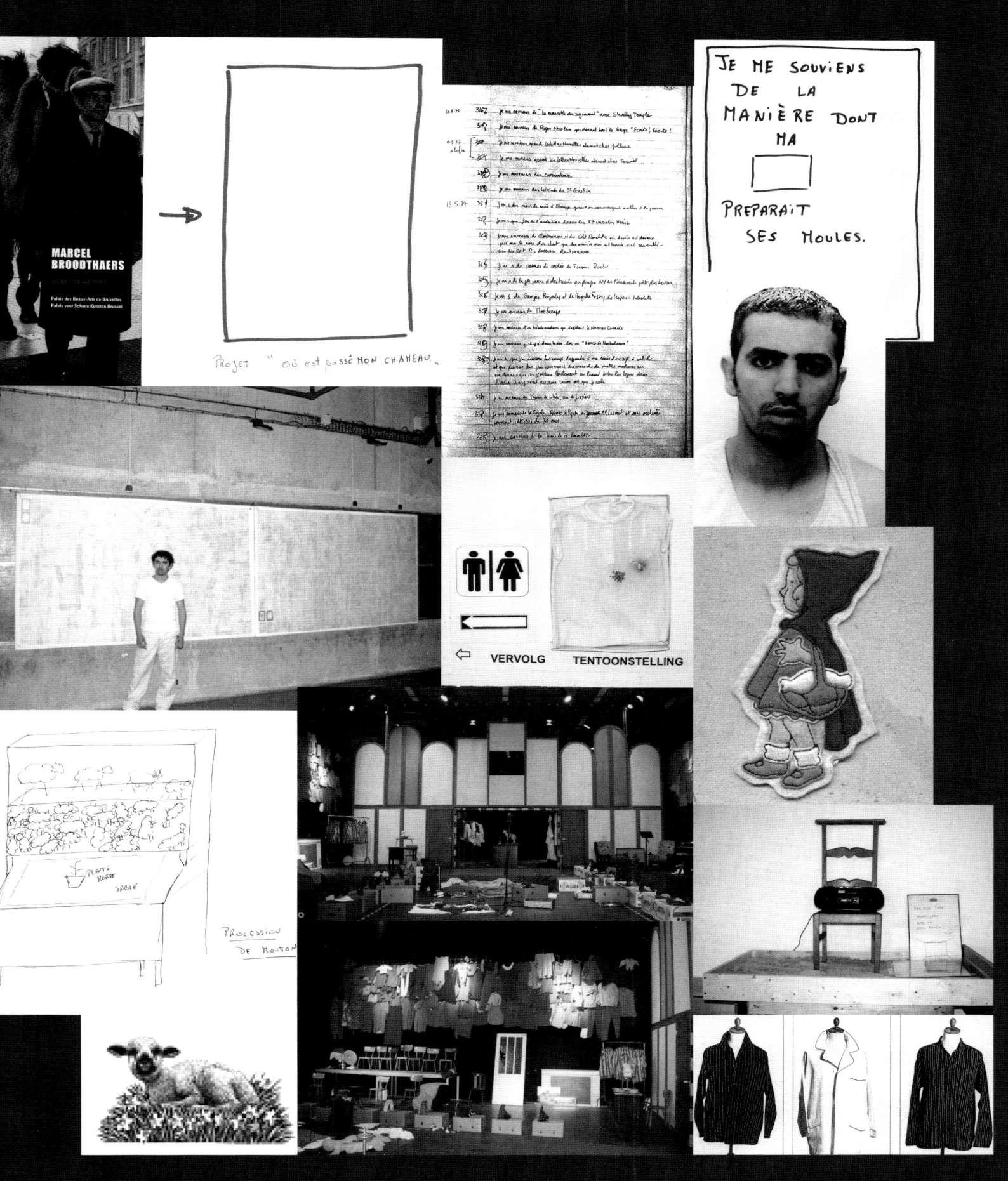

WHEN AN OEUVRE IS MORE THAN THE SUM OF ITS PARTS

A MINIATURE CULTURAL SOCIOLOGY OF THE FLEMISH PERFORMING ARTS IN 2003

RUDI LAERMANS

I.

The landscape of Flemish theatre and dance today makes a rather remarkable impression – it is even something of a unique sociological phenomenon. There are rich and poor institutions, large and small theatres, canonical companies and symbolic lightweights. There is nothing unusual about all that, and as in every social world the quantitative and qualitative differences are responsible for envy or jealousy and regularly produce frictions and clashes, not to mention open or furtive forms of lobbying. But the unusual feature is that, in spite of all this, it is hard to draw the line in Flanders between establishment and newcomers, centre and periphery. Large houses like the Koninklijke Vlaamse Schouwburg (Royal Flemish Theatre, Brussels) or Het Toneelhuis (Antwerp) almost greedily absorb up-and-coming theatre talent; Rosas supports young choreographers via the non-profit subsidiary Werkhuisproducties; Victoria and Beursschouwburg regularly reassess their functioning in the light of new developments; fresh graduates come knocking on the door of Stuk (Leuven) or Vooruit (Ghent), whether they have a project subsidy or not; Alain Platel gives other choreographers an opportunity with Les Ballets C de la B; and so on and so forth. There is no shortage of examples. And the conclusion is invariably that the performing arts in Flanders are not immediately caught up in a bitter struggle between pretenders to the throne and those who occupy it.

The pioneers of 'the new Flemish wave' of the 1980s are the official residents of the centre and, partly thanks to the 1993 performing arts decree, they have been that for more than a decade now. So most of them do not behave like quasi-monarchs with their own court and a territory that has to be fiercely defended against possible intruders. What is alive in the entire landscape of Flemish theatre and dance is a strikingly strong awareness of the double danger of organizational institutionalization and artistic routinization. This climate of 'anti-institutionalism' that is so difficult to explain, being both very diffuse and extremely effective at the same time, seems to me to be the hallmark *par excellence* of the current Flemish theatre and dance scene. That is in line with notably low thresholds in the social intercourse between the established companies and the newcomers, as much as, for example, between artists, critics and the core public. Relations at work in most of the companies are also egalitarian and democratic, not to say cooperative. The director or choreographer is not an omniscient master, but rather a coach who bears the final artistic responsibility.

An open climate of discussion has its disadvantages too. Mutual criticism is a possibility, nay, a necessity – but a lot remains unsaid, simply because consultation or cooperation implies dependence, in the present and above all in an unknown future, and entails a lack of critical distance at times. Differences in power certainly play a part here, albeit in a more subtle and less visible way than in a cultural field with a clear-cut dividing line between a self-protective establishment and an offensive periphery. That is what makes it so difficult for newcomers to position themselves in Flanders. They lack strong symbolic fathers and mothers who deliberately stifle their artistic potential. They are more likely to be cuddled to death, because they receive attention – from established institutions, but also from the daily press and the advisory committees to the cultural policy-makers of the Flemish Government. There is a manifest concern for entrance and promotion opportunities, and most thinking, discussion and decision-making is done with a view to a simultaneously flexible and sustainable Flemish theatre and dance landscape, much less in terms of international export or safe investments. A major factor here is the growth of the Flemish cultural budget, which is why it may be a temporary situation, even though it has been going on now for a decade.

As a result of the 'anti-institutional' consensus, Flanders has no stark *artistic* polarization between the generation of the Eighties and their successors. Yet if both generations share the same attitude, it is interpreted in widely divergent ways indeed – albeit without much conflict or struggle for legitimacy. The differences primarily have to do with how the specific artistic practices of those involved are described, given concrete shape and situated vis-à-vis other cultural practices. They are not unrelated to the more general shift from a modern to a postmodern culture, from a modernist to a postmodernist interpretation of what was once Art with a capital A. But since such general considerations have not found deep roots in Flanders, I shall immediately clear them away and limit myself to noting a few striking differences between the generations of 'the Eighties' and 'the Nineties'. (From here on the inverted commas will be dropped and readers are asked to supply them for themselves.) I shall not mention any names after this but, for the sake of argument, my generation of the Eighties consists of Anne Teresa De Keersmaeker (Rosas), Jan Lauwers (Needcompany), Lucas Vandervost (De Tijd) and Luk Perceval (Toneelhuis); my generation of the Nineties comprises Olympique Dramatique, Haute Coiffure, Benjamin Verdonck, De Zweep, De Queeste, Heine Avdal, Amgod, Charlotte Vanden Eynde, Kris Verdonck and Cie Buelens Paulina. This idealtypical classification is far from conclusive; there are several transitional figures and companies, such as Meg Stuart (Damaged Goods), Dito'Dito, and of course Tg. Stan.

II.

In artistic terms, the spirit of 'anti-institutionalism' appears among the generation of the Eighties in the striking way they manage to deepen and renew both their theatre or dance idiom and the craftsmanship they acquired in the meantime. Sometimes this is a gradual process, but it is just as common to find proverbial breakthroughs, performances in which a new step is taken in a remarkable way. Risks are not avoided, and occasionally the generation of the Eighties still comes up with mediocre or simply bad productions. But thematically and stylistically these also bear the hallmark of their maker. That is the decisive point: the generation of the Eighties consists of artists who are deliberately building up an oeuvre. They do not want to become imprisoned in it, hence their constant search for something new, but every new production is always an affirmation of an artistic calling with a romantic slant. Artists have something to say, they have a personal vision (that is their authorship), and, performance after performance, they search for the appropriate formal means to flesh that out. (That trajectory creates the oeuvre.)

Content plus form, culminating in a powerful dramatic or choreographic expression combined with a unique signature – that is what the generation of the Eighties is after. At the same time, practically every one of their performances shows a strong awareness of theatre or dance, opera or 'the performing arts in general' as specific media. Their boundaries are meticulously explored and shifted, above all in the direction of 'visuality'. That is regularly done with a view to maximal expression, without the kind of transgressions that by now are included under the label of 'performance'. Recognition of the medium-specific identity of theatre or dance can also be seen in the strong awareness of tradition of the generation of the Eighties. Classical repertoire (Shakespeare!) is a touchstone for their own artistic vision, while they also uphold the principle of a minimum of *métier* on the part of actors and dancers. A text is not mumbled inaudibly unless that is dramaturgically called for; a movement is not danced in a sloppy fashion unless that is specifically required by the choreography.

The generation of the Eighties forms the canonical centre of the Flemish performing arts, a position that the government and critics have consolidated in the last decade, and that has also received international confirmation. They are therefore heavyweights in institutional terms – which is just as true of the arts centres that were started up in the 1980s. An effective organizational institutionalization is in line with the steady growth in subsidies and infrastructure, even though this growth is very modest by comparison with examples abroad. Most of the generation of the Eighties use the surplus resources to improve the working conditions of the artistic staff, and above all to further highlight their own artistic trajectory. In most cases that is characterized by a fear of repeating themselves, i.e. of producing work which, in spite of its excellence, consists of variations on a recognized artistic identity. In terms of organization they have by now become an institute, but in artistic terms that is not at all what they want, in so far as institutionalization means routinization and complacency, self-affirmation and narcissism. It may look paradoxical, but it is the practice of the artists themselves that neutralizes the apparent inconsistency in the combination of organizational institutionalization and artistic 'anti-institutionalism': the oeuvre is not yet complete, the artist-author still has to produce his or her definitive work.

III.

While most of the generation of the Eighties subscribe, roughly speaking, to the modern concept of art, the majority of the generation of the Nineties adhere to an artistic practice that – however vague and inadequate it may be – can be characterized as 'post-artistic'. The generation of the Nineties are not authors who build up a coherent theatre or dance oeuvre either gradually or abruptly. They simply make production after production, they stroll from project to project, and they concentrate on the present without worrying too much about the past or the future. They seem to be not very interested, if at all, in a consistent artistic identity, and are guided rather by the possibility of working alone or with others, and today rather than tomorrow, on a specific project. If they are given the chance to do so, they often complete that project with a remarkable degree of enthusiasm and dedication. They do not complain that the stage is too small or too large, they are flexible and pragmatic, and they tailor their concept if necessary to suit the given work or theatre conditions. That makes them interesting partners for arts centres, especially the smaller ones, and for other organizations. The generation of the Nineties consists of context players who are readily able to adapt personal ideas and external questions to meet specific limiting conditions, without sacrificing any integrity or reflexivity in the process. They are not strategists but tacticians, and they excel in the art of appropriation: they are latter-day heirs of Situationism, but usually minus the revolutionary utopianism of that avant-garde movement of the 1950s and 1960s.

Project, concept, idea – performance after piece after production, most of the Nineties generation have no interest at all in developing a more general vision. They elaborate ideas, often in a highly consistent and rigorous yet context-sensitive way. Not surprisingly, they are not concerned with the formulation of a theatre or dance idiom of their own, a personal vocabulary or an individual approach to theatre or dance. 'Essayism' is perhaps the most appropriate word to characterize the artistic practice of the quintessential member of the Nineties generation. He or she does not worry about whether the performance is Art with a capital A or not, what matters is the creation of an interesting experience machine, an artefact that 'is well thought out' and manages to reach the audience. This generation is one of makers and doers, in the most literal sense of the word: they often resemble artistic engineers rather than artists *pur sang*. The work they produce is almost always aimed at an audience without being vulgar. It is often addressed to 'the man-in-the-street' from an honest democratic persuasion. That explains the numerous street and location projects in which the boundary between artistic and social work is often blurred, if not completely obliterated. And if

they simply work in an artistic setting, this usually results in performances that exploit the force of sentiment without much embarrassment. The performing artists of the Nineties do not make work for seasoned connoisseurs; they target that strange humanistic sensitivity that often comes across as inhuman. Their humanism and commitment are unmistakable, but in most cases unformulated: they do not argue, they infiltrate the body.

While there is still a canon, both a historical one and a professional one, for the preceding generation, their successors in the first place vie with their momentaneous 'self'. That is, as it is for the literary essayist, the source and touchstone of every activity. That is why they often write their texts themselves, even though texts written by others – occasionally even by classical authors – may be used also, but fragmented and disfigured, reduced or expanded, depending on the concept used. Diction is of hardly any importance, dialect is a usable form too, as are clumsiness and bleating, figuratively coming a cropper and literally bungling (but then playing at bungling, at times even very carefully contrived bungling). In more dance-centred productions that is reflected in a high degree of informality, an often theatrically exaggerated 'incapacity' – or 'unwillingness' – in the movements. That does have a model: not Art with a capital A, but simply soap opera.

The performing artists of the Nineties are not out to deliberately or critically break down the boundary between what used to be seen as high and low culture, art and kitsch. It is rather their manifest indifference towards that persistent institutionalized boundary that is typical, and so is their both reflexive and naïve attitude towards the difference between performing and visual arts. Their artistic practice is characterized by that easy – but not complacent – assembly of culturally heterogeneous genres or disciplines. Whereas the generation of the Eighties makes visual performing art, the generation of the Nineties shows a remarkable lack of concern for the history of art and pays little or no attention to the differences between installations and performances, video art and live art. They make neither theatre nor dance nor performing art in general, but simply explore the different forms of theatricality within our culture. Their practice is of the order of *the theatrical in general*, which is why it is difficult to pin down within the existing definitions and notions. But is it art to boot? Most of the time not Art with a capital A, that much is certain, but at any rate the *making* and *presentation* of it draws parasitically on the notion of modern art. The generation of the Nineties needs the generation of the Eighties – but the reverse, of course, is just as true.

H Y B R I D S

FROM UNDER THE BED A HAND

I felt a surge of unadulterated fear when the teacher of 'Shamanism Today' announced that we were going to do aura exercises. I didn't want to touch anyone's aura. But suddenly everyone was touching everyone else with their hands. Everyone joined in, deadly serious, eyes almost closed. Tania defined exact volumes around Renée, she even named the colours of her aura. But when Liliane and Nora touched one another, frisked each other even, the teacher intervened. She said that they must keep a distance of twenty centimetres from each other's body. Leen said that she could feel a bulge on my back, believing she had detected a certain obstinacy. I tried to feel her, too, keeping a scrupulous thirty centimetres away from her body. I shrugged my shoulders. I couldn't feel anything. She said: 'How is it possible that you can't feel anything with me!'

'No,' I said, 'I can't feel anything at all. Absolutely nothing. Sorry I am so sceptical. Normally I am quite good at this. Forthcoming, I mean.'

She said it didn't matter.

After that exercise, the teacher advised us to try it at home with pets or plants.

'Are you now saying,' I asked her, 'that pets and plants also have an aura?'

She confirmed this. She said that even wood has an aura.

'So can you sense aura with furniture?' I asked pointedly.

'Only if the furniture is made of unvarnished wood. Not impregnated or something like that.'

'So may I,' I now asked with a piercing voice, 'may I ask you this? Have you personally experienced that? I mean, have you,' and I pointed an offensive forefinger at her, 'have you ever felt the aura of untreated wood?' The penultimate word I chopped up into little pieces, *un-treat-ed*. The last word I pronounced loudly and harshly: *w-o-O-DD*. I repeated my question: 'I would like to make it clear that I am now asking about your personal experience? Have you ever felt the aura of *un-treat-ed w-o-O-DD*?' I myself was impressed by the construction of my question.

The only answer she could give was that I was not obliged to believe her. 'Everybody has his own truth. Have you?'

I said there was no reason to stare at me.

There was silence. I allowed the silence to hang in the air, until that stupid Leen, in her shiny leather trousers, asked me in a whisper if it was true that I had not felt it. She turned her pelvis offensively towards me. The aura of her body touched me.

It is the age of blond, jeans and flat bare midriffs. As Antwerp's greatest writer Jean-Marie Berckmans has been taken into hospital, I pay him a visit. In the cafeteria we drink ice tea and Coke. A certain Kristien approaches, dressed in a brand-new red jacket, and underneath something with spaghetti decorations. She recently performed work by Jean-Marie, and now she is 'doing' Peter Verhelst's *Sprookjesbordeel* [Fairy-tale brothel].

'Do you work in that brothel? Tell us something about it, why don't you,' I ask.

'I'm an actress,' she says. She says nothing.

I persist. Still she says nothing.

When I leave, I pat Jean-Marie amicably on the shoulder, but my hand clings to him. It stays put, resting exhausted on his bony shoulder.

Hugo: 'That woman in *Het Sprookjesbordeel* came very close to me. Shockingly intimate, some people thought. I didn't. I wanted to go straight back and try a different version.'

Ben: 'They refuse up-front to talk and then they send you away. Like in the zoo, behind rails. They wear overalls, hardly what you'd call sexy. You have to choose cards. You are blindfolded so that you are not sure whose hands you are in. You lie on a waterbed. It's all there in the script.'

On massage: first comes the palpation, the examination of the damaged structure. (Isn't everybody's structure damaged?) The hand wanders but it seems to register: the solitude and lack of fulfilment are exposed. The hand wants to know who the body is and interrogates it in intrusive fashion. Very philosophical: speak to me, says the hand, let me feel this. The patient experiences an inquisitive tingling, and eventually feels thoroughly understood. Replace 'massage' and 'hand' in the above by 'text'.

Leuven, May 1998. Kamiel Vanhole and I are organizing a literary meeting (*Literaire Living*) with Peter Verhelst and Leon Gommers. The motto of these 'livings' is: the reputation afterwards is more important than the advance publicity, which in fact also applies to *Het Sprookjesbordeel*. We have a chat about the role of blood and organs in Peter Verhelst's texts, *and* in Leon Gommers' kitchen. Leon, who is both cook and writer, has made a strange cake with chicken livers and honey. Peter confesses the most abominable thing he has ever done, which was to bite in a consecrated wafer. He praises the beauty of cancer cells. He tells us how lovely the wild arum is: that stalk form on a velvet flower in which you can see everything. Then he tells us this: as a child he was lying on his bed, almost asleep, when he suddenly felt a hand coming from under the bed and feeling in his direction. It was his father, merrily lying under the bed.

Luk: 'You can't explain it, wow, boy. Like things you sometimes dream. You feel liquid on your lips, strawberry coulis. Smells. Was there music? I don't know any more. You hear how that woman eats a strawberry, like a zip fastener.'

Tine: 'They eat close to you. You can feel the hair, the hands, the breath. You can't see anything but you can hear Peter Verhelst's text. You melt.'
Guy: 'Four slim lasses, dressed in black. A girl who gives you her hand and hustles you upstairs. Candles, ambient music, impressive. You go and lie on a wooden bed, blindfolded. You are surprised by the impact of a whispered neo- or postromantic text. Over the top. After that even chatted briefly with those ladies. You find to your satisfaction that they liked it too. Told Peter Verhelst that he should sell the concept. As a chill-out sensation for clubbers and discos.'

Listen with your eyes closed and you find yourself in a world of gold-sprayed bodies. Famous chocolate makers. Hairs you can count. Arabesques on tulle. Someone is running the show. Diary lying open, winking. You become as soft as butter and flexible. Peter says: 'It is the glad news. It makes people happy. People arrive as stiff as a board and they leave like ballet dancers.'
It is about language but not the language that is printed in a series of letters. It is a language that is spread over the body, spurted almost. At a time when an improper look or touch is taboo, while the iconography of sex is all around, neutral physical contact suddenly becomes explosive. The body, yes the body. Even doctors scarcely touch their patients. Doctor Verhelst has a fascination for bodies, bodily fluids and bodily openings. Peter Verhelst told me that as a lad he read New Age books and was mesmerized. Not that he understood them (who does?), but that he found them unbelievably nourishing. Did he read ethnography? He knows the metier like an anthropologist: it is all to do with metamorphosis, liminality, transition. He designs a contemporary *rite de passage*: not Western because of its focus on the body and yet very Western in its logocentric character. The body is lovingly doused in language, while it is hardly touched. Visitors tremble with emotion and poignancy. Peter Verhelst realizes that the ritual is efficient if something happens in the body. The body, yes the body.

KOEN PEETERS

It was as a poet that Peter Verhelst made his debut in the early 1980s. His poetry soon attracted attention — the anthology *Obsidiaan* (1987) has won several awards. His novels (*Vloeibaar harnas* [Liquid armour], *Het Spierenalfabet* [The muscular alphabet], etc.) have also met with success. In the key year 2000 Verhelst was awarded (among other prizes) the Gouden Uil for his 'stories brothel' *Tongkat*. The author was praised for his craftsmanship and sense of composition, but above all for his 'sensual firework'.

In 1997 Peter Verhelst wrote his first play: *Maria Salomé. Baconstudie / Kahloterreur*, about five mythological figures, which Jan Ritsema staged at the Brussels Kaaitheater. In 1999 he made *Romeo en Julia. Studie van een verdrinkend lichaam* [Romeo and Juliet. Study of a drowning body] for Ivo Van Hove and the Zuidelijk Toneel. A year later choreographer Thierry Smits staged the sequel to *Romeo en Julia* at the Kaaitheater: *Red rubber balls. Studie van een hangend lichaam* [... Study of a hanging body].

Also in 2000 Peter Verhelst was appointed writer-in-residence with Het Toneelhuis. His *Aars! Anatomische studie van de Oresteia* [Arse! Anatomical study of the Oresteia] was directed by Luk Perceval. He translated Martin McDonagh's Leenane trilogy into Dutch for a coproduction between Het Toneelhuis and Zuidelijk Toneel Hollandia. And at the request of Het Toneelhuis he turned his fairy-tale novel *Zwellend fruit* [Swelling fruit] into a 'stories brothel' at the Villanella production De Nachten.

Peter Verhelst also received commissions from other houses and companies. With Blauw Vier he and Peter De Bie created *COUPe ROYALe / Vorst in eigen nat*, a 'trail' through rooms with eating, actors, music and video (as part of the Time Festival). BL!NDMAN made a production based on his collection of poems *Verhemelte* [Palate]. And for De Roovers, Prometheus Ensemble and Muziektheater Transparant he wrote a libretto based on *L'histoire du Soldat* [Stravinsky / Ramuz].

In 2001 Peter Verhelst started working closely with choreographer Wim Vandekeybus. Vandekeybus used *Zwellend fruit* as the basis for *Scratching the Inner Fields* [Ultima Vez production]. Ultima Vez again set to work with texts by Verhelst to produce *Blush* (2002) and *Sonic Boom* (2003).

Peter Verhelst played a central role in Bruges Cultural Capital of Europe 2002. For this event he wrote the poem 'Op een dag' [One day]. It provided inspiration for the whole project and now also adorns the backs of the seats of the Concertgebouw in Bruges. His Philoctetes adaptation for Crew (and coproducers) was entitled *Icarus Man-o-war*.

In 2002 Verhelst also created an adaptation of *Zwellend fruit* with Het Toneelhuis. His fairy-tale novel became *Het Sprookjesbordeel* [The fairy-tale brothel], in which individual visitors had stories whispered in their ear, soundscapes by Eavesdropper could be heard and the senses of touch, smell and taste were titillated. The stories from *Het Sprookjesbordeel* are to be found in the *Mondschilderingen* [Mouth paintings] collection. At De Nachten (2003 edition) Verhelst presented *Body Bag*, a try-out version of the sequel to *Het Sprookjesbordeel*. Two actors received about ten visitors in their 'antechamber' and gloomy stories were dished up.   CVP

PETER DE BIE / LAIKA

PARADISE IS IN A CELERIAC
ON BEING INVITED TO PETER DE BIE & LAIKA

1.

You don't just go and see the productions — I prefer to call them 'happenings' — of Peter De Bie; it is more a question of making your way in, in both the literal and figurative sense. It begins with the location. Sometimes you make your way through different rooms (*COUPe ROYALe*). Or you are 'obliged' by the scenography to go and lie on your back, to see all kinds of soft erotic tableaux vivants pass over your head (*Undeuxdouce*). Or you take your place at a carefully laid table in a rotating dinner tent, the location of De Bie's first contribution to the theatre circuit, *Peep & Eat*. A kitchen revolves on its axis and the guests take their seats in small compartments round that kitchen. There are hatches at different heights in the kitchen walls through which you catch a glimpse of the diligent work going on behind the stove, you are passed plates by charming waiters, or you witness short, often exuberant acts. And the kitchen just keeps on turning.

My best and main memory of *Peep & Eat* is indeed the 'peeping': you sit at a table with complete and utter strangers and by the end of the evening you have the feeling that you part company more or less as friends, or at least as good acquaintances. You have, after all, been peeking at each other's plates. Not that you necessarily want to see each other again the next day: what happens belongs to the time-span of the actual performance; in other words, intense but brief. Admittedly, the fruity wines and the sultry evening air of Lisbon where I saw the show, helped. But therein lies part of the secret, I think: nothing is too artificial, conjured up only by its makers; it is rather the sort of theatre that, in a manner of speaking, can take you unawares, any time, any place. 'Those for whom food's already-artfulness is an opportunity, look to the arts of everyday life for a resource that they work on right where it is, taking the life world itself as their site of operation, or they divert it into the art world, or make the two converge. Recognizing what is already artful in life, they may curate it or they may collaborate with ordinary people.... It takes its cue from the already total performance of the life world,' as Barbara Kirschenblatt-Gimblett wrote in 'Playing to the Senses / Food as a Performance Medium'.

Peep & Eat is a performance that succeeds in creating possible interaction during the dining process and kneading a moment of collectivity into a ritual of solidarity. De Bie makes the guests, rather than the centrally located kitchen, the centre of the action and therein lies the clever paradox. The spontaneous, unexpected interaction of the table companions works perfectly alongside the more orchestrated performance of the actors. Meanwhile, you see the almost dancing hands of the cooks who work themselves to the bone to ensure everything is ready on time, whilst being watched and being happy to be watched. They sweat with a will. As well as all kinds of other tantalizing aromas, you almost believe you can smell their sweat. Reality and fantasy merge. The juices flow.

2.

'Well,' said Pooh, 'what I like best,' and then he had to stop and think. Because although Eating Honey was a very good thing to do, there was a moment just before you began to eat it which was better than when you were, but he didn't know what it was called.
—Richard Milne

It is tempting and only natural to describe De Bie's happenings from the standpoint of their culinary qualities. That is a little pitfall he dug for himself, because it happens not every day of course that you are served a delicious supper as part of a cultural event. Yet he certainly does not regard the gastronomic aspect as the core of his artistic activity. He started to make culinary productions to satisfy an ambition to create an alternative sort of entertainment. The main motive has always been direct contact with the public in a way that differs from the often more cerebral norm in the theatre of textual and/or visual language. (The same applies for that matter to most of Laika's productions, of which De Bie is a driving force.)

The fact that food is cooked, and eaten too, is just one of many ways of sparking sensory communication, which does not neglect the senses of taste and smell. Interestingly, as the master of ceremonies, or rather, as the catalyst, De Bie never rants and raves about food; in fact, the actual kitchen activity is a familiar occurrence and not difficult to summarize: someone prepares something for his guests and allows them to witness the process in celebratory fashion. No deliberate bungling or throwing in the name of (contrived) theatricality. There are, however, a couple of 'disturbing' or perplexing elements, like the intense colour of some dishes, the rather unusual receptacles such as kidney dishes and fish bowls, sauce that flows out of hypodermic syringes and a dark-red elderberry aperitif served in a plastic 'rubber glove' — all slightly kinky. Familiar ingredients are given possible new meanings, call up associations that couple enjoyment with the notion of transience, with the greed *and* vulnerability of our mechanism, but most of all these subtle interventions resemble a boyish prank, the stuff of a childlike imagination. You are reminded of the experiments you used to carry out in the chemistry lab, experiments with form and colour, which are sometimes echoed in language (Verhelst in *COUPe ROYALe*) or music (Vermeersch in *Patatboem*). And which, above all, are open to interpretation, your own interpretation. Which brings us back to that freedom when you make your way into De Bie's world: there is plenty to experience, but nothing is imposed. You put together your own menu.

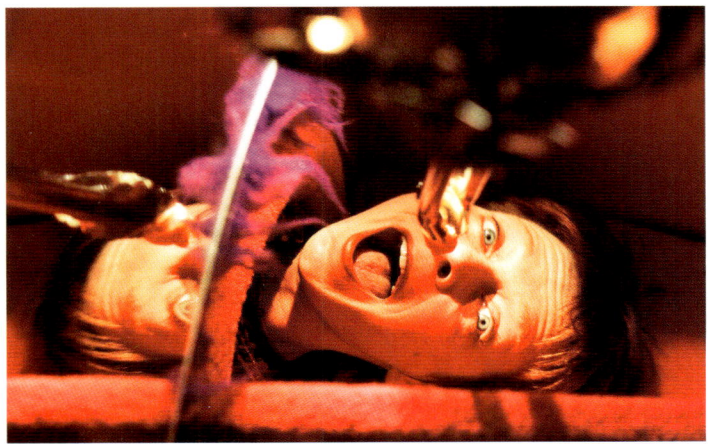

3.

I am amazed at the proliferation of commercial and media-led culinary information currently on the market: an inexhaustible supply of *Naked Chef* books and television shows, bulky gastronomic supplements accompanying newspapers and magazines, politicians who compile their own cookery books (usually with the obligatory over-aesthetized photographs). Where does such hype come from? You can only hope that people are keen to become more aware of their gastronomic culture and that they are beginning to deal with food and drink more creatively and more attentively. But if I am pessimistic, it is because I see it as the umpteenth (temporary) form of escapism, a pleasant way for the affluent to indulge themselves inventively on what nature has provided, but also as a springboard to social distinction.

Is Peter De Bie part of such a trend, or is he offering an alternative? Probably both. What is certain is that he manages to create a world that is all his own, recognizable and consumable certainly, but nevertheless set in a specific context and flavoured in such a way that our senses are not only catered for, but also sharpened and confused. I sincerely hope he doesn't bring out a cookery book, for he would be doing himself an injustice.

4.

Finally: I can picture the impressive stage set of the kitchen concert *Patatboem*, the floor and the costumes of the musicians and cooks, drenched in bright red. And all around the pots and pans, cutlery, washing-up bowl and instruments in shiny, sparkling metal.

'Heaven is a place, where nothing ever happens', an ironic song by David Byrne, is the closing song in *Patatboem*. The singer takes up her position at the washing-up bowl and picks up a celeriac (which contains a microphone). A saw, used just moments earlier to swiftly cut up the vegetables, provides the supporting, teasing sounds. The unbridled energy of cooks and musicians simmers on, in and above the pots and pans. Now there is that epilogue silence — 'nothing ever happens'. Two hundred spectators have seen their evening meal prepared under the on-and-off anarchic and dissonant and cradling sounds of Vermeersch and his band. What generosity! Paradise is in a celeriac.

PATRICK JORDENS

PETER DE BIE / LAIKA

Peter De Bie is a culinary artist: he makes theatre with tasty and colourful ingredients. By busying himself with food on the stage, he is looking first and foremost to address the senses in such a way that life is seen in an unexpected light. Furthermore, with this form of theatre he wants to encourage greater audience participation and thus provide a more intense experience.

Peter De Bie (1967) studied socio-cultural work in Ghent. Following a training course and later as a conscientious objector, he started to work in the documentation department at the Flemish Theatre Institute. He went on to become business manager of the Antwerp youth theatre company Blauw Vier. In the meantime he qualified as a chef and did the catering for theatre companies. He still does.

As well as being Blauw Vier's business manager, De Bie also became the driving force behind a series of productions in which gastronomy was coupled with theatre. De Bie believes that eating can lift a production onto a higher plane. In 1998 he made *PEEP & EAT*, an extraordinary eating event in which the kitchen becomes theatre and vice versa. The stage is a restaurant in which the waiters do not move, but on which a whole kitchen revolves on its axis. The audience sits in different compartments and can only occasionally take a peep to see for itself how De Bie prepares a gastronomic, four-course tour de force. The theatrical and visual surprises in this kitchen are a test for the senses. For his dishes De Bie experiments with colour combinations and surprising receptacles. *COUPe ROYALe* followed in 2000. Made in cooperation with writer Peter Verhelst, the cooks and the actors serve the public an eccentric banquet.

In 2001 Blauw Vier changed its name to Laika. De Bie is a core member of the artistic team. This company, which regards the world as a place of discovery, provided him with the scope he needed to develop his sensory theatre projects. The installation *Undeux-douce* was mounted in 2001 as part of Le Petit Bazar Erotik, a joint venture of ten international companies. *Laika Tafelt* [Laika dines] also appeared in 2001, a cookery book, which enables the reader to try out some of De Bie's unusual recipes at home.

In 2002 *Patatboem* was performed at the Centro Cultural de Belém in Lisbon as part of *Percursos*. Spread over several years, this project intends not only to show productions but also to intervene in the local cultural scene. The idea is that after three seasons, in 2004–05, this interaction will result in a production rooted in the Portuguese culture.   YB

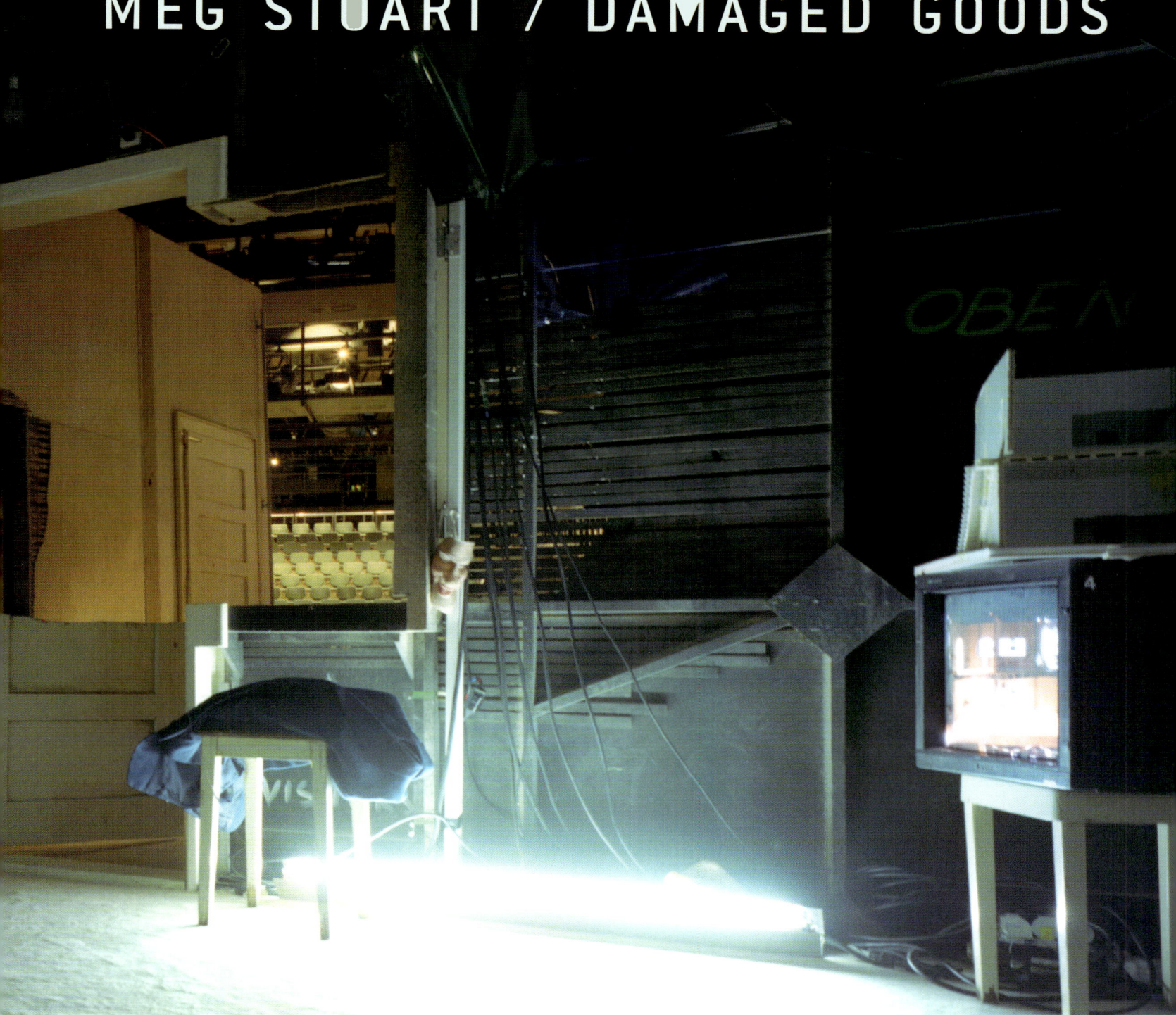

FRAGMENTS OF AN UNSEEN HOUSE

ON 'VISITORS ONLY' BY MEG STUART / DAMAGED GOODS

'In another moment Alice was through the glass, and had jumped lightly down into the Looking-glass room. The very first thing she did was to look whether there was a fire in the fireplace, and she was quite pleased to find that there was a real one, blazing away as brightly as the one she had left behind.'
—Lewis Carroll, *Through the Looking-Glass*, 1872

A knock at the door; the hostess admits a visitor. He stoops to get through the door because he is too tall, the door too low. Trying to enter the room next to it with five men doesn't work either, for this time the door is too narrow. On the first floor a man walks through the door and drops through a hole in the floor, despite repeated warnings. Elsewhere a woman puts the door firmly on the catch to keep unsavoury folk out. And when a girl starts running round in wild circles, sure enough a door falls down, right on her forehead, and she is taken away bleeding. However crazy the performance may be, at least the house looks a paragon of banality and normality, and reality happens neatly between four walls. At the same time a gap is constantly opening up between house and inhabitant, between perception and action. Is this a classic farce?

The house acquired a history of its own during the creation process. In the scenery workshop, the finishing touches are being put to the top floor; they're already clearing up. 'This is real Swiss design, not a fake. You can live in it. Actually they should have brought a container, put the whole house in it, and then let it out. This is not made for a single theatre production.' The 'fake version' is in the studio: a house with eight rooms spread over two floors, made of wooden strip frames spanned by coarse cotton, everything life size. So does fake exist in gradations? This may be fake scenery, but surely the real one is no less fake? What is more or less fake? Imitation scenery of an imitation house? Imitation which shows it is fake? The actual scenery is, it is true, shamelessly illusionistic, but apart from the image, the durability of the structure is a match for a real house. Why do we so readily see a house which happens to be built in the theatre as fake? And is there really an original of it, or at the end of the day is that constructed in our head?

House Rules
Art. 1. In the interests of order and security in the house, it is deemed necessary to monitor events with the aid of cameras. The pictures will be kept for no longer than 24 hours, with the exception of pictures that record an incident.
Art. 2. Physical violence, threats, intimidation and sexual harassment will not be tolerated.
Art. 9. Persons who seem confused and those who are clearly under the influence, as well as persons who cannot give any valid reason for being in the house, will not in principle be admitted.
Art. 13. Persons who refuse to allow themselves, their clothes or their luggage to be checked, will not be allowed into the house.
Art. 18. If you wish to know more about the house rules, or if you have any questions about them, kindly contact the caretaker.

'The house is so huge, you'll have to deal with it!' Monumental? It depends on how you look at it. As they had to be able to get it into the theatre, all in all the size of the house has been kept within certain limits: 13 m wide, 12 m deep and 6.8 m high, including an extra platform measuring 33 cm. The metal structure and the wooden joists supporting the upper floor, however, make the construction very heavy. In order to support the total weight of 10 tons, the whole structure is connected to a central pillar under the stage, so that the weight comes to 500 kg per square metre. An alternative and less expensive construction method spreads the weight over several points of support. It takes two stage managers, nine theatre technicians and six stage hands two days to construct it; it takes a day to disassemble it. No fewer than two trucks with a 15 m trailer and an extra 8 m lorry are involved in moving the hazardous load. What is the specific gravity of images?

Among the numerous photographs on the wall of the studio is a whole series by the American artist Gordon Matta-Clark, who in the 1970s let fly at derelict houses with a saw, making large openings in them. Gaping holes, spyholes, whole sections removed, strange perspectives which turn a house inside out. The house on the set now seems to be a collection of quotes, the gaping rectangular holes a sort of ready-made. A derelict house now devoid of a private space, a derelict house whose stories, memories and traumas leak out through the holes. Wherever it is, it is draughty.

Windows are too low, doors have been cut in half, the floor is full of holes, the path of our observation is uneven, expectations are scuppered. Is this really still a house? Literature about the working of the brain teaches us that the concept of 'house' must be stored somewhere in the brain as a set of encoded neural connections. Perception is also trained by an accumulation of experience, whereby surplus information is systematically forgotten and habits are established that reduce the need to recall a precise observation. A radically different arrangement of reality, like a cut-up house, nevertheless requires creativity and neurochemical activity to bring about new connections. For the record: memory, false memory, hallucination and fantasy have a similar structure in the brain, only the context in which they appear decides their status. And then language or images are not *per se* an adequate translation of that relationship. What should we think of excessive brain activity, a sort of immersion in one's own realm of ideas which has become so full that the hierarchy of all the stored memories blurs, irrespective of their origin? Is anyone still watching?

A part of the performance is always unseen, even if only because the walls of the house partially obscure the spectator's view. Does not our domesticating gaze also tear reality to threads? In search of an overview and insight we run after our own fictions and control mechanisms. In this mental theatre not only is reality veiled, but with every transformation the unseen performances multiply, for want of witnesses. It is dark in the auditorium.

JEROEN PEETERS

MEG STUART / DAMAGED GOODS

After training as a dancer at New York University and taking additional classes in release technique and contact improvisation at Movement Research, Meg Stuart (New Orleans, 1965) was a dancer and assistant choreographer with the Randy Warshaw Dance Company from 1986 to 1992.

At the invitation of Klapstuk 91, she made her first full-length production *Disfigure Study*. It was a powerful start to an impressive series of productions the choreographer made with her company Damaged Goods, which has been based in Brussels since 1994: *No Longer Readymade* (1993); *No One is Watching* (1995); *Insert Skin #1 — They Live in Our Breath* (1996) with visual artist Lawrence Malstaf; *Splayed Mind Out* (1997) with video artist Gary Hill; *appetite* (1998) with visual artist Ann Hamilton; and *ALIBI* (2001) and *Visitors Only* (2003), both in cooperation with scenographer Anna Viebrock, video artist Chris Kondek and composer Paul Lemp. She also created *Swallow My Yellow Smile* (1994), commissioned by the ballet company of the Deutsche Oper Berlin and, in association with graphic designer Bruce Mau, *Remote* (1997) for Mikhail Baryshnikov's White Oak Dance Project.

A recurrent feature in the work of Meg Stuart and Damaged Goods is the search for new forms of cooperation, presentation contexts and the 'crossbreeding' of theatre, architecture and visual art, heralded in the dance installation for the exhibition *This is the Show and the Show is Many Things* by curator Bart De Baere at the Museum van Hedendaagse Kunst [Museum of contemporary art, now SMAK] in Ghent (1994).

Together with Christine De Smedt and David Hernandez, from 1996 to 1999 Meg Stuart was also involved in *Crash Landing*, an improvisation project for dancers, musicians, video and sound artists and designers. *Crash Landing* ran into five editions: Leuven, Vienna, Paris, Lisbon and Moscow.

Between March 2000 and March 2001 Meg Stuart and Damaged Goods created *Highway 101*, in close cooperation with theatre director Stefan Pucher and video artist Jorge Leon. In conjunction with a partly varying artistic team, movement, sound and video material was developed with a view to a number of specifically chosen places. *Highway 101* thus gradually evolved into a continuous self-commemorative and redefining project, focusing on memory, the relationship with the audience and the use of space. In March 2000 Meg Stuart and Damaged Goods presented a first series of showings of *Highway 101* at the Kaaitheater studios in Brussels. Then it was the turn of Vienna (Emballagenhallen), Paris (Centre Georges Pompidou), Brussels again (La Raffinerie du Plan K), Rotterdam (TENT.) and Zurich (Schiffbau). The installation *sand table* and the solos *soft wear, private room* and *I'm all yours* were originally part of *Highway 101*, but went on to lead a life of their own and since 2001 have often been presented in a programme shared with writer, director and performer Tim Etchells (Forced Entertainment).

From 1997 Meg Stuart / Damaged Goods was one of the artists-in-residence at the Kaaitheater in Brussels. In 2001 the company took up residence at the Schauspielhaus Zurich, which is under the artistic direction of Stefanie Carp, Christoph Marthaler and Anna Viebrock. Since the 2002–03 season Meg Stuart and Damaged Goods have also been attached to the Volksbühne am Rosa-Luxemburg-Platz in Berlin.   MU

HOWEVER DIVERSE OUR BASIC PRINCIPLES MAY HAVE BEEN,

SINCE THE FOUNDATION OF DE FILMFABRIEK WE HAVE IN FACT

EVOLVED MORE AND MORE EMPHATICALLY IN
THE DIRECTION OF THE THEATRE. NOW WE

ALSO DARE TO ADVERTISE THAT AND INITIATE PROJECTS OURSELVES.

WITH OUR NEW NON-PROFIT HET SOORTELIJK GEWICHT,
WE ARE AIMING MORE SPECIFICALLY AT THAT NO MAN'S
LAND BETWEEN FILM, MEDIA ART AND THEATRE.

IMAGINE: WE MAKE A VIDEO INSTALLATION, BUT THEN ON A TWELVE-

METRE STAGE AND WITH A THOUSAND PEOPLE IN THE AUDITORIUM. ONLY THEN

DOES IT BECOME REALLY INTERESTING, ONLY THEN ARE THE RELATIONSHIPS

TOTALLY DIFFERENT, ONLY THEN CAN YOU THINK ENTIRELY FROM THE VIEWPOINT OF
MEDIA ART. THINGS LIKE THAT HAVE AN IMMEDIATE IMPACT ON THE

THOUGH WE CALL OURSELVES DE FILMFABRIEK [FILM FACTORY], UNTIL NOW WE HAVEN'T DONE ANYTHING ON FILM REALLY. BUT THE NAME VIDEO FACTORY WOULD CERTAINLY HAVE ATTRACTED TOO MANY PEOPLE WITH BROKEN RECORDERS HOPING FOR A FAST REPAIR SERVICE.

GUY CASSIERS ALWAYS INSISTS THAT HE WORKS WITH US **BECAUSE WE NEVER DO WHAT HE ASKS OR SAYS.** AND HE'S RIGHT, TOO! OTHERWISE HE MIGHT JUST AS WELL ASK A TECHNICAL BUREAU TO EXECUTE HIS OWN IDEAS.

UNFORTUNATELY, ALL TOO OFTEN WE ARE STILL THE **CAMOUFLAGED SUPPLIERS** OF **MEDIA ART FOR THEATRE.** EVEN THE ULTIMATE IN-CROWD, THEATRE PEOPLE AS MUCH AS PRESS AND DECISION-MAKERS, HAVE SCARCELY ANY INTEREST IN WHO MAKES WHICH CONTRIBUTION TO SUCH A **HYBRID PRODUCTION.**

WE LIKE TO UNDERMINE THE IDEA THAT EVERYTHING HAPPENS DIRECTLY ON STAGE; WE THREATEN TO DEPRIVE THE AUDIENCE OF **THE TYPICAL 'LIVE'** FEELING AND IN SO DOING INDEED SHARPEN THAT FEELING. MORE THAN THE CAMERA FRAME OR THE FILM SCREEN OR A COMPUTER MONITOR **THE STAGE** IS AND WILL CONTINUE TO BE OUR STARTING POINT AND OUR DESTINATION – **OUR FRAME OF REFERENCE.**

OUR RADICAL MENTALITY HAS EVERYTHING TO DO WITH OUR STATUS AS SUPPLY COMPANY; IF WE DON'T GET UP ON OUR HIGH HORSE, NOTHING INTERESTING EVER RESULTS, BECAUSE NO DIRECTOR IS ITCHING TO COMMIT MOST OF HIS BUDGET TO NEW MEDIA.

MANY THEATRES TRY TO DO IT THEMSELVES AND THEN A MONTH BEFORE THE PREMIÈRE THEY PHONE US WITH A WHOLE HOST OF TECHNICAL QUESTIONS. THEN WE EITHER LAUNCH A COUP OR DECLINE THE OFFER. THEY MUST BE PREPARED TO OVERHAUL THE ENTIRE PRODUCTION.

THE NORMAL PROCEDURE FOR A THEATRE PRODUCTION IS THAT A LIGHTING TECHNICIAN, A SET BUILDER AND A VIDEO ARTIST ARE SOUGHT. YES, EVEN THE LATTER HAS BECOME MORE OR LESS STANDARD BY NOW. BUT IF IT'S ONLY A MATTER OF PLAYING THE OBLIGATO VIDEO PART, WE REFUSE THE INVITATION SYSTEMATICALLY. THAT IS JUST OUR WAY OF DOING THINGS. THE SEPARATION OF TASKS MAKES IT IMPOSSIBLE FROM THE OUTSET TO INTEGRATE INTERESTING MEDIA ART INTO A PROJECT. WE SEE MULTIMEDIA ART NOT AS THE SIMPLE SUM OF SEPARATE PARTS, BUT AS AN INTEGRATION PROCESS.

TOO MANY THEATRE PRODUCTIONS STILL MAKE DO WITH A SCREEN AT THE BACK OF THE STAGE, SHOWING IMAGES LIKE WALLPAPER, OR ARTISTIC CLOSE-UPS OF THE ACTORS, LIKE AT A POP CONCERT. RATHER THAN THE PURELY ILLUSTRATIVE AND DECORATIVE APPROACH, WE LIKE TO APPLY A VISUAL LANGUAGE THAT ACTUALLY STARTS FROM THE SCRIPT AND SOMETIMES CONSISTS LARGELY OF SCRIPT.

WHY DO ALL THOSE DOPEY ACTORS HAVE TO LEARN ALL THOSE SCRIPTS BY HEART, WHEN ALL YOU NEED TO DO IS PUT A **TELEPROMPTER ON THE STAGE?** AND, IN CASE YOU DO PUT ONE THERE, WHY SHOULD THE SCRIPT BE THE SAME EVERY EVENING?

MECHANISTIC DEVICES CAN IN OUR VIEW GIVE A MUCH

CLEARER AND MORE HONEST PICTURE OF EMOTION THAN WHAT YOU GET WHEN YOU START FROM A PSYCHOLOGICAL INTERPRETATION. **LIKE MARTIANS,** WE TRY TO **EXAMINE THE EMOTIONAL MAN,** RATHER THAN CHEAPLY PILE ON FAMILIAR EMOTIONS.

WE ALWAYS TRY **TO CREATE SOMETHING THAT MAKES US SUPERFLUOUS.**

AN AUTOMATON TO BY-PASS HUMAN AUTOMATISMS. BETTER TO GENERATE SOMETHING SPONTANEOUS THAN TO DIRECT

EVERYTHING WILL BE ALRIGHT, THE WAY OF THE WEED, THE CUTTING: THOSE ARE **NO LONGER CHARACTERS,** BUT PEOPLE WHO HAPPEN TO FIND THEMSELVES IN A STRUCTURE, WHO HAVE LITERALLY BEEN DROPPED INTO A SCENARIO. AND, WHAT'S MORE, SOMETIMES **THEY ARE AWARE OF IT, TOO.**

FILMS ARE MADE TO GENERATE ABSENCE, TO MAKE THE PUBLIC FEEL **SAFE** AND TO GIVE IT THE IDEA THAT IT CAN NEVER BE TAKEN BY SURPRISE. THIS IS ENTIRELY AT ODDS WITH WHAT THEATRE MEANS TO US. THERE IS A NEED FOR **NEW VIEWING ATTITUDES,** NEW WAYS OF READING A PRODUCTION. THE PUBLIC IS NOT EXACTLY OUR FIRST CONCERN. WE CONCENTRATE ON THE **INTERACTION WITH THE ACTOR OR PERFORMER** TO BEGIN WITH, AND WHETHER THE AUDIENCE CATCHES ON OR NOT, WE'LL FIND OUT SOON ENOUGH.

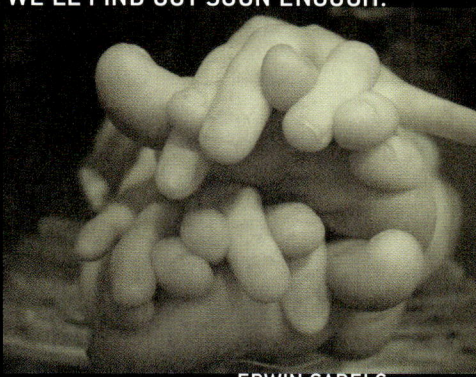

EDWIN CARELS

D E F I L M F A B R I E K

De Filmfabriek [The Film Factory] is an independent production house that seeks out the place where film, digital media and theatre meet. De Filmfabriek sees itself as an artists' collective or as a think-tank for cultural projects rather than as a commercial company. The collective currently consists of Peter Missotten (video artist), Bram Smeyers (director and graphic artist), Kurt d'Haeseleer (video artist) and Wies Hermans (graphics and interactive programming). They mount their own productions while also developing the concepts and productions of others. De Filmfabriek works with (among others) William Forsythe, Guy Cassiers, Wim Vandekeybus, Ictus, Needcompany and Laika.

Nostalgia for the soundness and the traditional methods of the theatre world was an important motive for Peter Missotten when setting up the company in 1993. The very first Filmfabriek project was *The Mind Machine of Dr. Forsythe* (An-Marie Lambrechts, Anne Quirynen and Peter Missotten, 1993), a video installation with nine dancers from Ballett Frankfurt, six sheets of glass and as many cranes. De Filmfabriek made the promotional clips for Forsythe's choreography *Eidos/Telos* (1996). Several dancers from Forsythe's company took part in *The Way of the Weed* (1997), De Filmfabriek's first (digital) long-playing film.

Other long-playing films they have worked on include *The Cutting* (2000), a Filmfabriek project based on a scenario/theatre script by Paul Pourveur, and *Goldfish Game* (2001) in cooperation with Needcompany.

The cooperation with director Guy Cassiers is a constant in De Filmfabriek's activities. Since Cassiers has been director of the ro theater (Rotterdam), De Filmfabriek has taken full charge of the theatre's house style, including flyers, posters, the website and a CD-ROM with eight interpretations of eight plays. They won the TheaterAffichePrijs 2003, a Dutch award for the best poster design for theatre. Furthermore, they also designed the scenery for Cassiers' *Lava Lounge* (2002) and *The Woman who Walked into Doors* (2001), a ro theater and Het muziek Lod coproduction.

A recent Filmfabriek project is *S*CKMYP*, a digital lounge film by Kurt d'Haeseleer to a text by Peter Verhelst and with music by Köhn. *Bonte Was* [Coloured laundry], an interactive language course in Dutch for non-native people with just a basic schooling, was developed at the request of the Flemish Government.

There was a two-day retrospective in de Schaarbeek Halles (Brussels) to mark the European festival Temps d'Images in August 2003. And at the end of that year the première took place in Rotterdam of *De dood van een prinsje* [The death of a little prince], a video performance by Peter Missotten based on a text by Maurice Maeterlinck (in cooperation with the Toneelacademie, Maastricht). JJ

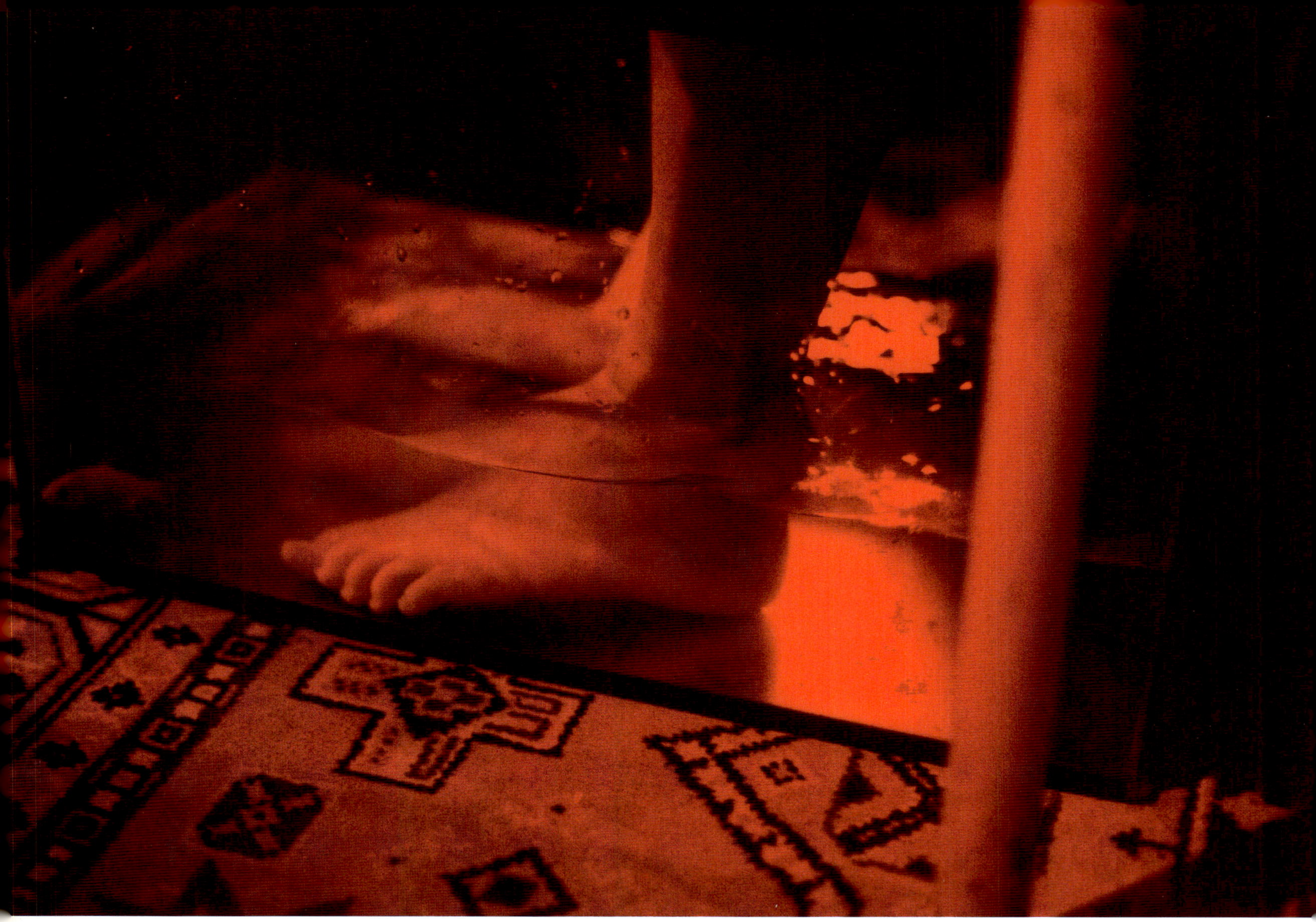

DÉJEUNER SUR L'HERBE

We have two kinds of cheese, four different sorts of bread, aubergine caviar, smoked salmon, dried apricots, artichoke hearts, strawberries, chocolate, tomatoes, Aquarius water, a can of Coke, a can of vanilla Coke, twenty three-ply napkins and a potato peeler. We sit at one of the 'Ponds of the Drowned Children' (Etangs dits des Enfants Noyés) in the Forêt de Soignes in Brussels. We keep our clothes on, it is Ascension Day, the weather is wonderful and we laugh at the name of the ponds. It's all a question of translation. The Flemish miller Verdoncken wanted to divide his land among his five children. The Frenchman who had to record this associated the man's last name with the word verdronken – French: noyé, i.e. 'drowned' – hence the name of the ponds. So no drama involving children. No horror in that forest. Only the idea of it. It says much about the phenomenon of fear, and about fairytales – two elements in Inne Goris' installation Zeven [Seven], in which Goris divests fairytales, and dissects the fear, the isolation and the solitude that proliferate in fairytales.

Inne Goris likes the Ponds. She often goes there, she wants to map out a theatre trail there one day and when she was making Zeven she went there to find out just how afraid you can be in a wood. In the installation there is a little wooden box that treats the public to a video of fast-moving images. Trees, bushes, shadows, a tattered piece of red cloth – a reference to the fairytale Red Riding Hood. 'I imagined that everything I saw had a meaning. A broken twig, wind in the branches, undergrowth in the shape of a cross. It worked.'

As well as Red Riding Hood, Inne Goris plucked material from Cinderella, The Little Mermaid, Sleeping Beauty and Little Red Shoes, all stories she had been storing up for a long time when working with young children at the BRONKS youth theatre in Brussels. As a source of inspiration for productions. As a bedtime picture book. Above all, she wanted to make a production without actors, because she was actually a bit fed-up with them. So she started looking for a writer who could draw atmospheres from the original stories and for a designer knowledgeable in the same field. Peter Verhelst wrote; Michiel van

Cauwelaert built. Frames provided Goris with her starting point. A canvas on which she would map out Zeven. Dominant. So as to create freedom. For herself. For the public.

'I want to build up my productions as associatively as possible. Because that's what I like myself. I remember, for example, Wim Vandekeybus' What the Body Does Not Remember, productions by The Wooster Group and Needcompany's Ça va. They are pretty much the first productions to have struck home. The Wooster Group's production was in fact an adaptation of Chekhov's Three Sisters, a work I took in hand in the autumn of 2003.'

I ask why those productions made such an impression. She talks about Ça va. That she remembers above all the image of a man standing in the middle of a stage and a woman who walks round him. Then the woman throws herself into his arms, the man lets her drop to the ground, the woman walks away. The scene is repeated. 'Setting things in motion, tells you more than just saying a script. Or so I thought at the time.'

In Zeven Inne Goris sets silence in motion. The silence that cries out between the lines of the fairytales of Andersen, Perrault and the Grimm Brothers. It is the silence that hides among the trees, the silence of solitude, the silence of beauty or of insanity. Seven different rooms provide seven different perspectives. Video images, a bare white space, a pompous tent with a stretched ball gown, a bed with pine needles on the sides and a soft voice whispering in the pillows. And in between little details. For example, you suddenly find yourself standing in front of a telescope that provides a view of a dwarf waving. Somewhere hidden in the top of the hall where the installation stands. 'Zeven is an offer,' she herself says. 'The spectator can tell his own story.' You are given ingredients. But you do the cooking yourself. I remember seeing notebooks lying around in the installation in which you could jot down your thoughts. I remember writing: 'And, Inne? Have the lambs stopped bleating?' I remember hoping she would appreciate this reference to The Silence of the Lambs. I remember a

hospital bed with a rosy apple on the bedside table. I remember archetypes of spectres which fed fairy stories and the clinical way these words were presented. In text. In image. In detail. I remember the absence of boys' figures in the installation. And I remember the sensuality that it aroused.

Inne Goris invariably rejects fairy stories in which boys play the lead role. At the same time she also cuts out the happy endings. So there is no release whereby fear is allowed to leave the building and life to become comprehensible. By cutting in this way, Goris inserts a loop which links content and spectator. The key word is the solitude in which Goris chisels her female characters. Snow White sits between seven strange little men who do not know her at all. Sleeping Beauty lies in an abandoned, overgrown palace courtyard. The Little Mermaid has lost her tongue. 'If they want to solve it, they have to do it themselves,' says Goris. She cuts herself when buttering a nut bread roll. Her finger in her mouth, she flicks through the files she lugs from one rehearsal to another. 'It is work I have to do, to be able to stand aside prepared,' she explains.

She reads out a quote to me by Leyla Berg, a Jewish writer: 'I read The Little Match Girl and Little Red Shoes over and over again. How unpleasant it is to be a girl.' She laughs. 'Why do boys never have to lay the table?' she goes on to ask. And again she quotes, this time from *Le sabotage amoureux* by Amélie Nothomb. 'There are three sorts of people. Girls, women and idiots.' She then tells me that her mother always said that it is not nice to be a woman and that men are bastards. And that when preparing *Zeven*, she thought: 'Damn it! Fairytales about men are not exciting. And in all the other fairy stories they come and save the women. The question is whether that is so much more exciting?'

We fall silent. For the first time in my life I drink CocaCola Vanilla, and fail to see the attraction. She says that after *Zeven* she can feel breathing down her neck people awaiting more of the same. She says she doesn't want to continue down that path. She doesn't want to stay with a format at all costs, just because it happens to be good. That with *Zeven* she thinks she conjured up a world that is part of a trend we are beginning to see in the performing arts. That for that reason *Zeven* deserves to be revived. But that she has her doubts if she should continue down that road. She says she is hatching a new idea for an installation. Inspired by *Out of the Dust*, a book by Karen Hesse, it is set against the background of the Great Depression in the United States. But that she will probably choose for the girl again. That girl is taught to play the piano by her mother. Later on, the daughter accidentally sets fire to the mother, and as a result she is foisted off onto the father. 'The book begins like this,' Goris quotes: 'My father wanted a boy. Instead he got a long-legged girl.' I detect a pattern and ask her if her productions include much of her own life. And silence falls again. 'It is very strange,' she then says. 'I never think about it in rehearsals. But if I line it all up, I am usually shocked. It is indeed always about me.'

We look through the rehearsal book again. I note with interest that it contains almost exclusively photographs or illustrations of paintings of women. Cindy Sherman, Louise Bourgeois, Paula Rego and Marlene Dumas. I say that there is a great deal of explicit biography in the work of those women. Inne says she knows that, but that she herself is still too afraid to communicate her life so directly. That perhaps the embarrassment is too great. That she may perhaps do so one day. I say that that might well be a weight off her shoulders, and that it might also give her considerable artistic strength. And I think of *Déjeuner sur l'herbe*, Manet's painting that confronted the man in the street with the fact that nakedness in a painting is not necessarily only allegorical in character, but also amazingly powerful and real.

I ask her what else she is going to do. She says: 'Start up projects with the new non-profit Zeven. Because that is precisely what I do. "Zeven", you see, doesn't just mean "Seven" [in Dutch], it is a verb.'

ROEL VERNIERS

INNE GORIS

After reading applied social and cultural studies, Inne Goris trained as a drama teacher and director at the Maastricht Toneelacademie. At the same time she worked for BRONKS, the children's and youth theatre in Brussels. She led educational and theatre workshops based on improvisation and montage, activities in which under fives and older children take centre stage.

Inne Goris' journey took her from teacher to maker. Several initiatives made a lasting impression, not least a project she set up in 1996 together with visual artist John Körmeling and 77 infants. An exhibition at the Museum voor Hedendaagse Kunst in Antwerp (MUHKA) showed the results of these months of work.

Meanwhile, Goris continued her investigations: theatre with and for children, projects in which drama lessons are the engine for research into different subjects: language stimulation in the context of bilingual Brussels, the importance of the body if you have no words, how bookish language works on stage and how you can bring prints to life.

Niet in staat tot slechte dingen? [Incapable of bad things?], her thesis project in 1997, is a stylized collage of the cruelty to which children subject one another. Not reality theatre, but a streamlined and form-conscious project with ingeniously devised patterns of movement, snippets of text and rhythmical music, in which the border between 'perpetrator' and 'victim' becomes blurred. Inne Goris does not aestheticize violence, neither does she try to make it look 'real'.

After seven years she left her familiar haunts in search of a more solid artistic basis for her ideas. She did not really succeed until she showed *Zeven* at the BRONKS Festival in 2001. At the same time, she worked on several projects with choreographer Wim Vandekeybus, acting as director's assistant and dramaturge of *Scratching the Inner Fields* with his company Ultima Vez.

Zeven [Seven] was produced by BRONKS. It is a cross between an exhibition, a show and an interactive sensory walk, which leans towards the darker side of the Cinderellas and the Sleeping Beauties of this world. Seven rooms evoke seven fairy tales, all named after girls, but the question is whether these girls really play the lead role. *Zeven* is poignant images, snippets of text, poetry alongside repetitive phrases, film and music, narrow rooms, and so on. It couldn't be further removed from Walt Disney. LA

ART BASICS FOR CHILDREN

I have always had some difficulty with children theatre, by which I mean theatre for children, made by adults. (I have often thought that the main thing children learn in the theatre is to applaud.) And even if I have produced a number of scripts intended to be put on for children, there has always been a degree of resistance, something inside me which refused to submit to the child. They are so different, I conveniently thought for so long. But that is not the case. They are the same. They are people too. But they have not figured it all out yet. They don't know the tricks yet, the dodges. They still have no knowledge of the overwhelming number of written or unwritten rules, spoken or unspoken laws, agreements and conventions designed to ensure we don't constantly bash each other's brains in. They don't know them. So they cannot contravene or break them either. They simply stumble across them. I see them busy and I think: don't do that, I had just started to like you. Don't say that, you seemed so sensible. They do what they can. Apes ape apes.

'Papa, I want to go with you and see what you and mama do ... Rain and Drumming and Übung and Wortel van Glas [Carots made of glass] and so on ... but the best I have seen was De Drie Biggetjes [The three piglets] by [the female group] K3. All children agree on that. And the stupidest wolf ... looked like you! Honestly! Its voice and everything ... and it was also the funniest.'

Acting for an audience of children is easy. They are easily satisfied. Provided there is enough colour and movement in it and you don't make it too difficult, then they whoop together as loudly as the crowd at Rock Werchter. What they really want is to be grown-up. That is their whole *raison d'être*. Being together and thinking the same way are part of that. They do their very best to grow but often it's not at all nice to look at.

'Boys are so stupid and irritating. They spend all their time pestering us and pinching our bottoms and that sort of thing ... Except when we do tournaments at Beersel castle. Then we are all dressed as knights and princesses and they protect us. Then they are cool.'

But sometimes it *is* nice. To look at, I mean. Really, really nice. When they play for themselves, not for a public, outside in the garden or in a corner of the house. When they are practising quietly and not trying to compete with the rest of the world. *'You are the daddy and I am the mummy and you are the dog. And you came home and I was angry and the dog still had to be fed, okay?'* The dog is usually the little brother or something else they would have preferred not to have around, but who is around and who they have to allow to join in, because an adult has told them to. (I knew a boy who always actually chose the role of dog and in that way, sneakily, acquired a position of power.) But what is so nice is that they don't play for results. They start and they end up where they end up. There is no plot, no grand preconceived plan and so their concentration is high. They lose a shoe during the game and they don't notice. They are constantly in search of solutions for the looming problems and they are not afraid to intervene in a big way or to give their story a sudden twist. Those are the times I believe they are at their best and when I wonder if all that is not much, much more important than going and looking at a story with an ending that is enacted for them and which if it was made by adults often serves above all to please the self-invented child in the adult. (Spare me the child in the adult.)

'I have chosen three images that are typical of me. Two pigs and a little Japanese woman in a kimono. Afterwards I thought that perhaps I might have chosen other images – a little boat or something or a dolphin. I do find it strange that I chose two pigs. The Japanese woman and one pig and then a dolphin as well, instead of another pig – that would have been better. But they were two very different pigs – one was big and the other was a piglet – it was really sweet. But I think now that I should have chosen a dolphin instead of that large pig perhaps? Next time I'll give it more thought.'

Gerhard Jäger says: 'ABC originated from my own love of books, combined with the fact that I became a father.' That is a wonderful base on which to build. He added children's books, videos, CD-ROMs and other material to his collection of second-hand books and he wondered how he could make that collection of use to a young public. That is rather different from walking them through a play. Jäger wanted to pass something on. Something he had. If making theatre for children comes anywhere near that notion, then I usually have the least difficulty with it. Passing on something we are engaged in is probably the most sensible way adults can relate to children. Gerhard Jäger and his team have made a place where children can wander freely. Where they come across Oskar Schlemmer, and Calder and Eames and Karel Appel. The film *Der Lauf der Dinge* by Peter Fischli and David Weiss, which bowled me over a few years ago, bowls them over too. (There is a difference of forty-three years between my daughter and me and we talk about the same film, without my having to bend or she to stretch.) They learn to paint Chinese characters if they want to, or to build their own house, once they have studied the houses of the world. They look at photographs of Stonehenge and play with boulders in the sandpit, paint an animal with its eyes closed, organize a dream landscape or cook a meal and eat it. The guides don't take the lead as they do in museums, they follow. Everything that is available is made by adults in an adult way. I mean that it has been thought about and carefully executed. This is an adult world, which is made accessible to children. Here curiosity is shared, about what surrounds us, about who we are. And not so much as a hint of entertainment anywhere, because there is no reason to while away the time.

JOSSE DE PAUW

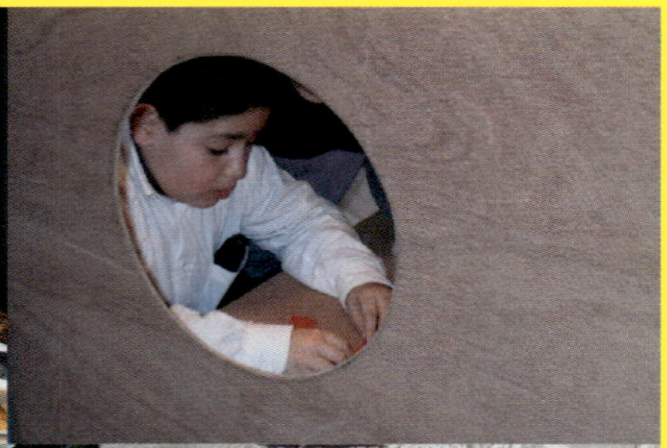

ART BASICS FOR CHILDREN

Art Basics for Children (ABC), an initiative of the Austrian artist and cultural philosopher Gerhard Jäger, is a young organization working out of Brussels. The work carried out in this laboratory focuses on the study and development of the artistic experience and aesthetic education.

ABC is best known for its mobile studios, which provide everyone aged four and over with an introduction to or a more in-depth knowledge of different art forms. The studios are specially designed activity stations, equipped with books, CD-ROMs, objects, videos, sound recordings, themed packages including all kinds of material, etc. The visitor can explore the tour at his own pace or under the supervision of an ABC-trained guide. ABC endeavours to stimulate the individual visitor's imagination with a view to bringing him or her into contact with the history of art and culture.

Jäger presented his first installations in the form of try-outs at the 1998 BRONKS Festival. June 1999 saw an extended sequel in a school in Schaarbeek (Brussels). ABC was again invited to the BRONKS Festival the following year. In the autumn of 2001, at the request of HETPALEIS, the non-profit ABC put together an exhibition route in the Antwerp youth theatre, where this interactive exhibition and mobile books and multimedia library remained for two seasons. A travelling version of the studio can regularly be seen in theatres, schools, cultural centres, museums, hospitals and the like. For the 'Rosas XX' exhibition marking the dance company Rosas' twentieth birthday, ABC created an interactive dance studio. The *ABC van de Dans* [ABC of dance] provides children with all kinds of materials and sensory stimuli, including a film projection of Bauhaus dancing practice that encourages them to dance and move. During the summer of 2001, ABC organized a workshop devoted to stories of the children of asylum seekers at the 'Klein Kasteeltje' asylum centre in Brussels. The experience prompted ABC and the asylum centre to join forces and create a permanent studio, which opened in October 2002. Constant improvements have since been made to it.

In addition to the studios, ABC also feeds the discussion about art and education with debates and research. Children's workshops are organized and together with (future) teachers the non-profit organization wants to support research into the practice of art education. During the 2002–03 season, ABC worked specifically on integrating architecture into education, carrying out a study at the request of the Flemish Ministry of Education and working with students of architecture on new activity stations and architecture boxes that can be loaned.

Close collaboration with BOZAR will begin in September 2004. ABC will support and advise the Paleis voor Schone Kunsten/Palais des Beaux-Arts in Brussels on a new education department, it will be responsible for the BOZAR Studios from the point of view of both their interior layout and objectives, and it will create an ABC media lab, an interactive project concerned with film/image and sound.

Finally, there are ABC's Kamishibai shows. 'Kamishibai' is a traditional Japanese narrative form in which a narrator slides prints in and out of a minuscule theatre, often mounted on top of a bicycle, to illustrate the story. Since 2002 ABC has regularly sent narrators out onto the street with bicycles. YB

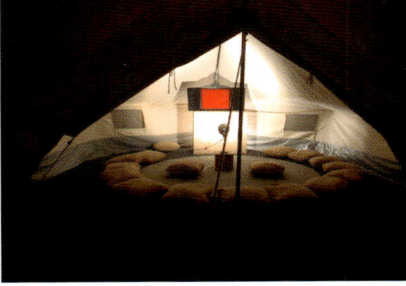

LABYRINTHORIUM

POKING THROUGH THE FOURTH WALL

JORIS JANSSENS

Leafing through this book, we come across not only plays but also exhibitions, installations and films. We lose our way in a labyrinth, and exchange the plush of the theatre seat for that of the brothel. We make a journey. The evening-length show proves to be just one possible format for directors, dramatists and choreographers to enter into dialogue with their audience. Performers no longer play exclusively in the dark auditorium, but increasingly outdoors: in the park, in the shadow of the cathedral, in taxis, on a bicycle. They build small huts in city squares or do fancy cooking on revolving stages. A crate in front of the NATO headquarters may serve as a podium.

What we see on and off stage is the result of what are sometimes radical choices, with divergent causes and effects. Although this book is out to highlight that colourful variety, it is still possible to trace a few connecting threads. Where do the hybrids come from and where are they going? In the following we shall try to come to grips with questions like these by investigating how performing artists understand and present their own practice, and how in doing so they play variations on the most fundamental conventions of the theatre.

1.
A recurrent feature in the discourse on certain performing arts (particularly contemporary dance) is the use of scientific metaphors. The 'social-artistic laboratory' Les Bains::Connective, which the reader will come across in the pages of this book, is an example of this. They are not so much concerned with the finished product as with initiating processes that allow the audience to take a look behind the scenes at informal previews and in workshops. They do not eschew the artistic risks, and failure is not ruled out as long as positive lessons can be drawn from it. The artistic practice is also treated as a process in *9 x 9,* a performance that can teach us something about how masses behave, move and look. More generally, the arts centres describe their artistic productivity in the same way, and in the municipal theatres, workshops, academies and training centres, too, productions that are ready for staging – if they ever get that far – are preceded by previews, try-outs, discussions and accompanying publications. What used to be peripheral phenomena have increasingly come to have a finality of their own in the last few years.

'Public research' is also the main point in the programme of the current team in the Nieuwpoorttheater in Ghent. It is noteworthy that rather anti-intellectual noises can be heard inside this arts centre. Elsewhere in this book, Enrique Vargas, artistic director of this year's Time Festival, says that 'rationality and science are myths' and that 'rationality murdered millions of people'. Even though his age and provenance distinguish him from most of the other subjects in this book, Vargas is nevertheless in place among our other 'hybrids', because in spite of the rational connotations that the academic imagery evokes, Vargas' 'theatre of the senses' is prototypical of many other cross-fertilizations that can be seen in our theatres and festivals today. 'The performing artists of the Nineties do not argue, they infiltrate the body,' writes Rudi Laermans in his essay – a claim that is given an exuberant reception below by Michel Uytterhoeven. The academic imagery seems to turn into its opposite. Still, there is no contradiction here. Vargas too is out to generate a certain consciousness on the part of his audience. You undertake a personal journey of discovery in his labyrinths. In this sense what is at stake in Vargas' labyrinths is closely related to that of the podium practice that describes itself as scientific. Science is empirical, and empirical means perception, but there are other roads to knowledge besides word and image. The sensory artists are not bent on hedonism, but they want their public to produce a new form of knowledge, an unconscious knowledge of a different kind. Not by detached, intellectual contemplation, but by smelling, tasting, hearing and even touching they want to activate traces of memory, spasms, atavisms and indescribable sensations. For the rehearsals of *Visitors Only* Meg Stuart not only invited a neuropsychologist, but paid equal attention to paranormal phenomena and hallucinations. Some commentators developed a discussion of ghosts in the slipstream of her *Highway 101.*

Labyrinth or laboratory? In both cases the performing arts are not geared to provide entertainment for entertainment's sake. They are a knowledge discipline in the widest sense of the word. After all, there are two halves to every brain. The left-hand side is the realm of Apollo, of reason, logic and science. The right-hand side is the domain of Dionysus, of magic, art, mystery and madness. Narrow threads connect the two halves with one another. Dionysus is the god of wine and theatre. Perhaps the return to the senses is a return to the time-hallowed, festive roots of theatre.

2.

Back to the roots, then? But in that case why do so many 'performances' look so little like theatre? I think that we may call both Apollo and Dionysus to account. Some artists want experience, others prefer rational understanding, but both persuasions seem to demand a fiddling about with fundamental conventions of theatre. For instance, there are very many variations on one of the basic rules of the theatre: that of the fourth wall, the imaginary wall in the black box that divides two kinds of perception and two roles from one another. The audience watches the actor and the actor knows that he is being watched. The audience is here, the actor is over there. Variations on this (spatial) convention can assume divergent forms. They may be aimed at reflexive insight or at very direct, sensory experiences.

What is perception? What neuropsychological processes take place in our brain? Where are memory, trauma, or our image of ourselves located? What role is played by old and new media if we attribute meaning to what we see? These and other questions are raised by a good many contemporary dance productions, as well as in the work of Meg Stuart and Damaged Goods, for example. To look for an answer to these questions, to acquire insight, they develop an arsenal of strategies, at times playing variations on the convention of the fourth wall. This was particularly the case in *Highway 101*, a performance that was not put on in theatres. In various places in Europe, performers and audience followed a route in what were often disused industrial buildings. The spectators gradually came to literally assume the position of the performers: they were thus able to look back on where they had been and watched previously. Stuart enables the spectators to see themselves in their memory. The security cameras and monitors that she placed also led to confusion. Meg Stuart: 'Is it real or is it not real, live or pre-recorded? Which of all these moments is the present, what are we certain of?' In this way Meg Stuart introduced different reflexive moments into the viewing behaviour of her audience.

Benjamin Verdonck brings about a similar confusion in viewing behaviour in some of the 'theatre presentations' from his 'Publieke Domeinen' [Public Domains] cycle. He walks through a crowded shopping street, dressed as Santa Claus. But it is 15 December: he has got the date wrong. Or he sits in a shopping centre as a beggar, with a sign next to his cap reading: 'I need no money.' The reaction provoked by such actions from passers-by is in the first instance a feeling of recognition. Only later do they realize that something is not quite right. By deploying theatrical elements in a non-theatrical setting, Verdonck deconstructs our gaze: he brings about a small disturbance of our automatic patterns of looking.

While Meg Stuart and Benjamin Verdonck problematize our perceptions, others focus precisely on the primary force of the gaze. The Giants from Royal de Luxe, who descended on Antwerp for four days in 1998, were able to look at the public and blink. According to Stefan Crets, that is what made them so human and familiar: 'People set off not just because of the size of the colossus that was driven through the city but above all because of the opportunity to see a living giant. They are seeking an encounter with that body whose chest moves when it breathes, whose head turns gently, and especially whose eyes can look at you – eyes that are big and never stop looking round with a constant astonishment and openness. So it is a question of the encounter with a human being, mysterious and strange, but recognizable and poetic.'

In their search for direct experiences, other artists even block out visual perception altogether. Enrique Vargas' labyrinths are murky. In *Het Sprookjesbordeel* [The fairy-tale brothel] you are blindfolded. Because vision is limited, the other senses have to cope with it all. The makers of the labyrinth and the brothel want a more direct contact between one actor and one spectator. That is why they communicate through the senses of smell, taste and touch, the primary media that precede language. In the case of both Vargas and Verhelst, the actor actually touches the spectator, thereby breaking a taboo of the theatre: he pokes his hand through the fourth wall. Other artists address our senses too. Human hair was burnt in Meg Stuart's *Insert Skin #1. They Live in our Breath* – a penetrating smell that instinctively recalled concentration camps. But the smells may be pleasant, too. It is not fortuitous that so much is cooked and eaten on and around our podia. Peter De Bie and Laika put on culinary performances. Children could cook together in the studio of Art Basics for Children in HETPALEIS. In *La Cuccina dell'arte*, the latest production by Circus Ronaldo, pizza dough is used for juggling. And in the *Pagnol Trilogy* by De Onderneming you are served not just soup, a beer and sugared almonds but also a full meal. In her contribution to the present publication, Ellen Walraven offers a clear description of how De Onderneming makes the spectator an accomplice in their performance through the use of such props.

In addressing the sense of taste and smell, many artists want to get the audience more closely involved in the performance. By comparison with traditional theatre, they stage a different, less passive relation between performer and spectator. Digestion, for example, is a very active and physical way to process the information provided. The sensory dramaturgy is less aimed at filling out a character, a story line, or the interaction between characters. It is about the relation between a performer and the audience.

At the same time the culinary mise-en-scène entails a different construction of the relations of the spectators to one another. In the theatre we look at the stage, not at our neighbour, but eating is something we do together. Table manners intrude on the etiquette of attending a theatre performance.

3.
Some sensory performances do provide moments of reflection afterwards. The Art Basics for Children route contains various meditation areas. *Het Sprookjesbordeel* has a chill-out room. You do not applaud after the experience. You immerse yourself in silence to process the experiences, to digest them – sometimes literally.

When it comes to sensory dramaturgy, the difference from Pieter de Buysser's pieces seems large at first sight. However, Lampe – the hunchbacked servant of Kant, a character, a non-profit organization and an alter ego – is in the dark too. He tries to explain in words why it is so dark but he stammers. He does not turn out the light, but he does question the Enlightenment. 'I don't know. I see off and remember. Remembrance is rethinking the event, rethinking the experience, the unlimited experience that opens me up like a tomb.'

4.
Many performing artists are very critical of the fact that theatre is essentially a viewing situation: they problematize or censor the gaze. They address other senses than seeing and hearing. Here art and science enter into an intimate symbiosis. On the one hand, neuropsychological insights can teach us a lot about the relativity of our perceptions. Scientific insights thus put pressure on the basic principles of theatre. On the other hand, many performing artists target experiences that precede language and intellectual insight: Dionysus criticizes the limits of intellectualism and rationality. Science draws attention to the limits of theatre and vice versa.

Whether they have their sights set on experience or understanding, the performing arts are in both cases a knowledge discipline that is critical of its own presuppositions. Artistic choices in theatre and dance in the last few decades have often been motivated by a critical attitude towards their own traditions, which is why the performing arts are often called self-reflexive. That term seems less apt to describe the hybrids under discussion here. It disguises the fact that for many of them appealing to the senses is a strategy to say something about the world in which we live. Dance as an artistic investigation of bodiliness is still often a critical commentary on the movement vocabulary that was handed down within the discipline. But the dance of Meg Stuart, Christine De Smedt, Ben Benaouisse or Charlotte Vanden Eynde is also about codes, conventions and practices taken from everyday life. About how we know we are under scrutiny every day and about how we adjust to the perceptions of other people. About the different roles we play every day: at work, in the street, and in front of the bathroom mirror. In that way, too, they take up their place in a postmodern dance tradition.

So identity and the production of meaning are the key words. The relation between how we see and experience ourselves and others, how we recognize ourselves and lose ourselves again in a flux of images, how we are thrown back upon ourselves and belong to real and imaginary communities, is an important focal point for the performing arts as a knowledge discipline. In our media society, identity and cultural diversity have become marketing labels, and the notion of what constitutes theatre has become so eroded in the process that it is precisely the theatre that can raise pertinent questions about our position in the world as human beings. When all is said and done, Arnold Schwarzenegger is more 'theatrical' as a politician than as an actor.

'Many meanings … are shifting today. What are time or body, masculinity or femininity, waste and beauty, stone and the sky, the street and the landscape, skin colour, machines, etc. for us? Who makes, manages, produces "meaning" and its representations? "Tradition" slows down and no longer preserves properly, and that results in all kinds of conservatisms and fundamentalisms. A large part of the production of meaning is commercialized: advertising shows what body, time, pleasure and work can mean. The institutions that are traditionally in charge of Knowledge, such as the academic institutions, generally react very sluggishly and continue to work in the "humanities" with nineteenth-century maps and territorial divisions. In this context art has developed to become one of the few places where – among other things – work is done relatively intensely, with a sense of urgency, and to some extent freely or autonomously, on meaning and representation. This seems to be the main – or today perhaps even the only – reason to assign a (significant) social importance to art' (Bart Verschaffel).

5.

For decades hybrid artistic practices such as performances, happenings and environments have been escape routes from dramatic and artistic practices that were felt to be bourgeois. That is also true of our hybrids, our nomads and other members of the generation of the Nineties. This book offers elements for a new story about the social relevance of the performing arts that has nothing in common with conveying a political content to an already convinced audience. Within the wider context of the media and spectacle society, performing artists can produce alternative insights. They stage new social interactions that break down the traditional hierarchical relation between artist and spectator. They speak in public space, where they reach a new audience or function as small disrupting influences in the world of shopping malls, petrol stations or other public spaces that have been taken over by big business. 'Ethical management' is also important for some of the items in this book which take the relation between the organizational and artistic aspects of their work to extremes (De Onderneming, Les Bains::Connective, *9 x 9*, etc.). Old and new platforms are engaging in a 'glocal' (global/local) debate with the neighbourhood and the whole wide world at the same time.

This is essentially a story of small-scale politics that has little in common with some of the macropolitical discourses that exist today on the performing arts and the creation of communities. The micropolitical strategies outlined here are not based on opting for the large number of spectators, the grand gesture to counter disillusionment, or a certain populist politics on the cultural demands of the 'man in the street'. But they do reflect an awareness that all choices – including artistic ones – are essentially *ethical* choices.

LITERATURE
- P. de Buysser, 'Het theater van de ongrond', *Dietsche Warande en Belfort* 146, no. 5 (October 2001), pp. 599–609.
- S. Crets, '"De Reus" of: de fabricage van de stad', *Cultureel jaarboek Stad Antwerpen 1998*, pp. 9–20.
- N. Decock and M. De Pourcq, 'You do the work and the work does you. Enrique Vargas' "labyrinth of the senses"', *Janus* 12 (2002), pp. 41–46.
- E. Jans, 'Geven is een mooi, kwetsbaar en subversief gebaar', *Etcetera* 20, no. 87 (June 2003), pp. 32–33.
- R. Laermans, 'Media Magic', in *Media mediations. On Vincent Dunoyer and others*, Maasmechelen: CC Maasmechelen 2003, pp. 76–81.
- J. Peeters, 'Strategies of Adaptation. Some Points of Entry and Exit concerning Damaged Goods' *Highway 101*', *A-Prior: Meg Stuart* (Autumn–Winter 2001–02), pp. 68–81.
- B. Verschaffel, '"Onderzoek": over Kunst als Kennisvorm', in B. Balcaen, W. Davidts, D. de Clercq *et al.* (eds), *B-sites. Over de plaats van een kunst- en onderzoekscentrum te Brussel*, Brussels: Brussel/Bruxelles 2000; Ghent University: Vakgroep Architectuur & Stedenbouw, 2000, pp. 46–53.

A PLEA FOR TAKING RISKS

DEFINITIONS AND COUNTER-DEFINITIONS IN THE DEBATE ON PUBLIC PARTICIPATION

MANU CLAEYS

In allocating cultural subsidies, a democratic government has to justify the choices made, which obliges it to reflect on what it considers really important and why that is. So it weighs the investment against the expected return. Traditionally it was enough to point to some more or less clearly defined cultural added value for both the government and the population. In the past few decades this was accompanied by a growing concern for social justice. The extent of public participation was also weighed in the balance. It is a concern that became increasingly visible in the whole Flemish cultural field, but nowhere was it debated so vigorously as in the world of theatre and dance. 'Public outreach' even became one of the key concepts in the Decree on the Performing Arts of 18 May 1999.

This is hardly surprising, for anyone who stages narrative or movement art will come upon a government that demands a social return on investment than those who express themselves artistically in a book or on canvas. There are several reasons for this. The most important is probably the budget: because there are considerable overheads (building, personnel, production) and there is little money to be made, the sector is relatively heavily subsidized, which naturally attracts attention. There is also the inherently social character of the activity: people spend a few hours together, enter into an intense and direct exchange with the artists, and make themselves visible as a cultural minority. That gives rise to both expectations and fears when it comes to the formation of a community. And finally there is the work of art itself: because of its specific nature, it belonged to the field of the avant-garde for a historically longer period and more often in the last two decades than works of a literary, musical or sculptural nature. It is easier for the latter to reach a large public through reproduction (literature, music) or collection-building/speculation (visual art), for which they can appeal to the publishers, labels and galleries that operate on the free market. For dance and theatre, on the other hand, mass consumption or large profits are practically ruled out and a certain marginality is a constant. Whether they like it or not, this preserves them from as-similation by the commercial logic and from recuperation by the corresponding glamour circuit. It makes them genuine free havens, less disposed (tempted, forced) to conformism or compromises. But it equally makes them dependent on and in the end accustomed to government support.

It is above all these factors that have won the sector a position of prominence in the debate on the social relevance of art and culture. The performing arts became the touchstone for everyone who had something to say in that debate. It was not uncommon for them to be cast in the role of scapegoat.

A long time ago it was all much simpler, because it was the patron who paid. There was hardly any question of a social engagement within a structured cultural policy, and even less of having to account for how funds were spent. From the end of the eighteenth century, however, elected administrators began to engage in more explicit attempts to turn the arts into an instrument of the common good. The main reason to do so proved to be the need to create a national soul within the new nation states. In order to assimilate as many citizens as possible into that nation-building story, the cultural thresholds must not be too high. Official art was therefore almost always reduced to edifying entertainment, popular theatre, heroic novels and gripping painting. And the Arts had to be Fine in the sense of decent, idealistic and sacred.

The situation changed at the end of the nineteenth century. The subsidized arts were supposed not only to bring hearts together (by working on the emotions), but also to elevate the mind (refinement). That is why the idea of disseminating culture was particularly prominent among progressive circles for whom the German *Bildungsideal* (humanist ideal of education) was the norm. Some of them interpreted this in a traditional, 'bourgeois', patronizing way with respect for the canon and High Art (education, training). Others – the Modernists – put the emphasis on the individual quest with scope for critical reflection (emancipation, maturation). Not only *could* modern art be unruly – it *should* be. Taking risks was a part of the game, and since realism infiltrated the arts, ugliness and the unfinished became aesthetic categories. At the same time the specialization and autonomy of the arts increased, as they did in the field of administration and the academic world. Much art was self-referential (art for art's sake), and artists increasingly positioned themselves in relation to other artists, which gradually turned works of art into material for connoisseurs. The emphasis in art gradually shifted from an intense representation of reality to a somewhat curious mental exercise.

Cultural policy followed these trends, albeit with a time-lag. It was above all in the second half of the twentieth century that attention was focused on the non-commercial artistic discourse that was less accessible in terms of form and content, that paid no heed to the premodern concept of good taste, and that openly opposed direct serviceability to anyone at all. From now on the core of cultural policy consisted of subsidizing art that was recognized as autonomous and thus by definition could not be instrumental. The Theatre Decree of 1993 conferred a far-reaching autonomy on companies and arts centres. The politicized Cultural Pact (meant to protect ideological and philosophical minorities in Belgium) had had its day too; independent advisory or evaluative committees no longer had to reflect the political balance, but decided for themselves on the basis of expertise which applications for subsidy should be granted.

The sector was thus liberalized and freed from traditional religious and socio-political barriers. This brought cultural policy to the brink of a nervous breakdown. After all, the possible return on investment had by now not just become risky because it was potentially subversive – it was simply no longer possible to gauge exactly what politicians in particular and the wider community in general could expect to get back from artistic experiment (which is the way with experiment). Postmodern trends within the art world did not make matters any easier in that respect, because the Modernist suspicion of paternalism eventually turned into an anti-Modernist fear of it.

While the possible edifying effect of art was initially supposed to be real, even though it was elusive and unpredictable, the recent discourse has been marked by a cultural relativism that not only preaches an equality of visions and expression outside relations of power, but often even degrades art to a noncommittal, ironic activity. As a result, expertise turns out to be suspect, pretentious, intolerant and finally redundant, and it becomes difficult to confer the authority to grant subsidies on it.

If it is true that by now the government has come to recognize the autonomous, non-instrumental character of art, it is also true that from the mid-1980s the democratization of society, the sociological disintegration of the intellectual élite and the rise of right-wing extremism have encouraged the re-emergence of a call (and one which has been getting louder and louder ever since) for a legitimation of what is considered, and rightly so to some extent, as government subsidy for a highly educated minority. On no account may the policy be lacking in democracy, and that is what it looks like today.

Finally – or should we say: to crown it all? – cultural policy has fallen into the clutches of an increasingly powerful market logic and the sights of an increasingly dominant commercial entertainment sector. Viewing ratings have become more important, not only because what cannot be enjoyed immediately on a mass scale smells of élitism, but also because there are performing artists who do manage to reach a large public but are still apparently in need of subsidy in a small linguistic area. Think of the growing success of the boulevard comedies, musicals and cabaret.

As a result of all these factors, notions such as accessibility, low thresholds and public outreach are once again at the centre of cultural policy, just as they were two centuries ago, though in a different context and for different reasons. In the meantime, official policy has followed a route leading from entertainment sponsor via edifier of the people to subsidizer of the avant-garde, with the accent gradually shifting from *assimilation* via *education* to *emancipation*. It is now looking for a balanced synthesis, a meaningful correction of the urge above all to subsidize forms of cultural expression which have little immediate appeal for the vast majority of the population, in other words: a wider *participation*. By now those in positions of authority who still honestly and wholeheartedly support the value of artistic autonomy are also frenziedly looking for ways to redefine the cultural policy in a way that is friendly to the public, if only to head off populism.

An obvious way to do this is to widen the concept of culture itself. The anthropologist Rik Pinxten (Ghent University) noted that in the last twenty years many European ministers of culture have indeed moved from an arts policy to an anthropological working definition of culture as 'everything that can be learnt'. It is a logical step, for culture certainly is a wide and vaguely defined term. However, it is important not to lose sight of the specific function of culture in the narrow sense, for to dissolve art itself in the broadening of the term is a fatal move. In the enthusiasm of the moment, there is a political tendency to want to impose measures from above to widen the field of the arts, or – and I don't know which is worse – to marginalize the impact of culture in the narrow sense to such an extent that art is no longer given a central position or role. So there is suddenly much less scope for artistic autonomy, an emancipatory vision of the arts or a critical maintenance of quality, in spite of protestations to the contrary. It is a pity, because an uninspired Minister of Art can never be an inspiring Minister of Culture.

When many in the cultural sector continue to stress the specific function and thus place of art within cultural policy and maintain that the achievement of artistic objectives is the decisive norm for the evaluation and funding of companies or arts centres, that does not mean that they do not pay heed to the political demand to reach a larger or more diverse public. What it does mean – and let us be honest here – is that that question reflects in the first instance a social concern and takes sociological facts as its point of departure. In the last resort, it has little to do with artistic motives.

That said, a misunderstanding needs to be cleared up. There is nothing performing artists would like better than packed theatres. They are by definition constantly searching for an updated interaction with a public that keeps on changing and hopefully growing too. They do not wait for a government to put the question of the public on the agenda. So in raising the question of the public recently, it was the government that homed in on an awareness that is very much alive in the sector, and not vice versa. It stimulated the search – which is welcome – and linked a discourse and concomitant policy to a process that was already under way in the field.

A crucial moment in this process is 1993, the year in which Antwerp wanted to be cultural capital and the organizing team made radical choices based on a strong belief in the autonomy of art. The emphasis was not on a nostalgic looking backwards, but on reflection, challenge, and the question of whether 'art could save the world'. It was precisely the radical nature of the choices made that activated the debate on the social impact of art, on what was popular or élitist, on how the public space could be won back, and on how to involve as large a section of the population of Antwerp as possible without lapsing into superficial animation. Artistic interventions took place on boats, at busy intersections, beside the canals and in the parks. This all rose to a crescendo after the cultural year and with the arrival of a new generation of performing artists. More and more often they left their own premises to explore the limits of theatre practice and reaching the public. Companies like MartHa!Tentatief, Woestijn 93, Aksident, Theater Tol and De Onderneming put on their work in the zoo, the living room, the factory, the sculpture park or the café. The urban activists of City Mine(d) presented their stories from a traffic island. Mohamed 'Ben' Benaouisse gave a performance in a convent. Hut dweller Benjamin Verdonck took up residence on neighbourhood squares. I visited *Het Sprookjesbordeel* in the basement of a school.

The most exciting thing about all this is the presence in the street, where, as the French director Michel Crespin recently remarked, you come across both intellectuals and workers and where theatre and real life can interact (*De Standaard*, 5 July 2003). The risk of failure is not small, because the chance passers-by are either very demanding, or not demanding enough. They come and go, child or pensioner, speaking dialect or standard language. They are not motivated, but they are inquisitive and have to be sucked into what is going on at every moment. Too much text or plot is out of the question, anticipation and visual spectacle are de rigueur. In fact, street theatre cannot be much more than entertainment. It is theatre in the broad sense, broadened for the unknown, 'found', and therefore broadest audience.

Precisely because the annual Street Theatre Festival in Ghent wants to be more than that, for some time now it has increasingly come to exchange the street for the limitations of non-conventional sites such as a football field, a tent or a warehouse, in search of, indeed, a smaller audience.

This brings us to the crux of the matter, the tension between culture in the narrow sense or art, on the one hand, and the public in the broad sense or the anonymous public to whom those who grant subsidies are accountable, on the other. In this connection, in his *Het cultureel regiem* [The cultural regime] (2002) Rudi Laermans pointed out the difference between quality and quantity that all too soon changes into an opposition between the two in the present-day discussion of cultural policy because, instead of aiming at a balanced synthesis between maintaining the supply and stimulating the demand, it always runs up against an opposition between meanings to which the cultural sector attaches importance, on the one hand, and the statistics to which the government gives priority, on the other.

This opposition was expressed most vigorously in a broadcast of the Canvas channel programme *Nachtwacht* on 28 September 2002, when in a discussion of cultural participation Patrick Janssens, then chairman of the Social Progressive Alternative (sp.a), considered that anyone who receives public money has the moral obligation not to work selectively but to reach as wide an audience as possible. Earlier that year, during a cultural afternoon organized by the sp.a at Vooruit (15 May 2002), he bluntly told the assembled cultural sector: 'If you come to the government asking for money, tell it who is sitting in your auditorium.'

It is a position that does not do the debate much good, not only because you never hear the same moral argument when investment subsidies or risk coverage are asked for by and granted to factories, temporary loans to farmers, tax benefits to enterprises, allowances to priests, scientific funds to astronauts, donations to parties or grants to writers, but because in this form it boils down to a party ideological standpoint, it ignores what it is that makes art art. Such pronouncements arouse artists' suspicions. After all, they get the impression that politicians are not really interested in their art or their motives, but in something else. That was why the writer Pol Hoste asked during the same afternoon session whether Patrick Janssens had a view on the relation between artist and society.

In the publication *Wie slaapt vangt geen vis* [He who sleeps in the morning may go begging the day after] (2001), Patrick Janssens made it clear that when it came to the allocation of government funds for culture, the so-called 'Matthew effect' [cf. Matthew 13:12: 'Unto every one that hath shall be given, and he shall have abundance'] worried him. 'I do not think that everyone has to share in quality theatre,' he explained, 'but I do think that the opportunity to do so, the interest in it and the eventual result should not be socially correlated.' So far so good. It is a justified concern, and one that is shared by many in the cultural sector, not least by the generation of the Nineties. But it was then followed once again by the *parti pris* that coming up with a solution for it was 'part of the responsibility of a company'. That position is never supported by any arguments, because any attempt to provide them would immediately reveal its impracticality. Typical is the suggestion that Patrick Janssens made in *Het groot onderhoud* (April 2002; the title is an untranslatable pun meaning both 'the overhaul' and 'the long talk/conversation'), a workbook in which the sp.a wanted to test its ideas on the world of today: 'The theatre must make efforts to reach all kinds of people instead of everybody having to make efforts to reach the theatre. But we cannot allow this to lead to a drop in the quality of the theatre' – in other words: run with the hare and hunt with the hounds.

It is typical of the present, but unfortunately it is not good to keep separating in this way the discussion about public outreach or the social composition of the public from the substantive debate about what art demands and does. 'The essence of my argument is the equitable distribution of public funds,' Patrick Janssens stressed in a newspaper interview (*De Morgen*, 16 September 2002), thereby adopting the statistical approach of a sociologist who does not venture to apply qualitative arguments and thus shows that he has no affinity with the field. He avoids a discussion of the character of the experience of art, of the complex trajectory covered by an individual who is interested in art, and of the value that a society attributes to the mere presence and activity of the recipient of the subsidy. Instead of an intellectual framework in which the artistic ambitions of the sector are situated in an engaged and informed manner, in the end the most we get is a superficial, sometimes even cliché-ridden view of art.

Whoever opts to stay on the surface in the debate on content and to emphasize objective, statistical criteria (viewing ratings) is on safe ground. After all, such an analysis looks up to date because there is nothing patronizing about it and there is no question of interfering. The autonomous citizen is not told what to find interesting, the autonomous performing artist is not told what to put on. But behind the laid-back liberty lurks a fake autonomy for the artist. With respect to both form and content, the artist is as autonomous as the television broadcasting company that is forced by its policy plan to enter into the logic of the viewing ratings.

Perhaps the distinction between meanings and figures came precisely because art has achieved such an autonomous status in the last few decades. To openly argue for serviceability or even good taste in art is *passé*, and there is hardly a politician who would risk it. But you can still talk about a moral obligation to be at least broad in your outreach. It is another way of instrumentalizing the arts sector within a political project, which glosses over or even denies the fact that the call not to work selectively and to return something to everyone inevitably has consequences for artistic autonomy, because programming for a wide audience means programming in a different way. You can't have it both ways. It is impossible and in a certain sense too easy to evaluate companies in terms of quantity – art is precisely the cultural field par excellence where that does not apply – or to limit their social relevance to the size or composition of the audience. When politicians or bodies that grant subsidies consider an applicant not relevant artistically, perhaps they should have the nerve to say that straight out and to explain why they think so, without thereby operating as the ultimate arbiter. The Flemish Government's new Arts Decree, in which a broad advisory committee stands above the specialist evaluative committees, already creates scope for that, and it would certainly benefit the debate.

A motive often operates here that is more important than the qualitative instrumentalization of the arts, which has been abandoned by now: to limit the potential damage within a specifically defined democracy. Don't ask what art can do for you or what you want to and can do for art, ask those who make art why you, he and she are not in the theatre and tackle them about that. That too belongs to the essence of the discourse of redistribution, in particular a negatively inspired attitude that is no longer based on the emancipatory value of art but on fear of (patronizing and thus insulting) a voter who turns his back on the politicians. Politicians want to legitimize themselves vis-à-vis the 'man in the street' who is not subsidized to do his thing. 'Social relevance is above all a political argument,' commented Johan Thielemans in an interview (*De Standaard*, 24 June 2002). 'Something that politicians cannot sell is an important group of the audience suddenly having nothing offered to them because it has been scrapped for purely qualitative reasons.' Because they do not recognize or cannot explain the use factor or the indirect, slowly percolating return on investment in art, and such an explanation runs the risk of coming across as an affront to the cultural capacities of many voters, they fall back on what is measurable and throw the ball back into the court of the sector again. Accessibility is called in as the minimum. Counting heads is an important activity in a democracy, after all, and 'élitist' remains a dirty word, even in a world where a football ticket costs more than a theatre ticket and the expensive Beckham label has more prestige than the sale-price Beckett label.

To remain stuck in the contradiction between the statistical language of the politicians and the language of meaning of the cultural field is fatal to the discussion on public participation because it will lead to confusion about what may and what may not be expected from the performing arts in that context. It puts the cultural sector in the narrow sense in an impossible, schizophrenic situation. On the one hand, the social relevance of art is made to depend to some extent on the composition of the public, which leads to a lower appreciation of the artist (failure to fulfil expectations, too difficult, not profitable, too élitist, too inaccessible, etc.) and to the erosion of the right to unconditional experiment. On the other

hand, too many demands are made on the artists, in the sense that they are supposed not only to prick consciences and hold a mirror up to society, but also to aim for a socially mixed audience that is not to be found anywhere else in society – nor in the governments, parliaments, cabinets, party offices and local councils that we all subsidize – and is, according to Professor Christian Kesteloot, largely a romantic myth, or as a demand 'more of a remedy for the symptoms than for the causes of the problems' (*De Morgen*, 17 June 2003). They have to get rid of a socio-economically driven inequality and a cultural segregation produced by education and the use of the media at the level of art, as well as to legitimize themselves to a public that in nine cases out of ten is not really concerned with art at all. Perhaps a surplus of good political intentions is obstructing the cultural expertise here, but it is more likely that it is an abdication due to a politics that refuses to recognize its own structural failure in this area, and it is certainly a pure Catch-22 situation for the artist who is unable to win this battle.

'Culture is often used as a lightning-conductor,' Rudi Laermans comments in the margin of the discussion in Antwerp on the funding of the new Museum aan de Stroom (*De Morgen*, 4 June 2002). To reduce the risk of being struck by lightning, the cultural sector has no alternative but to throw itself fully into the discussion with those who, for whatever reason, create unrealistic expectations about what an artistically desirable and socially acceptable relation is between maintaining supply and encouraging demand. In its search for ways out of the ambiguities and misunderstandings, the sector must also (be bold enough to) scrutinize its own views and make them clear where necessary. Thus far and no further, this is what we can and want to do, this is what we can't and don't want to do, these are our limitations and our potential for this and that reason: that is what the discussion must be about. The development of a discussion of (artistic) underestimation and (social) overestimation seems to be called for.

The provocative view put forward by the then Minister of Culture Bert Anciaux in September 2000 is a good basis for that. 'I have got acquainted with the ascetic élite,' he said in his invitation for the State of the Union. 'Its social relevance is zero,' was the verdict. The minister's pronouncement was certainly courageous, but was it also true and wise?

It is certainly true that the increased autonomy of the companies and the transformation of the large theatres into nuclei of innovation was partly at the expense of the idea of dissemination and democratization on which the expansion of the cultural centres was based, but this trend by no means conceals a deliberate strategy of exclusion. Patrick Janssens nevertheless seems to imply the opposite when he says that he does not think 'that you can reserve such an important cultural factor as art for a specific group' (*De Morgen*, 16 September 2002). Formulated like this, it looks as though an élite deliberately follows a specific, preferably ascetic course to stop the rest from following. That is a gross misrepresentation of the special nature of art which, although it can be uninteresting, cannot be undemocratic. 'Art is the denial of equality,' wrote Alain Finkielkraut in *L'imparfait du présent* (2002). I would prefer to say that art is one of those areas where it is not only legitimate but also necessary to go beyond equality (Janssens' redistribution) or tolerance (Anciaux' community-forming). Artists simply do not set out from patterns of democratization (political), edification (education) or social welfare (therapeutic).

So 'socially irrelevant' is most probably supposed to mean: irrelevant in quantitative, i.e. electoral or sociological terms. The ascetic élite can only welcome this and probably live with it. That does not mean that artists are not politically or socially committed, nor that they shun trends towards democratization, edification or social welfare in their work or any consequences in that direction. What it does mean is that they do not want to be forced into the position of administrator, teacher or social worker.

Artists want to see their social relevance interpreted and appreciated in a different way from what some politicians envisage, so they approach the question of the public in a different way and aim to cater for different needs from those prescribed by the political agenda. This does not imply that they should adopt an attitude of modesty in this respect – on the contrary, for they react only too often in a defensive, almost apologetic or self-effacing manner that reinforces that underestimation even further. It is much more fertile to go on the offensive and to define the social relevance of their artistic project by emphasizing its inspiration and impact.

Jan Lauwers, a committed member of the ascetic élite, was led this spring to situate the strength of what he produces in its useless, impractical character. By criticizing the notion of utility, he wanted to protect his theatre from the tyranny of the socio-political or commercial logic. 'The present-day discussion is about economics and structures, but never about art,' he said in this connection last year (*De Morgen*, 14 September 2002). He is right in taking umbrage, but anyone who flirts with the category of the useless as a legitimation becomes very vulnerable. An echo of this analysis can be heard in the claim by Eric Antonis (and others) that 'by definition art does not need to be socially relevant' (*Knack*, 31 July 2002), or in the ironic discourse of the Postmodernists. Calling one's own position into question can be refreshing, but to minimize one's social relevance or to create (and confirm) the impression that art is an innocent pose or a luxury item – like concern about the environment – that can at most offer a corrective or compensatory alternative for after working hours, is not only lacking in ambition and too noncommittal but above all risky. It hardly rids the term 'arts subsidy' of the somewhat dirty, begging, undemocratic echo that it now has for many people. It is more advisable to drop legitimations or apologies of that kind and to use a language that can also be understood by the sceptics.

That language must explain why the superlative of socially 'useful' or relevant – i.e. 'necessary' – applies to interesting art, and why a large public outreach is irrelevant in this context, and thus irrelevant when it comes to the allocation of subsidies as well. The comparisons that both Lauwers and Antonis made with scientific research were more on target. 'Not everybody understands the black hole in space,' Lauwers remarked. 'There's no need to, but a few people should be working on it. Well, I think that the same applies to theatre.' The artist is 'the research department of society,' said Antonis, and he added that 'if you only invest in the production department and not in research, you end up always making the same thing'. That already sounds pretty different from 'useless' and 'socially irrelevant'.

Since the clearing away of misunderstandings is a priority, it is good for the sector to come up with alternative definitions – in other words, to interpret non-artistic terms such as return on investment, relevance, diversity, social mix, thresholds or public participation in their own way. In doing so they can outline a route focusing on artistic 'added value', 'core business' or even 'unique selling proposition'.

An interesting starting point for a specific determination of such definitions and counterdefinitions is offered by the debate between Gert Verhulst (Studio 100) and Barbara Wyckmans (HETPALEIS) in the *Nachtwacht* broadcast of 11 January 2003. Wyckmans claimed that the shows of studio 100 [a company producing children's programmes, shows, songs and the like, which also runs the fun-fair *Plopsaland*] were not theatre but circus spectacles, that they followed stereotypical and predictable patterns in which there was no room for gaps, for stimulating the imagination, or for Fear. Not true, replied Verhulst, because they had a ghost in the Christmas show. Precisely, rejoined Wyckmans, a stereotype, and all ends well as we have a false security forced upon us. Does it all have to end badly, then? asked Verhulst. He wanted people to feel contented when they went outside again. That was what they had paid for. Besides, it was a large-scale, expensive show – it needed 70,000 visitors to break even – and so they had to play it safe and avoid too many oddities, because 'we want to put on theatre for a large audience'.

Verhulst argued several times that it was a good thing that this kind of commercial theatre existed, 'because it guarantees diversity'. That is a debatable point. It is true that Studio 100 puts on shows that HETPALEIS does not. Seen in that light, then, there is a larger choice. According to a counterdefinition suggested, but not formulated, by Wyckmans, those shows actually encourage homogeneity, fill in patterns, stimulate uniform thinking, and imprint the dominance of the soap structure in people's heads (the Belgians already watch more TV soaps than all other Europeans). Precisely because the widest possible public is targeted, it is staged in an unambiguous, closed way, confirms existing roles, and offers a feeble sort of humour. The public outreach may be larger, but the diversity within that public becomes smaller as the production becomes tamer. An essential element in Verhulst's argument was the logical, correctly made connection between the cost price of the show and the envisaged size of the audience, on the one hand, and the need to play it safe, on the other: if you cannot count on subsidies and still want to stage an ambitious project professionally, the threshold must not be too high, otherwise the audience might stay away. It is an honest train of thought for someone who wants at least to break even, but when your priority becomes satisfying the customer in search of relaxation with escapist pleasure and contentment ('feeling good'), you have, when all is said and done, crossed the threshold of the amusement industry, which is a part of culture in the wide sense of the word, but where different criteria apply from those of the arts sector.

Taking risks is an essential feature of the productions of HETPALEIS. Diversity is immediately taken to refer not to the differences between the companies, the genres presented, or the composition of the audience, but to the differences in what goes on in the heads of the spectators. 'We are caught up in the idea that a community consists of people who have something in common,' claimed cultural philosopher Eric Corijn at a colloquium organized by Agalev on cultural policy (28 September 2002). But

how do you create coherence on the basis of what makes us different from one another? How do you organize your community while leaving scope for individual autonomy and creativity? How do you learn to live together without a pre-shaped identity, without escaping into McWorld or Jihad, without populist illusions? That is the question of diversity facing the performing arts, and companies like HETPALEIS are engaged in a practical search for it by appealing to the imagination. Anyone who does that may provoke the consternation or even irritation of the audience. What they present should not be difficult, but it should be difficult to place. That is what theatre-lovers come for.

During a press conference of the Kaaitheater on 19 June 2002, Marianne van Kerkhoven alluded to precisely that distinction between 'difficult to place' and 'safe': 'I think that the difference between art and entertainment lies precisely in the fact that in art artists do what they feel they should do, produce what has never been produced before, while in entertainment a few artists create something that corresponds to the expectations of an audience that wants to see what it already knows in a new variation.' This is a very sharp alternative definition of the notion of innovation.

In the same text she indicated what she saw as the basis for tolerance: 'Being able to imagine something or somebody differently, differently from the familiar world that we see around us.' That too is a part of the artistic alternative definition of diversity, which in the first instance is a sociological rather than an artistic term. 'So this discussion is not just about the autonomy of the artist, but about that of the spectator as well,' Van Kerkhoven continued. 'It is because the spectators are prepared to do their part of the imagining in connection with what they see and hear that the artist can afford to be less explicit or unambiguous, much more complex, more indirect, and thereby more fertile.' So that readiness contributes to determining how far the artist can go.

If artists are to venture and be able to be implicit, this entails a certain respect for the assumed competence of the potential audience. How competent do you expect it to be? It is a never-ending question. Many would-be artists fail precisely here: they underestimate the audience, show too much, get bogged down in explanations, pay too little attention to form in relation to content, and eventually drive the vast majority of the public in the same, predictable direction. Gone is diversity, while diversity or heterogeneity is the essence of the many reactions that an interesting work of art provokes. As the philosopher (not by chance) and art critic Frank Vande

Veire formulated it: 'You have to be thrown back on yourself by something that is hard to place' (*De Morgen*, 2 August 2003), and 'we should concern ourselves with what is so sublime about the work of art – with ourselves, in fact' (*De Morgen*, 7 August 2003). Deep down the experience of art is an individual one that cannot be delegated and can hardly be shared. Because our selves are essentially different, the confrontations with ourselves are different too. So welcome to diversity, and may the sector pay the most attention to that kind of mix. Promoting public participation means the opposite of asking the audience to clap their hands together, to shout the same answer, or to press the 'horror' or 'excitement' button en masse by being able to recognize a ghost or an adulterous player in reality shows. It is much closer to what music reviewer Didier Wijnants proposed as 'basic principles' for the concerts at Jazz Middelheim: 'Was there enough risk? Was the equilibrium sometimes at risk? Was it also a challenge for the listener?' (*De Morgen*, 12 August 2003).

At the Agalev colloquium Eric Corijn pointed out the urge of the powers that be to keep the oppressed in the same position. He saw populism as characterized by 'a supply culture from a single centre via marketing', and the same applied to the world of entertainment. In art, on the other hand, it was a question of what he called decentring, the ability to adopt different positions. People who can do that can get a grip on their lives, because art teaches people to deal with real complexity instead of with a reduction of complexity.

The government also recognizes this point in the Policy Memorandum on Culture 2000–2004 when it links the acquisition of cultural competence to enlarging the field of possibilities and the chance of an autonomous existence. But at the same time that government loses some of its political control over an emancipated cultural public that does not reduce or allow itself to be streamlined. That is the subversive side of art, and perhaps theatre is the subversive art form par excellence because of the unmediated, open interaction between the artist and the public. Perhaps that is why the performing arts find themselves in the eye of political storms more often than the other arts do. For many performing artists the *real* challenge in the whole debate on diversity is the struggle to reach a larger audience with subversive innovation instead of a reinforcement of the status quo, to be able to voice criticism instead of commentary. Their call to detach the demand for a broadening of their public from the tendency towards a levelling of the public is also a call to abandon the discourse of populism.

The debate between Gert Verhulst and Barbara Wyckmans was not just about two ways of presenting theatre; it was also about two different ambitions for creating a favourable climate for their own type of theatre. Wyckmans wants to reduce the number of children and young people that keep getting fed the same cultural menu on television and on stage. She calls them 'deprived'. With that in mind, HETPALEIS has a separate unit to create a climate for those productions within a wider setting and to back them up via school visits, educational play-and-learn material, workshops, etc. The field of education is the pre-eminent partner for this in-depth approach. Verhulst would also like to see a more varied menu. He commented in *Nachtwacht* that it should not all be Disney or Barbie and that it was a good thing that there was now a local cultural industry as well. His productions are also accompanied by play and reading material, but the preferred partner in his case is not the school but the media. The accent is therefore on 'breadth', on publicity and promotion by means of 'kids marketing' (newspaper supplements, songs, merchandizing, related products in the shops). Studio 100 is itself a media company, by the way, so that it is in a much better position than HETPALEIS to influence the climate. It is no accident that many subsidized companies dream in secret of similar access to the mass media.

Studio 100 aims at participation and is therefore closer to the dominant educational model than HETPALEIS, which still strives for emancipation. The modern notion of emancipation replaced the premodern one of assimilation, but has itself recently been replaced by the new, postmodern slogan of participation. Wanting to increase public participation is a noble ambition, but within a populist context or a commercial logic it soon becomes confused with social justice, an increased market share, or cultural relativism. In that context value judgements are easily disposed of as the imposition of a vision, for people are intelligent enough to be able to decide for themselves what they find exciting, beautiful, important, etc. Anyone who suggests the opposite is accused of casting doubt on the principle of equality and of not being a genuine democrat. That is true not only in the new educational model or in the discussion of subsidies for the performing arts, but also in political campaigns or the legitimation of entertainment journalism. For instance, former VRT [Vlaamse Radio- en Televisieomroep, i.e. Flemish public broadcasting network] anchorman Stef Wauters considered that intellectuals 'should show more of an interest in what interests people' instead of imposing their own interests (*Humo*, 18 March 2003).

It is increasingly common for dissident intellectuals to be forced on to the defensive by remarks of that kind. Rudi Laermans offered a sociological explanation for this: 'The bourgeois élite and the middle-class public no longer exist. There is a new class of the more highly educated, progressive and politically correct people which adopts a predominantly anti-intellectual stance. It thus forms a mirror image of right-wing thought, which equally defends what is popular and populist' (*De Standaard*, 17 October 2002). So from now on this new class models itself on the classic opponent of the intellectual and artist instead of forming a counterweight to that faction. That is one of the reasons why the unconditional subsidizing of the autonomous artist is once again under pressure and more attention is being paid to the public outreach.

Laermans' new class has detached increasing cultural participation from the *Bildungsideal*. The belief in a progressive policy of the dissemination of culture was reconfirmed, but this time without the educational or emancipatory ambitions. Culture in the broad sense has come to occupy centre stage, and there is suddenly less room or even understanding for the specificity and the importance of culture in the narrow sense (art). The same trend is taking place in politics at large, where populists increasingly adopt a broad definition of democracy. At that level, too, a shift is taking place from education or emancipation to participation, to a quantitative democracy in which only the will of the majority ([the] people, the village street, the citizen) counts and the path of least resistance (the customer/voter is always right) is chosen. 'But in that case it is an apolitical, shallow democracy stripped of any ideology,' Marc Reynebeau correctly pointed out, 'in which there is no longer any other voice, any different opinion, any choice, any nuance, and thus any debate' (*Knack*, 9 July 2003). There can be no genuine democracy without debate. Socrates already knew that you cannot just reduce a democracy to the will of the majority, and he immediately added that within a democracy every member was equal, but not every opinion. The same is true of philosophy or of art, where radical logic and aesthetics operate and not a political correctness that rules out all public discussion of what is true, beautiful or good.

The triumph of the ideal of participation, the abandonment of the policy of *Bildung*, and the populist proneness to anti-intellectualism are perfectly in line with the commercial logic. It is not entirely surprising that 'quantitative democrats' are sensitive to (or are easily pressurized by) the democratization arguments of cultural producers who claim to offer what the market demands. 'The commercial sector seems in this way to achieve what the government, after decades of failed attempts to make culture accessible to all, has never managed to achieve,' writes Joris Janssens (*Courant* 63, May–June 2003). The essentially anti-political form of political populism, 'we say what you think', finds here an anti-artistic form of cultural populism in 'we show what you want to see'. Socially relevant then comes to mean catering for the taste of a wide audience, and the fact is systematically glossed over that this is a democratization of entertainment, not of the enjoyment of art. Once again the notions of art and culture are confused with one another.

Cultural populism is sustained by the socialist idea of redistribution and the liberal idea of the market. Both logics are concerned with the power of number – whether social or economic – and not the cultural emancipation or (promotion of the) autonomy of the individual who creates or participates. It is precisely that autonomy that coincides with what art sets out to be. To clarify and preserve that, we need a third logic that does not reject the striving for diversity or the growth of participation but gives them an artistic interpretation of its own, a logic that holds on to the desire for emancipation and is therefore less noncommittal than in a sociological or economic context because it cannot be quantified.

Art is like love or qualitative democracy: participation means more than being present, it means working with full dedication. You do not become a dedicated spectator, a good lover or a fully fledged citizen just like that. It calls for effort and guts, active participation and a willingness to experiment, as well as wisdom and strength of imagination. Every visit to the theatre is in fact a small workshop in which you learn to cross thresholds and, as Van Kerkhoven put it, are prepared to do your part of the imagining. Preparedness is not the same as capability. In a lecture at a conference on Culture and Participation (7 December 2000, Ufsia, Antwerp), Bruno Verbergt made a subtle distinction between raising neoliberal cultural competence and promoting cultural participation that is not about the acquisition of cultural capital but about the exchange of symbols. In his view, art creates 'meaning of a symbolic kind, in other words, meaning that can succeed or fail, where there is essentially a random factor present, essentially a tradition, with codes and rituals, which are experienced instead of consumed'. That is why experiencing art is more about doing than knowing, more about sharing than appropriating, and the promotion of participation is more about initiation than acquisition. The preparedness to experience art is about being willing to do, share and be initiated. Financial thresholds are the lowest obstacles. The physical ones are higher, not to mention the mental ones.

The artist takes risks, too, if only to remove the potential passivity of the participant. The artist throws down the gauntlet, undermines certainties, investigates what can barely be shown. The artist develops new perspectives, works on a different language, fulfils unprecedented ambitions and in doing so breaks with the normative framework and dominant discourse. Perhaps the asceticism lies in this avoidance of a sense of contentment ('feeling good'), because the stories and images provided by an artist have an alienating effect. This is where the social commitment and thus relevance of the artist lies, not in trying to find ways of getting a large or a varied audience into the theatre. Attention to sociological number or diversity can be regarded as an interesting instrument, but it is not a goal in itself. There is therefore no contradiction between asking for government support and wanting to lay claim to maximal artistic freedom, for the whole point of the subsidy is to guarantee the latter. A government that calls this into doubt should say so clearly.

Marianne van Kerkhoven correctly pointed out the connection between the readiness of the spectators to play their part and the opportunity for the artists to work in a less direct, explicit or unambiguous, and therefore more fertile, way. In assessing artistic merit, that implicit quality is probably the decisive element. Art is not a treatise, a punch or an open door. So in giving the sociological notion of diversity an alternative artistic definition, particular attention should be paid to the ambiguous, the ambivalent, the fluid. After all, the puzzling element lies not only in what is said, but also, and even more, in how that is done. That is why an interesting work of art is, in the last resort, 'difficult to place' rather than 'difficult'.

This has its consequences for the new interpretation – its artistic counterdefinition, we might say – that we can give of the somewhat misleading term 'élitist'. The charge of élitism usually refers to the feeling that a large group of people is being excluded. In the context of art, however, this is not a strategy but a consequence. Once again we can compare this with the environmental situation, since political ecologists are often accused of the same: they are élitist and thus unpopular because they translate the luxury concerns of a minority into a language that the ordinary man cannot understand. For the sake of convenience, the fact that the ecological message is not so difficult in itself, but is difficult to place because

it is troublesome to bear (asceticism seems to be called for here too), is passed over in silence. It is not what is said that is difficult, but the readiness to be receptive to what is said. So simplifying the message is no solution, because the consequences it entails for the individual remain the same. (What is élitist about campaigning against the pollution of the air and for the preservation of green space or for less consumption?) Nor is making the message easier to bear a way out, because that means messing about with its essence. For example, whoever defends the narrow morality of viability cannot at the same time advocate the broad morality of sustainability.

You can also reverse the charge of élitism. You can want to be so non-élitist as to convey a contempt for your public and for what you produce. You can be so focused on the public that you insult it by underestimating its intelligence. In the end you harm yourself as an artist too, because you water down and perhaps enfeeble the character of your work.

Anyway, what is wrong with cultivating different speeds in the appreciation of a work of art? Nothing. On the contrary, artists are by definition not public friendly. Each time, the indefatigable search for new ways of looking alienates a part of their following. It's part of the game. Élitism is inevitable and even necessary here. That is why art has always been a question of minorities. To claim the opposite is demagogy.

To improve the chances of the artistic experiment's success, what you need in a certain sense is not a sociologically or culturally diverse public, but a relatively homogeneous one. Compare it with the circuit of alternative schools that are also subsidized by us all. Anyone who joins it appreciates the feeling of being surrounded by well-informed, highly motivated, like-minded fellow travellers who work just as hard to make something of it. Diversity is thus not always a bonus, and sometimes it has adverse effects. In exploring the unknown, a homogeneity in the will to take risks is a minimum. A politician who insists that 'the money from us all' be used for artistic products that we can 'all' enjoy is therefore both unrealistic and counterproductive.

Following at a distance, education in the wide sense can benefit from the course that has been run and from the experiences of the radical innovators. The same is true of sport, science, journalism and art. Every time there is an élite searching for an added value, inquisitive, exploring the terrain, bringing things into focus, breaking new paths. They are prepared to make great efforts and even to take personal risks to do so – the kind of risks that you do not impose on anyone who is reluctant.

Those people who 'create difficulties' are a welcome target for the defenders of equality, but it is ridiculous to expose this kind of hierarchy or to increase the tension between the different speeds. What is called for here is to recognize the expertise and to accept the hierarchy, because the alternative is a travesty of democratization based on envy, fear, arbitrariness and indifference. The latter is the worst conceivable breeding ground for art.

The fact that a hierarchy exists is not the responsibility of the cultural sector in itself. It is not for the theatre company to abolish the 'Matthew effect' referred to above or the existence of invisible cultural ceilings. It is not the artist's job to be concerned with the size and composition of the audience. The artist cannot be held accountable for the competence and mobility of the reader, spectator or listener. That would be a gross overestimation of the artist's capacity.

There is a lifelong trajectory for everybody that leads to the development of certain cultural tastes or competences. It is up to the government not to target individual artists or theatre companies in the debate on diversity, social composition or accessibility, but to address the whole of society and how it is organized. Anyone who wants to reduce cultural segregation and increase cultural participation must start early enough and above all invest in education and combating poverty, as well as paying special attention to youth work, the heritage, the media, libraries and museums, to encouraging socio-artistic projects and the amateur arts, to investing in a qualitative broadening of the programme, a correct price policy, arts education and specific educational projects, targeted promotional activities, and so on and so forth – in other words, to the setting up of an adequate framework to create the right conditions. But that is another story.

(IM)MOVABLES

LES BAINS :: CONNECTIVE

And I think the birds in the field, they don't sow, they don't mow and it is beautiful weather again, I direct my steps towards South Station and it is warm and I sit at home in a chair which my father made and in which I occasionally fall asleep because next to me is a mountain of clothes I never wear and piles of books I shall never read but which I cherish as objects which have to be stacked and are part of an unwritten past, I want to travel and to the sun not too far but to sort myself out and eventually to write those first lines of that all-embracing best-seller after which I can lead a life of leisure in an innocent landscape and wonder in amazement why anyone still writes novels, a question I am unable to answer and I find myself in the shopping centre called Zuidstation (or Gare du Midi or South Station if you prefer) where you can also take trains at given times, it is busy here and the crowds of people weigh like lead in the heat, I drink a cup of coffee and in the queue somewhat unexpectedly bump into Bernard Van Eeghem, that congenial 'bon vivant' and 'touche à tout et ne réussit à

rien', just back with bag and baggage and boots from abroad and a bit lah-di-dah (sometimes) and as usual looking slightly dishevelled but not without some taste, he says it is not raining and I agree, nodding, I ask where he has been and he mutters something unintelligible, I ask him what he said but he looks the other way, does not listen and asks are you coming with me I have to go to the swimming pool, I smile at him and say a swimming pool, that doesn't seem a bad idea but where are my swimming trunks, and he says we'll buy some here in the little shop round the corner, and he says it is not a real swimming pool, but a swimming pool where all sorts of things happen, contemporary and the different disciplines all together and all separate he says and I think breaststroke, butterfly stroke, back stroke and crawl, cutting through the water like butter and I spontaneously name all the swimming pools I know, can you swim I ask him but there is no water only art he says and are you coming with me he chuckles and there goes my super-fast train and I hesitate, concede and to-

morrow is another day and why not I think and outside it hasn't stopped drizzling I hear, the tepid rainwater is beneficial for the dull skin cells and I say just tell me where we are going and watch out for the tram thank you he says you are not the only one who has saved my life, so far everything is fine and we walk day-dreaming past and round building excavations and cranes, how that is I don't know but he says I knew the swimming pool as a dance-hall long ago but what is long and much later I saw the unsurpassed 'The Little Mermaid' there by the Roovers, he bends down a moment, thinks hard and a taxi speeds past, honks and where is it going to, he blows his nose and says that the absent water was audible again then, I say the water in that swimming pool is on the run and he smiles and says now you are quoting Paul Snoek, yes the Vorst swimming pool is a 'ruin of the sea, surrounded by all the names of the water' but then without water I suggest politely, he says the water here is art in all its supple end forms, last year even with 'Sauna in Exile' the building was poetical in the extreme,

that is to say a little like what it served as and I interrupt his train of thought saying you see like a swimming pool I say and no he answers, the architecture of the swimming pool was respected as such but there were performances with dancers who came into the cold zone from a wooden sauna container and began to steam under a revolving spotlight, you had to take your clothes off and put a bathrobe on, Anja Kowalski sang a song in a room alone for you, there were installations but everything was well integrated as is possible in a swimming pool and perhaps only in this swimming pool but suddenly the taps of heaven open so wide that we quickly take shelter in a coffee-house nearby, we drink fresh mint tea, I ask him if it is far now and he is able to say a little more, I am still hungry, I begin to feel real hunger, he says a connective and a laboratory where a lot can be done but because of a lack of funds is restricted, also the social plans for the area are not shaping up without difficulty, you can also rehearse there if your work is in some way related and parallel to what they have in

mind, congruent, he mumbles but I am not listening any more and look out of the window, it is raining and raining and a scooter glides across the square through a smooth puddle, I ask again if it is far now, four more highwaymen he says and laughs exposing his uncared-for teeth and says that he rehearsed with Q-02 in the swimming pool, I say wow and I believe you and he says yes of course nothing more and nothing less, tell me ha ha who consists of words ha ha and I start, are we going to that swimming pool or not I try and he of course tells me that we are nearby that we will just wait till the rain stops but that rain keeps falling and we order another mint tea and then another and another and then, I name aloud all the swimming pools I knew as a child and later had holidays at the sea or feet in ice-cold mountain lakes and in a refreshing fast-moving river, I have been through it all he says but now I am old, we order a hot espresso and walk reluctantly through the waterfall across the square and after going along rue Mérode for a bit we turn left into rue Berthelot and I see, oh sign-

board, a diver in profile, I am wet through and Bernard Van Eeghem has suddenly disappeared, submerged perhaps and I am alone, what is a swimming pool without water and full of art, wet through as I am and I swim away and ring the bell at number 34, inside everything is dry, I type the word water and a little later the word later and female dragonflies creep inside my obliging pores like words, as if I become   BERNARD VAN EEGHEM

The former municipal public baths in Vorst (Brussels) houses a 'socio-artistic laboratory'. Les Bains::Connective is an experimental workplace, where visual artists, musicians, performers, scientists and botanists can set to work, for longer periods of residence or as a temporary stop. Les Bains calls itself a 'connective', because none of those artists is part of a single team. They work separately, but do that in the same location, in an open network and with a similar experimental attitude, which aims not so much at ready-made productions but at the process of artistic research.

Artists have inhabited the baths since 1997. At that time it was used by the Antwerp non-profit organization Krul – among others Lawrence and Vincent Malstaf and Liv Hanne Haugen – as the location for *Liquid Quantum Garden*, a cross-over project for dance, performance, music and installations. In those days the swimming pool was a near ruin after an eventful history. The plans for the building date from the 1920s, but it was not built until the 1950s. After the municipality decided to sell the baths in the 1980s because the running costs were too high, it was converted into an up-market nightclub. Clashes with local residents brought this part of its history to an end in 1991.

After *Liquid Quantum Garden* Krul signed a tenancy agreement with the owner for a period of eleven years. The gradual renovation of the site is part of that agreement. This is done through voluntary work and as part of specific artistic projects. For *Sauna in Exile*, for example, the changing cubicles were patched up. Although buildings are usually renovated completely by the time productions are staged, for Les Bains::Connective the building is also work in progress. It is an integral part of its artistic operation. As is the occasional function of guest-house. Indeed, other artists who sometimes make use of the space pay no rent, but in exchange help with the renovation work.

As well as *Liquid Quantum Garden*, larger-scale projects like *Too Much is Not Enough* (2001) and *Sauna in Exile* (2002) in which codes, borders and expectations are examined, have also been mounted. For Les Bains these larger public events are less important than the continuous activities comprising small-scale music and dance improvisations, workshops, lounge evenings and renovation weekends for volunteers. 'Musiclab' is a platform for improvised, intuitive and experimental music, including workshops and improvisation sessions. Sometimes the infrastructure is opened up for visual artists, who want to explore the building's potential with interactive installations. Members of the 'connective' have also tried by means of several projects to involve the neighbourhood in its artistic activities.

Its approach involving both – Dutch- and French-speaking – communities in Brussels means that under the existing regulations Les Bains::Connective does not really qualify for culture subsidies. Structural support is not forthcoming, although, a couple of years ago, a grant from Brussels Cultural Capital 2000 drew the attention of a wider public to Les Bains::Connective.   JJ

119

B S B (B I S)

Renovation work on the Beursschouwburg is now beginning to make good progress. With every visit, a little more of the scaffolding has been taken down, more of the building's features have been revealed and you can form a better picture of what it will look like once it is finished. It is now becoming clear just how much of the complex is taken up by what architects call 'circulation areas': those that serve no specific purpose other than that you have to go through them. It is apparent even to a passer-by on Ortsstraat that this is above all else a building to walk through: the wide façade only has doors, and behind them a staff entrance, a wide, steep stairway and a high passageway leading to the Karperbrug.

The explanation for this lies in the rules and regulations for the design competition, which specified that the slightly lopsided ceremonial stairway dating from the 1940s should be preserved. This requirement was prompted by a fear of the reactionary Brussels planning permission policy, but also by a fascination for the whimsical route through the complex which was heterogeneous even before the building was enlarged. Because vital parts where work was to be carried out could not be reached via this existing route, the logical consequence was that a new passageway should be added to the already elaborate circulation system. A whimsical circulation system, not altogether lacking old-fashioned charm, supplemented by a wide, efficient link: it is an urban metaphor well suited to Brussels that shores up the new Beursschouwburg.

It is not an inviting café that draws the passer-by over the threshold but, as in a picture puzzle, the far ends of a route. Comparisons with the Stuk in Leuven are inevitable; that, too, is an arts centre that was created by making an urban route through an existing building complex. There, too, you have to go well beyond the threshold before you reach the café; the gigantic letters on the pavement are not a shop window but a clue as to where you should look for the entrance to the route. There are other similarities as well. In both complexes the main 'rooms' have a distinct décor, autonomous with respect to the architecture of the route. The grey gunite of the passageway, the white distempered stucco and brickwork along the ceremonial stairway or, in the Stuk, the red wire-cut brick, convey neutrality and sobriety. The frivolity the rather eccentric 'rooms' allow themselves is literally cheap: the gold on the brick in the auditorium is paint, and the chic chequer-board pattern in the café is created using garage tiles. It is ironic chic that endorses the sobriety with a smile. With it both art centres reflect the values that were celebrated thirty and forty years ago with the building of the cultural centres. The government and the designers who worked for it would not have accepted that all the money invested in cultural infrastructure smacked of luxury, and so concrete and brick predominated.

Of course there are also any number of differences between the Beursschouwburg and a 1960s cultural centre. The individuality of the rooms and their interwovenness with the fabric of the city complete the scale of values and in an arts centre, unlike in a cultural centre, art is not only distributed, but also produced. That is why the Stuk is crowned with a sawtooth roof, an icon that spells 'production', and also in the passageway of the new Beursschouwburg the footbridges and hatchways are reminiscent of a factory. But they are more than icons: loading and unloading work really does have to be done in the passage. The Beursschouwburg is the metropolitan version of its extensive Leuven relative. Space is at a premium in Brussels, and all activity has to be concentrated. Whereas in a conventional theatre every effort is made to separate technicians, artists and visitors, the narrow confines and the enclosed character of the Beursschouwburg are the ideal pretext for leading everyone through the passage and provoking encounters, rather like when actors perform in the street. The street belongs to everyone. The new Beursschouwburg will be a non-hierarchical 'meeting place' in a more substantial way than the average cultural centre ever intended. The passage can rightly call itself a 'street', a 'public' space, even if the option of allowing passers-by through from Ortsstraat to Karperbrug would seem to be aiming too high.

In their conceptual clarity and boldness the Stuk and the new Beursschouwburg allow a glimpse of what might be called a typological or even ideological quality: a trail along which the social task of an arts centre is echoed in its architecture. It is nice to state that here, because the success of the arts centres and subsequent building plans were received with concern in an earlier VTi publication, *Alles is rustig* [All is quiet]. Building is slow and expensive and its results are lasting – which arouses suspicions in people who are used to being at the core of current artistic events and breaking through the rigidity with spontaneous stimuli and minimal means.

Could the reluctance to build, apparent from *Alles is rustig*, explain the appeal of BSBbis, the temporary premises in Kazernestraat that replace the Beursschouwburg for the duration of the building work? A two-storey garage; downstairs dark; upstairs, spacious and empty because of the enormous joists and monitors; robustly stayed by the upward spiralling circle of a climbing car, elegantly denoting expansion and restlessness: the aura of this body cannot fail to strike anyone who has shared in our post-industrial era. And then the interior, which can be erected as quickly as it can be dismantled, is as inventive as it is efficient and uses its fair share of recycled materials – beer crates, sandbags, glasshouses from the DIY shop! This is real, it is a breath of fresh air, it smacks of adventure! The removal of the hierarchy between culture producer and consumer, which is achieved in the new

Beursschouwburg after much deliberation about the route-ing, is more or less automatic here – there is simply no other way.

In *Jaarboek Architectuur Vlaanderen 00–01* [Flanders architecture yearbook 2000–01] Anne Malliet expresses the expectation that the interior of BSBbis will be more durable than was intended. I do hope she is proved wrong. The crates have to go back to the brewer, the sandbags to the Civil Defence, the glasshouses to the back gardens of Schaarbeek or possibly to the loft of a trendy yup. Perpetual adventure – be it James Bond or Tin Tin – is dull. If at a later stage the building becomes a designer shop or a gallery, we will look round it hesitantly and argue as to exactly where those sandbags were.

Camping is good. Without the comforts of home, you see everything more clearly, it makes you a different person. But in time the lack of comfort begins to gall, and you want to go home to do what you could not do in your bivouac. Of course house and bivouac are related. At the camp-site you try to guess how your neighbours live at home. But you can get it terribly wrong! Anyone who visits the Beursschouwburg in its temporary accommodation might expect that 'at home' they are building a radically modern complex: a stack of plateaux like the garage, but with more technical facilities to enable any conceivable application. Totally wrong! The affinity is not the preference for a certain type of space, but the preference for spaces with a handicap: spaces which don't make it immediately clear how they should be used, and which require creativity on the part of programmer and artist.

The Beursschouwburg's new accommodation will not arouse in us the same emotion as the encampment in Kazernestraat. Apart from the obvious difference in terms of comfort, of spatial typology and the intensity of the aura of the old, there is this. In Kazernestraat the decision to maintain an existing body was a pragmatic and obvious one: after all, it cost nothing. Maintaining the existing complex body in Ortsstraat is a voluntaristic decision, one that has required considerable investment and, so far as the rather odd ceremonial stairway and the excessive platforms alongside are concerned, nothing short of a bonus to the actual programme of the arts centre. Therein lies the luxury of this sober, cheerful but thriftily executed new house. It is this luxury the new Beursschouwburg will have to show itself worthy of. The circulation areas – the spaces that serve no specific purpose other than that you have to go through them – will be the challenge after the move. Then we will see just how refreshing the holiday in the garage really was.
BSB and BSBbis: it is one project.

PAUL VERMEULEN

BSB (bis)

According to the original plans, the long-awaited conversion of the Brussels Beursschouwburg was to be carried out in several stages, so that it could continue to operate, albeit with the occasional location project. When in the year 2000 this proved unrealistic, temporary accommodation was sought. October 2000 brought the announcement of the move to a former furniture depot at no. 37 Kazernestraat. Comprising two floors and a total surface area of 2,400 m², this building provided sufficient space for production, presentation, café, offices and storage. The cultural potential of this industrial building had been discovered at the beginning of 1998. Plans to convert it into a Centre for Cultures during Brussels Cultural Capital 2000 came to nothing because of a lack of financing. That year Els Dietvorst (*Terugkeer van de zwaluwen* [Return of the swallows]) and Els Van Riel (*Bewegend portret* [Moving portrait]) used the crude, industrial space for a public presentation of their projects.
The Beursschouwburg was to use the space for a period of eighteen months from the beginning of 2001. B-architects, also involved in converting the building in the A. Ortstraat, bore the temporary nature of the building very much in mind. On the ground floor they built a room with walls of sandbags and scaffolding, which also served as a barrier against noise nuisance from concerts. Above that the Beursschouwburg team was given four glasshouses as office space, while a large open space with sawtooth roof (and natural light) was available for rehearsals, performances and exhibitions. In terms of furnishing the building, extensive use was made of recycled materials, either brought with them from the old Beursschouwburg or rescued from the scrap heap. Additional constructions, for instance those made of brickwork with protruding mortar, are in keeping with the rough character of the building.
The neighbourhood project *Terugkeer van de Zwaluwen 3* by Els Dietvorst was warmly received when the BSBbis opened in February 2001. Choreographer Tom Plischke & Friends were given ten days to explore the building's potential experimentally. The big difference between the Beursschouwburg and BSBbis in terms of atmosphere, appearance and scale did not result in an abrupt change in the programming. The new potential of the building and particularly of the circulation spaces was explored as part of the project.
The public had no difficulty whatsoever finding its way to this forgotten area behind the Anneessensplein. This is to the credit of the inventive communication and the speed with which the Beursschouwburg team reacted. Even in 2001 the café introduced longer opening hours to satisfy the demand for more meeting places. During the indoor concerts of the tenth edition of 'Klinkende Munt' in July 2001 the public could walk from the Muntplein to BSBbis past refreshment tents reminiscent of those used in marathons.
Meanwhile the old building has not been forgotten. Photographer Jan Kempenaers documents the developments at the site in the monthly magazine. As work fell behind schedule the date for returning there was moved to November 2003, while the official opening of the 'new' Beursschouwburg is planned for 5 February 2004, the arts centre's 39th birthday. In the meantime there is a growing body of opinion that a permanent cultural use should be found for the building on Kazernestraat.
NW

P . A . R . T . S .

OPEN LETTER TO A DANCER AUDITIONING FOR P.A.R.T.S.

P.A.R.T.S., or Performing Arts Research and Training Studios, is an environment constructed for you to learn. Not only to learn to dance, but also to learn something *about* dance. But, remember, no environment *per se* contains information. The environment, as the systems theoretician Heinz von Foerster said, is as it is. It is *your* interaction, *your* negotiations with that environment that will constitute what learning means for you.

Your attendance at this school will be a licence for confusion! Your nervous system will be assaulted by the newness of encounters. Since all nervous systems are organized so as to compute stable realities, yours will also look for assurance. But you will understand that it is this that makes up your programme for the coming years: a never-ending oscillation between perturbation and the self-assurance of your newly found internal organization.

You are the life vessel of all manner of know-how, histories and disciplines. You might be fond of gardening, of art or skating, of hiking or climbing trees. You might have done military service or escaped it, danced in the streets or in 'conservatoires'. Like all training courses, PARTS will privilege a certain type of knowledge and discourage other types. It is a regulative system, based on inhibition and repression, in synchronism with the demands of the contemporary dance scene. PARTS originated from this scene and is led by people who are deeply involved with it — not only the choreographer Anne Teresa De Keersmaeker, but also the organizers in her entourage. It inherited its myths, dreams and paradoxes.

If the word 'inhibition' sounds scary to you, then remember that – on a deeper level – it is innate to all learning, whether learning to drive a car or to do contact improvisation. What we call efficiency and fluency is the result of a successful repression of irrelevant responses (leading eventually to the degeneracy of neurons so as to facilitate forgetting) and the synaptic activation of others. Remember, though, that a training course will only ever be a tiny part of *your* larger history.

PARTS is a school that does not dedicate itself to the glorification of one dance technique, but to the transmission of several. Each approach presupposes a specific conception of physicality, the stage, the eye of the beholder, aesthetics and politics. Thus you will understand that it is incorrect to say that the contemporary dance school has freed itself from the dogma of the 'old school', where dancers' bodies were squeezed into the tight mould of the one and only sacred technique. Because this typifies the new dogma of your postmodern condition: your own endless motility, the fallacy of your versatility, the phantasm and pleasure of your malleability.

But you will realize that technicity is not what ultimately matters, however painstakingly acquired. What matters is that you change, and the question of what you change into is secondary to the force of that change. It starts with your transformation and you will learn that the audience that awaits you needs your expertise in change if, in its turn, it is also to be transformed. Your experience anticipates their own productive confusion. Just as you will want to have changed when you leave the school, they too want to be altered in some way when they leave the theatre.

Not coming from a pedagogical background, the founders of the school described it as first and foremost an 'artistic project'. This means that you will engage in an educational project whose approach goes *beyond* pedagogy. The stage is the ultimate proof of fulfilment. The stage: the organizing principle that gives direction and endows everything in the curriculum with a sense of finality. It may be no coincidence that now with the first generations of graduates the school is more active than any other of its kind in presenting their work at festivals and international theatres. In this respect, PARTS sometimes resembles more a studio than a training course – a workplace that lives in close and – for a school – unparalleled symbiosis with the contemporary dance scene.

But this goal may be too far ahead, for you are just about to audition. After all, destinations are one thing; finding *your* destiny is another. Good luck on the journey!

MYRIAM VAN IMSCHOOT

Founded by Anne Teresa De Keersmaeker in Brussels in 1995, PARTS runs professional dance courses. PARTS, short for Performing Arts Research and Training Studios, is not a purely technical course but sets out to make dancers and choreographers familiar with the contemporary performing arts scene and with every aspect of the creative production process. The curriculum combines intensive dance training with a sound theoretical basis comprising sociology, philosophy and history of theatre and dance; attention is also given to other artistic disciplines (especially music and theatre). The first part of the training imparts the necessary technical baggage, covering the modern, the postmodern and the classical. In the second part, students are given the opportunity to explore the subjects in greater depth and to create their own work.

The training is international in scope, attracting students from all over the world, with English as the language of communication. The teaching staff are also recruited internationally. Auditions are held in more than fifteen cities in Europe and further afield. As well as being home to celebrated companies like Rosas, Ultima Vez and Damaged Goods, the success of the first batch of PARTS graduates has also helped make Brussels a magnet for young dance talent from all over the world.

PARTS uses the same premises as De Keersmaeker's company Rosas and the contemporary music ensemble Ictus. The infrastructure – a former bleachery in Vorst – comprises ten professionally equipped dance studios, of which five are at the permanent disposal of the school. The student productions are mounted in the Rosas Performance Space – a professional auditorium with 400 seats.

The work of each new batch of students is presented at regular intervals in Brussels. The 'SUM/SOME of the parts' festival held during the opening weekend of Brussels 2000 featured work by (among others) Tom Plischke, Arco Renz, Salva Sanchis, Riina Saastamoinen, Muketsi Kuna, Gregory Maqoma, Moya Michael, Sharon Zuckerman and Charlotte Vanden Eynde. The largest presentation project to date took place in France. Entitled *PARTS @ PARIS* (2001), the Théâtre de la Bastille and the prestigious Festival d'Automne invited De Keersmaeker and PARTS to take up residence there for a month and give more than forty performances.

Even if Belgium is not awash with stages for contemporary dance, there are opportunities for the former students of PARTS to develop their careers. Some have worked with Jan Fabre, Meg Stuart, Wim Vandekeybus, Sidi Larbi Cherkaoui, Jan Decorte, Michèle Noiret and Anne Teresa De Keersmaeker, while others have also staged their own work. Rosas and PARTS support the graduates with the subsidiary Werkhuis/producties and the international network DÉPARTS. JJ

CONCERTGEBOUW BRUGGE

CONCERTGEBOUW

1.

When Aladdin ordered the genie of the magic lantern to build a palace, he asked that the ninety-ninth and last window be left unfinished so that the king, the father of his bride, could decorate it at his discretion with gold and precious stones.

When the Concertgebouw in Bruges opened on 22 February 2002, it was not finished. Everyone who had set foot inside had the feeling he could add something to it. The story of the 68,000 terracotta tiles went round the world: however new, the building immediately had a history; a story that anticipated the thousand and one nights which would follow.

2.

Music and architecture have something in common. Unlike all the other arts in which frontality is important, music and architecture are all around us. We are in their midst. They are the two arts 'which enclose man, or rather which enclose the person in his work, and the soul in his deeds and in the productions of his deeds ...' (Paul Valéry).

3.

There are innumerable theatres which have *not* been built in the history of the stage: Edward Gordon Craig's theatre, Adolphe Appia's, the Piscator theatre designed by Walter Gropius, Jan Joris Lamers' transparent theatre, and so on. Bruges built its Concertgebouw at the very beginning of the twenty-first century. The Festspielhaus in Bayreuth was built for performances of the work of a single artist; the Radio City Music Hall in New York with its 6,200 seats was designed on the basis of impresario Samuel Rothafel's fantastic vision. In Bruges the architects Paul Robbrecht and Hilde Daem built a theatre for the residents: for the many spectators and the many artists who (will) spend their thousand and one nights there.

4.

The building has no threshold; when you open the glass doors, the square outside flows into the entrance hall. It is large and spacious inside, but the sensation cannot be described as massive or monumental. You can be together there and also alone. You can choose. No particular attitude is imposed on you. When you sit in the auditorium, you find a line of verse by Peter Verhelst on the back of the seat in front of you: specially for you, only for you. When next time you return and sit down in a different place, you read another piece of the story. And after that another. And then one more. Ninety-nine times and more. The poem is never completed.

5.

The auditorium, it is said, is built like a horn, like the cup you make with your two hands when you put them to your mouth to make your voice carry. Simple. Organic. Human in scale. And yet it is big. Bigger than you can ever imagine. Like the theatre of Epidaurus where the voice in word and song, in tones and melodies wells up from that flat disk below and along the walls of the funnel. The origin of the world from sound, the primal scream with which everything began, the Om of the Hindus, the word that was in the beginning. First came the ear, only after that the eye. The eye which always needs the frontality vis-à-vis what it sees, *and* the proximity *and* the focus. 'Theatre is perspective. Making theatre is not staging something, but determining the point from which something has to be seen ...' (Bart Verschaffel). Theatre is adopting a standpoint.

6.

There are windows in the large concert hall; the theatre looks outwards. The light which filters in makes the theatre into a working space, a daytime space. The light also places the building in the outside space, in the city. It makes people curious about life. About the sounds in the street. What is behind that window? *'Let the sunlight in, open that door, open it ...'*, sings Bluebeard to Judith in Bartók's only opera *Duke Bluebeard's Castle*. *'Is it true, is it not true: was it inside or out? An old story, but what does it mean? ... The play is about to begin. The curtain of my eyes rises ...'*, sings the minstrel in the prologue to the same opera.

7.

Bluebeard's castle sighs, the walls weep or bleed, the space lives. Bluebeard *is* his castle. Every space has an inner self. In large buildings the massiveness and the publicness threaten to dispel that inner self. Rare are the monumental 'houses' that have a soul, but the Concertgebouw is one such. Bachelard described the *'immensité'* as *'conquête de l'intimité'* [conquest of the intimate]. In the chamber music hall the *intimité* is literally placed in the middle. The music as the core, as the central point. Just as the cavaliers in 'La Giralda', the bell tower next to Seville cathedral, ride up the gentle slopes, turning round and round that nucleus, that arrow pointing upwards to the space where Allah or God was thought to be, here too the spectators can walk round the music and embrace the intimacy of the music-making.

8.

The Concertgebouw is an open organism, it can as it were grow, change, fill up and empty again, acquire a history, I've like Bluebeard's Castle. The Concertgebouw is in fact a dramaturgy. A structure, a framework that is instrumental without being utilitarian, that is present without imposing that presence, that is autonomous and at the same time subordinate – to materials, to people and their activities, to time, to the space. 'The artistic act is always one of subordinating, not of dominating' (Kurt Schwitters). An act of unemphaticness, modesty, diffidence almost.

9.

'Do not forget that a theatre builds itself – by which I mean that the public is the architect of the auditorium and the performance is the architecture of the stage' (Herman Teirlinck). As in June 2002, in *SS*, the large-scale music-theatre production by Josse De Pauw and Tom Jansen in which fifty-five members of the Ghent Madrigal Choir appeared on the stage of the Concertgebouw, when one of the choir members bought a ticket for himself for the second performance and went and sat in the auditorium. He wanted to see the performance he was in as a performer through the eyes of a spectator. The border between stage and spectators' area is crossable, it is not a barrier. The curtain that goes up when the play begins is indeed 'the curtain of our eyes'. Paul Robbrecht and Hilde Daem have created a building and given it to the people of Bruges, who are writing their own production there – as performers and as spectators.

MARIANNE VAN KERKHOVEN

In its bid to become 'European Cultural Capital 2002', the Bruges city council seized the opportunity to broach a sensitive subject — that of introducing contemporary architecture into the historic city. The concert hall known as Concertgebouw was the largest of these projects. Its site was to be 't Zand, a large public space near the city centre. At the end of 1997, an international architecture competition was organized. And in January 1999 the international jury selected the project designed by Ghent architects Paul Robbrecht and Hilde Daem.

The building consists of a main building and a slightly separate tower, the Lantern Tower, which is linked to the main building by means of a walkway-cum-foyer with sloping floors. The Lantern Tower houses the Chamber Music Hall, with 320 movable seats on three levels. This hall takes the form of a *cortile* or inner courtyard of an Italian *palazzo*. It has a walkway that circles round the open boxes in a continuous spiral.

The Concert Hall in the main building has 1,300 seats spread over three levels. This room needed to accommodate not only symphonic music, but also congresses and performing arts events. Consequently, a stage tower had to be built and the acoustics required considerable fine-tuning. For example, the auditorium has slanting, oyster-shaped walls, rather like two hands held to the mouth to help the voice carry.

The architects have established links with the surrounding area in various ways. The building is covered with browny-red terracotta tiles — an ode to the brick bravura of St Saviour's Cathedral. When it is dark outside, the Lantern Tower lights up the square. It provides Bruges with a fourth tower, in addition to the historical triad of the Belfry, St Saviour's and the Church of Our Lady. Another link with the surroundings is a video wall above the main entrance on which performances inside and other events can be screened. There is a clear link with the city in the building itself, too: the backs of the seats in the Concertgebouw each bear a line from a narrative poem by Peter Verhelst about the city and its culture.

The first year of operation was rather exceptional, because the Concertgebouw's artistic and commercial management was in the hands of Bruges Cultural Capital 2002. At the beginning of 2003 a new team took over the helm, with Lieven Bertels as artistic director. The emphasis is on providing a wide range of music styles. The Concertgebouw is looking for an identity of its own through musical cross-fertilization.   EB

MUZIEKFORUM   GENT

F****?

(O N   T H E   M U Z I E K F O R U M)

'The best documented and computed project in local history', was how it was described in 2001.[1] It was the eve of the first public debate about Gerard Mortier's wild dream: a multifunctional arts laboratory for Ghent, an architectural landmark in the urbanized region between Paris and Amsterdam, a music forum for the twenty-first century. All in one.

The story of that Forum had small beginnings. Back in 1996, top musicians and local politicians joined forces to at last build an acoustically first-rate concert hall in Ghent. A 'Saturday morning work group' met to flesh out the plans. But too late, it transpired, for Bruges, nominated Cultural Capital of Europe 2002, had a new concert hall on its programme and a government is never keen to set aside money for two identical projects a stone's throw away from each other. Until Gerard Mortier appeared on the scene, as a *deus ex machina*. When Mortier speaks, people listen. 'If you don't do it, we will never find that money,' Mayor Beke is reported to have said.[2]

But Mortier did it. The plans for a concert hall were transformed into plans for a 'Forum for Music, Dance and Visual Culture', with office space, business lounges for the corporate sector and a film theatre. The roof was to become a *plaza*. Although the auditorium was slightly compromised (reduced from 2,000 to 1,800 seats), it would now be entirely modular in construction so as to accommodate every possible type of production. In terms of architecture, reference was made to the Guggenheim in Bilbao. A public series of studies – a novelty in Flanders! – was to colour the financial and artistic picture. And yes, 250,000 visitors a year was the target.[3] It was Mortier at his best: bursting with boundless ambition which automatically drew a cacophony of comment and criticism.

It was also the beginning of a crusade involving conferences, debates, meetings, recalls, reports, press communiqués and hearings. The debate was heated, the positions unassailable and such details as the building date disappeared into the background. In time the fate of the *Krook*, as the Forum came to be known, will gradually become clear, but even now the discussions about it have become a subject in their own right. Long before the first stone is laid, the 'best documented and computed project in local history' has also become the most controversial project. And thus a first objective has been achieved: the Forum is the talk of the town.

'THIS IS NOT A DEBATE!'[4]

Often a debate is not a real debate. Complex subject matter and vested interests are not conducive to that. 'The discussion is there for the form, the conflict thrives and is well protected. Subject to a few virtuoso pirouettes, the moderator can still try to bring about a confrontation of ideas, but is forced to slink off after a few attempts. The seventh-day feeling.'[5] The cultural decision-makers know the tricks of the trade and they do not always speak their mind. An interested layman has to interpret the facts and figures for himself and is likely to become more frustrated than satisfied. And public opinion, that strange creature, is spontaneously divided into believers and non-believers.

A debate needs to be fostered and nourished, as Mortier would undoubtedly agree. Hence this *tour d'horizon* of the Forum debate, inspired by the sms messages the public could send by way of interaction during the discussions at the Minard.[6] From there we step into the wood, in search of trees. Those who feel hungry can turn straight to the bibliography.

'PROJECT IS GOOD BUT WILL ABSORB TOO MUCH CULTURE MONEY'

First the figures. The cost of building the Forum was initially estimated at 50 million euro. It later transpired that that figure was 'exclusive': excluding VAT, excluding making the site ready for building and excluding redeveloping the surrounding area. Inclusive estimates are closer to 65 million euro plus, sometimes as much as 86.7 million.[7] And you don't need to be an experienced property developer to know Cheops' law: 'Nothing is ever built on time or within budget.'

Now the building costs rarely feature in the debates. People have accepted that the building will cost money. It is now the revenue that generates more commotion, and particularly the revenue from the predicted visitor numbers. The ultimate question was put to Guido De Brabander, Professor at the University of Antwerp: will the Forum attract 250,000 visitors? De Brabander watched and analysed, juxtaposed comparisons and variables, calculated three variants and finally diplomatically concluded that this is 'not very likely'. New projects, he added, 'place further limitations on that likelihood'. An impressive list follows of preconditions that need to be met.[8] Those backing the project were not very pleased. What did they expect? Enthusiasm and persuasion are Mortier's world, as is the canvassing power of a well-managed hype. Not the art of the possible, cold figures or spreadsheets.

Be that as it may, bare facts cannot be ignored. Since De Brabander's analysis the Concertgebouw has opened in Bruges, Ghent has welcomed Capitole and Handelsbeurs, while Flagey and Bozar have found a new lease of life in Brussels and even poverty-stricken Antwerp has been looking at how it can best *reposition* itself.[9] Whichever regions the Forum recruits from, and irrespective of dynamic visitor models, the competition has increased sharply in a very short period of time.

And exactly that is the vulnerable spot of the Forum. Not achieving the predicted audience numbers will create a deficit in the annual operating costs.[10] The Forum is 61% dependent on its own revenue and the quality of its marketing policy 'will be vitally important'[11] — it's make or break even. The scrapping of the business lounges for the corporate sector (good for 82% of the revenue) and the swapping of offices for workshops have only served to exacerbate that situation.[12] Extra subsidies will be hard to come by, the resources will have to be sought internally. Or how the concerns of big business can threaten the artistic core business.

'HELLO! IS THERE AN ARTIST IN THE HOUSE?'

Vooruit Director Erik Temmerman broached the question of that artistic core business: which new monopoly legitimizes the Forum? The monopoly of the arts centre within a larger cultural field, he reasoned, is extremely important. Financially, geographically and artistically. 'Otherwise you end up with a situation whereby the government is sponsoring competition.'[13]

At that Mortier referred to the role of the laboratory and to the study produced by culture scientist Rik Pinxten.[14] Pinxten gave the debate the chiasma metaphor, formulated the possibility of an 'artistic think-tank for auditory and visual awareness' and presented himself as a firm believer. Parading between quotes in his study, he made a plea for a new artistic dynamism and more 'interculturality'. No more exoticism and no more 'museumizing' of cultural products.[15] No more safe stories.

Reactions were divided. *'Ever been to the Vooruit, Mr Pinxten?'* a member of the audience sms-ed during the very first debate. Believers read it as a challenging declaration of intent, opponents as a woolly generality. Whatever the case may be, apart from Pinxten's study there was no up-to-the-minute inventory and analysis of the urban cultural perception, no measured consideration of the complementary functions of the existing arts centres.[16] The 'complementary' role, the Krook's new monopoly, remained the subject of heated discussion.

'LET THE FORUM BE THE CITY ITSELF'

And yet: sometimes a debate is genial and charitable. At an umpteenth symposium, this time at Victoria, Dominique Willaert called upon people to regard the whole city of Ghent as the Krook. Willaert dismissed the Forum as 'the megalomaniac and prestigious ambition of a privileged few'.[17] His idea was to weave a real network through the whole city, a 'spider's web' of little Krooks, sanctuaries without the jargon. With the new experience of the Ruhr region fresh in his mind, Mortier embraced

144

the opportunity. In interviews he had already leaked the odd idea in that direction. At the same time it was a way out of the Forum's greatest paradox: how to combine the large-scale with experiment? How to maintain contact from a lighthouse with the ground, with the amorphous, with the moist cultural mulch layer?[18]

The separation of the Forum *idea* from the Forum *building* was later rejected. The image of the lighthouse in the spider's web is now widely known. A mist still hangs over the specifics of that form, just as it does over the financial picture and the artistic content. Despite all the debates. In situations like these Mortier is at his best: 'Mist appears after a beautiful clear day when the energies begin to work.'[19]

To be continued.

KRIS MOTMANS

I wish to thank the Flemish Theatre Institute and the non-profit Forum for placing their inexhaustible archives at my disposal. My thanks also to everyone who took time out for a discussion about the Forum.

LITERATURE

• *Project Oprichting van een Forum voor Muziek, Dans en Beeldcultuur. Beperkte offerteaanvraag. Samenstelling beoordelingscommissie.* Ghent: vzw Forum voor Muziek, Dans en Beeldcultuur, September 2002, 30 pp.
• *Verslag vergadering Vlaamse culturele sector, vrijdag 7 juni 2002, stadhuis Gent.* Ghent: vzw Forum voor Muziek, Dans en Beeldcultuur, June 2002, 31 pp.
• *Verslag vergadering Gentse culturele sector, dinsdag 11 juni 2002, stadhuis Gent.* Ghent: vzw Forum voor Muziek, Dans en Beeldcultuur, June 2002, 41 pp.
• Daan Bauwens and Elke Van Campenhout, *Forum voor / over stad / Cultuur / Arch / Tectuur. Verslag debat 23 november 2001.* Ghent: vzw Forum voor Muziek, Dans en Beeldcultuur, n.d. [winter 2001?], 15 pp.
• Guido De Brabander and Sandra De Cock, *Haalt het Forum 250.000 bezoekers? Eindrapport in opdracht van de vzw Forum voor Muziek, Dans en Beeldcultuur Gent.* Antwerp: UAMS Universiteit Antwerpen, August 2001, 125 pp. + appendices.
• Hildegard De Vuyst (ed.), *Alles is rustig. Het verhaal van de kunstencentra.* Brussels: Vlaams Theater Instituut, 1999, 182 pp. + appendices.
• Pascal Gielen, *Kleine dramaturgie voor een artefactenstoet. Omtrent Gent Cultuurstad.* Ghent: Dienst Culturele Zaken, 2000, 111 pp.
• Dirk Holemans, 'Cultuur als levenskunst', *Oikos* 21 (autumn 2002), pp. 75–85.
• Dirk Holemans, Dirk De Corre, Dominique Willaert, Gerard Mortier, Koen Gisen and Patrick Allegaert, 'Het OIKOS-symposium: "Cultuur en Stedelijkheid"', *Oikos* 22 (summer 2002), pp. 9–55.
• Rudi Laermans, *Het Vlaams Cultureel Regiem. Onderzoeksrapport in opdracht van het Ministerie van de Vlaamse Gemeenschap, Administratie Cultuur.* Leuven: KU Leuven, Centrum voor Cultuursociologie, 2001, 216 pp.
• Samuël Maenhout, *Musisch Forum. Een model voor cultuurparticipatie bij jongeren.* Ghent: vzw Forum voor Muziek, Dans en Beeldcultuur, June 2001, 138 pp.
• Gerard Mortier and Daan Bauwens, *Bouwen op braakliggend terrein. Programmatie, prijzen, organigram en werkingsmiddelen.* Ghent: vzw Forum voor Muziek, Dans en Beeldcultuur, June 2001, 33 pp.
• Gerard Mortier and Daan Bauwens, *Bouwprogramma voor Forum voor Muziek, Dans en Beeldcultuur.* Ghent: vzw Forum voor Muziek, Dans en Beeldcultuur, October 2002, 37 pp.
• Rik Pinxten, *De Krook. Studierapport in opdracht van de vzw Forum.* Ghent: Vakgroep Vergelijkende Cultuur-wetenschappen, Universiteit Gent, n.d. [summer 2001?], 52 pp.
• Letty Ranshuysen, *Een nieuw stadsmuseum voor Gent. Voorstellen vanuit het beoogde publiek.* Ghent: vzw Gent Cultuurstad, 2003, 119 pp.
• Jo Sanders and Karen De Man, *Kritische analyse van de nota Bouwen op Braakliggend Terrein.* Ernst & Young, September 2001, 56 pp.
• *Hoorzitting met de heer Gerard Mortier betreffende het project 'Muziekforum'. Verslag namens de Commissie voor Cultuur, Media en Sport, uitgebracht door mevrouw Mieke Van Hecke.* Brussels: Vlaams Parlement, stuk 815 (2000–2001), no. 1, Session of 18 July 2001, 12 pp.

NOTES

1 Geert Van der Speeten, 'Avontuur van een Muziekfabriek – Gent debatteert over het Muziekforum', *De Standaard*, 23 November 2001.
2 Mortier in an interview with Karel Van Keymeulen, 'Gerard Mortier wil de slag om Gent winnen', *De Standaard*, 11 February 2000.
3 By way of comparison: deSingel attracts 120,000 a year, the Flanders Opera 100,000, Vooruit 48,000. Figures taken from De Brabander.
4 The subheadings derive from sms messages sent during the Forum debate at the Minard. See note 6 below.
5 Patrick Allegaert in 'Derde Keer, Goede Keer', *Oikos* 22 (summer 2002), p. 51.
6 The sms messages were projected onto a large screen during the debate. A selection is included in the report of the debate.
7 See Wilfried Eetezonne, 'De Krook kan ook Krookjes worden', *De Morgen*, 6 May 2002. For the period 2002–04 the Cabinet for Culture earmarked a total of 87 million euro for cultural buildings, including 31 million for the MAS [Museum aan de Stroom: Museum by the river], 13 million for deSingel and 11 million for the Flanders Opera in Antwerp.
8 De Brabander, p. 118: 'Meeting these preconditions in no way implies that the maximum variant [in visitor numbers—KM] will be reached.'
9 On the situation in Antwerp, see Geert Van der Speeten, 'Een zaal aan de Stroom', *De Standaard*, 26 November 2002.
10 The operating costs are estimated at some six million euro per year. Ticket sales need to generate more than 2.5 million francs per year of that, but in his most optimistic scenario De Brabander arrives at only 2.2 million.
11 De Brabander, p. 83. Details of the calculations on pp. 112–114. See also the report by Ernst & Young.
12 Ernst & Young, p. 36, detailed calculation on p. 37. All parties were coyly silent on the subject of sponsorship.
13 Report Minard debate, p. 12.
14 The study was entitled 'Krook' ('a sharp bend, a curve in something that was previously straight'). Krook has since been the Forum's official second name.
15 On the (de-)museumizing of heritage, see also Pascal Gielen. The word 'strolling' (*flâner*) is used here, as with Pinxten (p. 21), in a positive and refreshing sense.
16 Rudi Laermans has since produced a study, but that is completely separate from the Forum. Hildegard De Vuyst's *Alles is Rustig. Het Verhaal van de Kunstencentra* has been published, too, but also in a totally different context.
17 Dominique Willaert, 'Vijf aanzetten tot reflectie', *Oikos* 22 (summer 2002).
18 Pieter T'Jonck, architectural engineer and lecturer at the University of Ghent, during the Minard debate: 'And – above all – is there any sense in building a hyper-flexible hall for the unexpected and unknown, knowing that this unexpected and unknown will always ask for a specific location?' Report Minard debate, p. 10.
19 Quoted in *De Morgen*, 6 November 2002.

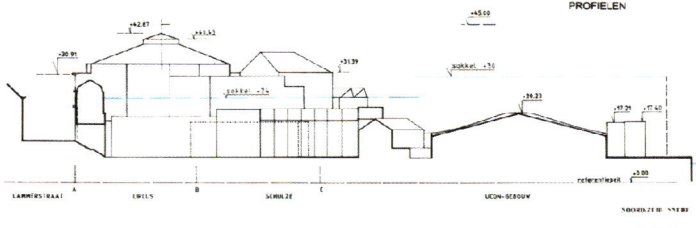

PROFIELEN

FORUM VOOR MUZIEK, DANS EN BEELDCULTUUR

The Forum voor Muziek, Dans en Beeldcultuur [Forum for music, dance and visual culture], alias 'De Krook', alias the 'Muziekforum', is the only virtual item in this publication. Underlying the idea for a Forum in Ghent is the demand for an acoustically perfect concert hall able to accommodate large orchestras. In 1997 Ghent city council set up a steering group and a project group led by Daan Bauwens. The chosen site is a centrally located piece of ground near 'Het Zuid', namely the Waalse Krook. In 1998 Gerard Mortier joined the artistic working group. At the beginning of the year 2000 Bert Anciaux, then Minister of Cultural Affairs in the Flemish Government, announced that he was setting aside an operating subsidy to set up a project secretariat. Gerard Mortier became the project leader and Daan Bauwens the project coordinator. The brief of the new non-profit Forum voor Muziek, Dans en Beeldcultuur was to develop a general vision that would embed the Forum in the Ghent, Flemish and international artistic scene; to come up with a proposal for its programming; to carry out a study into its social and economic viability; and to prepare an architectural competition.

As well as a study of the building programme and of the artistic and business aspects of the Forum's operation, a number of research assignments were contracted out concerning the Forum's aims and objectives (culture scientist Rik Pinxten, Ghent University), a culture participation model for young people (Maenhout), a feasibility study vis-à-vis the strength of public support for the project (De Brabander, De Cock) and a critical examination of the Forum's own proposals by Ernst & Young.

In terms of the aims and objectives, the idea is to get away from the old norms of the classical Western canon and to arrive at a dynamic, permeable and kaleidoscopic project. This is inspired by Pinxten's study, which focuses on the chiasma model of the chaos theory. The actual operation and philosophy are compared to a group of birds in a tree, which, suddenly startled, take off in apparent chaos only to alight again on the branches, but in a different configuration. Core concepts include: multifunctional, interdisciplinary, instigator of interculturality, interaction, research, experiment, production.

All this has architectonic consequences. Instead of a shoe-box concert hall, architecturally shut off from the outside world, the Forum's main auditorium is to be multifunctional and modular and able to seat between 800 and 1,800, while the foyer is designed to inspire a new relationship between auditorium and city.

The project has triggered a great deal of discussion, not least about the specific use the building will be put to, and about its interaction with existing cultural institutions. The idea of a 'spider's web', a plea for a network of actors and for a fabric that is socially and artistically anchored in the city, is now preferred to the initial idea of a 'lighthouse'. This means that the original concepts had to be adjusted and ways had to be found of removing barriers to the public. A 'lighthouse in a spider's web' is the new working title.

An international architecture competition was organized. At the end of 2001, a jury led by the Flemish Government Architect bOb Van Reeth drew up the following short-list from 34 entries: Rem Koolhaas with his firm OMA (Rotterdam), Neutelings Riedijk Architecten (Rotterdam), Claus & Kahn Architecten (Amsterdam), Toyo Ito Architect & Associates (Japan), Samyn & Partners (Brussels). EB

THEATRE BUILDINGS

ON THE THEATRE INFRASTRUCTURE IN THE URBAN SPACE

VEERLE KEUPPENS

The city is a meeting place

Theatre can be put on anywhere: in any village, on any farm, on a deserted island. But the natural meeting place for performing artists and their audience – at least in Western culture – is the city. 'Artistic and cultural facilities are traditionally connected with the city, not just for the simple reason that the city's central function entails a differentiated supply of facilities, but also because properly functioning cities are characterized by the presence of large groups of people, including artists and viewers.'[1] 'In any case city centres play a key role as multifunctional public spaces and as forums for social and cultural life.'[2]

That is why the present article has little or nothing to say about the diffusion of culture and its specific embedding in the infrastructure of Flanders, but is almost exclusively concerned with the theatre infrastructure in the cities. This does not entail any value judgement – it is a choice that is objectively determined by the predominance of the cities in cultural production. The city's importance will increase further in the future. 'The 21st century will be the century of cities. For the first time in human history over 50% of the world will live in cities. In Europe already 70% of people do.'[3] Neither will this article be concerned with extra-mural theatre, which has little or no need of infrastructure.

Buildings as attractions

In the last few years cultural buildings have been given more and more priority on the political agenda. One of the reasons for this is the recent development of urban space. In an interview the urban geographer Irina van Aalst places this phenomenon in a present-day context: 'To begin with, the entire economic basis of the cities is changing. Factories and businesses are disappearing from the cities. People have money and more time off work, so there is a search for a different source of income in the field of consumption, entertainment and leisure. City administrators increasingly view these factors as a visiting card for their city, as something that distinguishes them from other cities with which they compete for consumers, residents or new, often cultural small businesses.'

The recent interest on the part of certain cities in new, high-quality cultural infrastructure and their choice of ambitious buildings designed by famous architects (the Concertgebouw in Bruges, the plans for the Forum in Ghent) also fit into the context of city marketing. But should we be worried by it? Can a 'more attractive' city, with a conspicuous cultural infrastructure, not be an ally in the attempt to interest more people in art? Of course, there is the risk that the maintenance of these buildings will be so expensive that in order to break even they will eventually have to devote themselves more to entertainment than to reflection, encounter, participation, discussion and information. Are there instruments to signal such threats in time so that they can be thwarted or avoided? A first requirement is that all of the parties who are involved in the building and programming of a theatre consult with one another to determine exactly what they want.

Which theatre for this city?

Theatre comes before the playhouse and is also possible outside that building. 'To create an event, you don't start out with a shell, you start out with an impulse, with the source.'[4] However, from the moment the decision is taken to build a theatre, the decision-making process becomes caught up in a network that involves many actors: the theatre companies, the public, the architects, the local government and so on. With a view to city marketing, the local government (and in its wake a proportion of the potential audience) will tend to opt for an attractive building on an attractive site. It is easy to reach agreement on this choice, because it appeals to the architects too and it can be used to tempt theatre producers. A second requisite – which will be put forward above all by the local authority and the planners – could be that the theatre building itself must form a part of the public space in the sense of being accessible to all. The era of closed theatres that are only open at night seems to be over: theatres are incorporated in the city passage, they fulfil commercial (bookshops etc.) and catering functions, but can above all also incorporate other cultural functions. Space can be created in the theatre building for exhibitions, workshops, try-outs and so on.

Moreover, it appears that a public tends to identify with a venue more than with the programming, and that imposes certain demands of comfort and accessibility on the venue. This factor should not be underestimated either. Theatre producers have different priorities for a theatre. For example, they will describe their ideal theatre building as 'open, transparent, technically perfect and therefore temporary (given the tempo of the developments) and comfortable'.[5] These are diffuse criteria, and perhaps they cannot or need not be compatible with one another. At any rate, they can best be seen from the perspective that a theatre usually survives the individual performing artist.

Social integration of the theatre in the city

Recently a good deal of attention has been paid to the function of the theatre in the city as an agent of social integration. Art, especially theatre, gives the voiceless a voice. 'Samuel Beckett spent his whole life dedicated to writing about the homeless and the elderly, people without glamour, whom we do not see on television, who have no place in the picture of our society. And why did the most important writer in French and English devote practically his entire oeuvre to people without a voice? Because finding a voice is the most important thing that can happen on this planet.'[6] What is more, nowadays urban culture is by definition multicultural. Both aspects pose particular challenges to an artistic form that is so dependent on language as theatre. The question can and must be raised of whether and how the theatre infrastructure can respond to those challenges. That question concerns what is embedded where and how. Is it important to establish theatres in deprived neighbourhoods? Is it best to use existing abandoned infrastructure (such as industrial premises) for that purpose – 'to prevent those places from dying', as Ariane Mnouchkine says? To what extent is it important for such initiatives to originate in the neighbourhood itself? Or is it enough for the theatre companies to show an interest in minorities and deprived classes? Should the programme of the theatre be adapted to that ambition? Does that not entail the risk that the representatives of a particular social class will only attend those performances that are intended for them?

Finally, we should not forget that the function of social integration involves much more than a (potentially paternalistic) interest in people with less opportunities. Every theatre building, and by extension every infrastructure for the arts, will need to be entirely accepted and cherished by its neighbours and by the urban population. Cities must be able to be proud of their theatres, the buildings must become a part of civic pride. In that connection it will be especially important for peer groups from the city to support planned infrastructure and, once the building has been erected, to be able to appeal to a large pool of volunteers to keep it going.

Performing in a building?

Ever since the Renaissance, Western culture has been a culture that is aware of its own history. Time and again it reflects on its past and tries to deal with its heritage in a deliberate way. The architecture of the theatre, whose modern form, the municipal theatre, originated – not by chance – in the Renaissance, is no exception. 'The history of the theatre in the West is marked by the emergence, the metamorphosis, the disappearance of different architectural types.'[7] Some time ago people came to realize that it was possible to sample that heritage as much as one liked: 'Today, theatre architecture no longer proposes an absolute model, but draws on this considerable heritage in search of examples that can be reinterpreted.'[8] Even more recently, people seem once again to be questioning the historical forms of the theatre building and searching for new forms for the future. As can be seen from this publication, the roads leading in that direction are very diverse.

Some will be inclined to turn their back on the theatre building and to opt for virtual or public space. Although a good many contemporary performing artists are doing that, it does not seem to me to be the essential point. As an art form, theatre has almost always taken place in buildings, one reason being that they can stimulate the concentration on the action. Buildings can also challenge, invite, clearly indicate what is being offered, offer security, intrigue, arouse curiosity, provoke a reaction. The Italian architect Aldo Rossi correctly saw a connection between architecture and the theatre by claiming that architecture is a stage that is waiting for an audience to bring it to life. Rossi does not issue any pronouncement on the precise form of that stage, but indicates clearly that architecture in general, and by extension theatre architecture, is a structure that can only function when it is experienced and used by people. A building that is rooted in the city, that is complex and transparent at the same time, that communicates what it has to offer, that is inspired by vision, offers a permanent challenge to (many generations of) performing artists.

1 I. van Aalst, *Cultuur in de stad. Over de rol van de culturele voorzieningen in de ontwikkeling van de stadscentra,* Utrecht: Jan van Arkel, 1997.

2 E. Corijn, 'Kan de stad de wereld redden?', in *De toekomst van het verleden, reflecties over geschiedenis, stedelijkheid en musea / The Future of the Past, reflections on history, urbanity and museums,* Antwerp: Musea Antwerpen 2000.

3 C. Landry, *The Creative City: A Toolkit for Urban Innovators,* London: Earthscan Publications, 2000.

4 G. Breton, *THEATRES / THEATERS,* Paris: Editions du Moniteur, 1989.

5 B. Pluijmers and M. Kapteijns, 'Meningen van theatermakers, architecten, vormgevers, beleidsmakers en vertegenwoordigers van nieuwe media', in *Theaters van de Toekomst,* 's-Hertogenbosch: Stichting Erasmus Prijs 2000, 2001.

6 P. Sellars, *City of Cultures. De Interculturele Dimensie in de Podiumkunsten: Los Angeles, London, Brussel, Montreal,* Brussels: Vlaams Theater Instituut, 1995.

7 A. Duivesteijn, 'Waar theater en architectuur elkaar ontmoeten', in *Allemaal theater,* Amsterdam: Stichting Het Theaterfestival, 1994.

8 Ibid.

THE DESIRE FOR THE PAST

CAPTIONS TO NON-EXISTENT PHOTOGRAPHS

8.54 am

Lille is not a city, but a type of climate. It is Sunday morning and ice cold. The place: an industrial wasteland, an infinite *terrain vague* between exhibition halls, Eurostar tracks and motorway exits. I repeat: it is ice cold. Breathing is an exercise in sculpting. I chisel breath. I see that I am the first. The caravans stand silently around the tent. They are still asleep. Yesterday evening I took a few night-time shots before and after the performance. Today I want to photograph the dismantling process. I wear layer upon layer of warm clothes — all of them variations on wool. Between six and eight hours it should take. I don't yet know that I shall be unable to keep warm, despite furious hoof-beats and clutching shoulders. Neither do I know that I will start to lend a hand before the first coffee break and that the photographs will just have to wait. That I will go and write captions to non-existent pictures. What I lose in prints, I will gain in impressions.

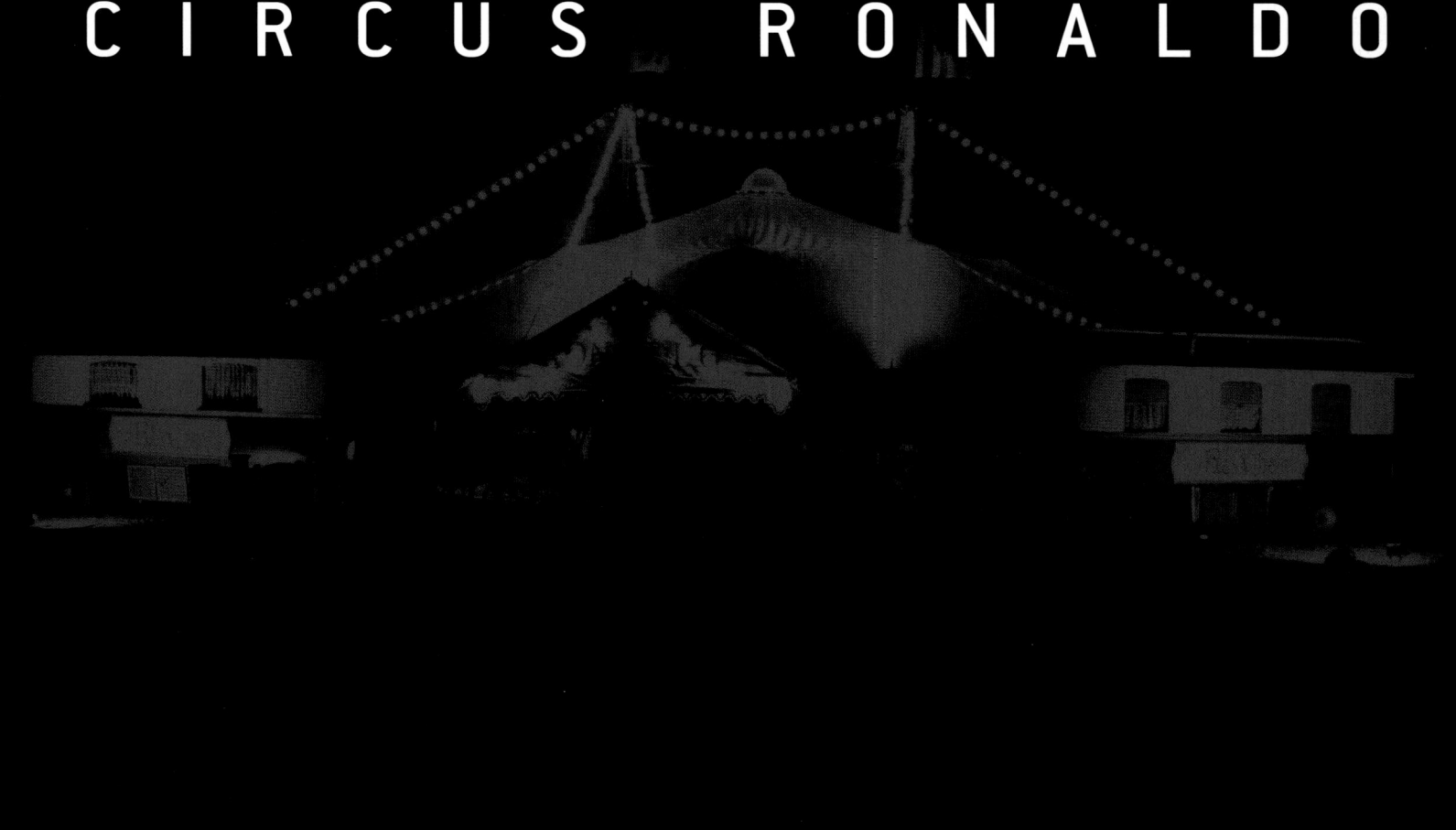

9.02 am

A large aperture, a long shutter speed. This darkness needs light. The tent-cloth blows over the gravel. The morning penetrates through the eyelets and the stitching. Knitting needles of light. I descry outlines. Johnny Ronaldo, the father, has already tried to explain it to me twice. Son Danny once devoted a whole evening to it. It is written down in three, four places. But I still don't understand it, that family history of the Ronaldos, *née* Van den Berghes. Yes, six, seven generations. A jumble of *commedia* and cowboys, of cabaret and acrobatics, of puppets and misery. Yet here in the half-light, I suddenly understand: the circular shape is unchanged, but the ring has become a stage – with puppet theatre. Circus and theatre and show in one. The Ronaldos combine the intimacy of a family circus with the poetry of *le nouveau cirque* and the burlesque of the street theatre. Now everything is sleeping. Spotlights, cables, planks. It is almost impossible to believe how last night this frozen still life was still so warm and glowing. I hear music again, the dog Italian of the actors, the roaring public. I press the button.

10.33 am

The first coffee break. The canvas walls are being removed, the seats are already in the lorry. Props disappear into trunks. Amongst them are museum pieces. I was planning to ask them about it. If an ancestry like theirs isn't something of a burden? But yesterday I was again struck by the roughness of the acting. Magnificent puppets from the interwar period fought each other mercilessly. Further damage was done on stage to a set hand-painted by the great-grandfather. Tongues of flame and fireballs shot across the historic tent. Circus Ronaldo is none too bothered about 'museumizing'. Clown Danny Ronaldo says: 'These things are made for it. They have to be able to withstand a few blows.' Danny has been performing in the same outfit for years. For years he has been doing his virtuoso juggling act with the same dirty, old balls. His spellbinding bicycle act was thought up by his great-uncle eighty years ago. There is something Dionysian, something moving about the matter-of-course roughness with which they treat that heritage. Is that nostalgia? No, that is poetry. There is more past in nonchalance than in nostalgia.

11.19 am

Why does the slipshod move us more than the perfect? For years circus was a universe of perfection: sequinned costumes, awe-inspiring splits, endless legs. Competition was an arms race towards the even more daring. But perfection bores: the public started eating popcorn. Even today's magical *nouveau cirque* (Soleil, Plume, etc.) is often no more than a well-oiled dream factory. Between deceitful perfection and honest shambles the choice is easily made. In Circus Ronaldo things fall flat, eggs drop, sometimes a fire is raging.

Karel – a one-time chauffeur, skipper and street musician who has become an actor, sculptor and jack-of-all-trades – is busy welding, Karel is. The bright blue light on this winter day, the sputtering of liquid metal, the glowing slag: it is very, very beautiful. Something tells me this is a quintessential image. Last night David Ronaldo knocked over a candlestand during his act with a whip. The candle went out, the candlestand broke. Not to worry. While the stage is dismantled, the lighting taken down, the canvas folded, the tent pegs hammered loose, here building, forging and welding are under way again. Circus literally means cycle. It never stops.

1.25 pm

Shows that are made in two months and that are still evolving two years later. Productions that grow spontaneously from the previous one. Children who sometimes join in and sometimes don't. Artists who come and go, always without a job interview: either you hit it off or you don't. Chaos is an ugly word for organic. Their best-known show is called *Fili*, threads. Threads to the past, loose ends today, ropes, cables, ribbons – oh, everything will be all right on the night.

This photograph. Abundant light: the whitish-grey air, the white tent-cloth. In the black: the minuscule silhouette of two masts and a man. And in between: a string of lamps. The acrobat has stepped all the way up the tight canvas like a man walking on water. He is now casually making his way along the crossbeam to disconnect the lights. Nobody looks, nobody sees. And yet there is considerable beauty here. One is reminded of [Jan Fabre's] *Man Measuring the Clouds* and [Jonathan Borofsky's] *The Man Who Walked to the Sky*. Again that feeling: this is an essential image. Nonchalance and enchantment, contempt for death and confidence. He unhooks the flex from one of the masts and then walks the tightrope with his string of glass globules to the other mast. He doesn't fall. *Fili*.

3.49 pm

A blurred image, a *flou bougé*. A birdcage is lifted up and carried to the lorry. You can quite clearly see that it contains a skull, a crowned skull. Death as a pet. During the show a shadowy procession filed past. A bed of nails, a set of razor-sharp sabres, the cage was carried like a banner. It reminded you of Bruegel, Bosch and Ensor. Sarcasm and *danse macabre* rolled into one. Circus is not for children, but for the dead ancestors. Their souls are here in the tent, the Ronaldos say, we are no more than a link, a piece of thread. We do our duty.

Mother Ronaldo did her set-piece last night: barefooted she climbed up the swords again, and once more she stretched out on the rusty nails. She has been dying in this way for years. But this morning I saw her step out of the caravan in her dressing-gown. In the freezing cold she called the dog. A yapper, too, is a pet.

6.24 pm

'*La commedia è finita,*' the ringmaster lied. The audience went on sitting, the orchestra went on playing. The show has no clear beginning or end. No clear border between audience and actors. Everyone is an accessory. When the crowds flock in, the performers are already acting; when the final applause is heard, a new party begins. A performance is a wave in the sea of everyday life. The transition between acting and living is a seamless occurrence. Inside the tent, the murmur of the outside world can be heard.

Everyone has gone now. I have been taking photographs of the caravans driving off in the dark. The industrial wasteland is once again an industrial wasteland. All that remains in the middle of the gravel is a circle with rather drier, trampled sand and around it, at regular intervals, inch-thick holes where the tent pegs pierced the ground. The image is too beautiful for words. The world as a trampoline. Lightness as a reverberation. The circus as a safety net. Yes, everything will be all right.

DAVID VAN REYBROUCK

The name Circus Ronaldo conceals a long history: a tradition of seven generations of circus artists, to which the family is proud to refer. It all began with Adolf Peter Van den Berghe, who was born in Ghent in 1827 and ran away from home at the age of fifteen to join a circus. As an acrobat he met the daughter of a travelling theatre company. Their marriage brought together the traditions of circus and theatre. As 'Variété-theater Van den Berghe', they and their children created a mix of theatre, circus and pantomime. Their grandchildren were less interested in circus techniques and the Variété became a popular travelling theatre. Jan Van den Berghe was the last director of the theatre, which did not survive the economic slump of the 1930s. In the 1950s his daughter's children, Jan and Herman Van den Broeck, made a comeback with variety music, and in 1971 the two brothers founded Circus Ricardo. Eventually Jan (alias Johnny) went it alone with Circus Ronaldo. He currently works together with his children David and Danny, the sixth generation, and even with his grandchildren, the seventh generation. Not all the employees are family members these days.

In the early 1990s, under the influence of the German Circus Roncalli among others, David and Danny Ronaldo began to allow more and more theatre into their circus. The fact that the first generation of the circus family had used this hybrid form motivated the two brothers even more. Separate traditional circus acts and exotic animals were sidelined to make way for more intimate shows with a clear story-line and well-defined characters. Circus Ronaldo presents shows with puppets, acrobats, masks and fire that reflect their own family history as well as the post-war Reizend Volkstheater [Travelling popular theatre] in Flanders, fairground artists and the Italian *commedia dell'arte*.

Recurrent themes in the shows are the life of an artist and the hope of recognition and appreciation. For years Johnny Ronaldo pressed a succession of ministers for subsidies for circuses, but initially his requests fell on deaf ears. In 1998 Circus Ronaldo was nominated Cultural Ambassador of Flanders. This brought greater fame and more extensive tours. Circus Ronaldo has regularly taken part in theatre festivals abroad since 1996. Finally, on 25 April 2001, a draft proposal was signed by the then Minister of Cultural Affairs of the Flemish Government Bert Anciaux and the Flemish circuses. Johnny Van den Broeck endorsed the memorandum, which sets out agreements regarding conditions for subsidies. His circus can now count on financial support from the government.   IT

I WAS THINKING ABOUT AN ARTWORK
BASHING THE BUSH ADMINISTRATIONS
ARROGANCE AND STUPIDITY
BUT I COULDN'T FIGURE OUT
HOW TO MAKE IT FIT INTO AN ART
MAGAZINE →

THEN AI GOT SO NERVOUS
I NEEDED COOL DOWN
                    BENJAMIN VERDONCK
SUNDAY AFTERNOON / JANUARY 2003

BENJAMIN   VERDONCK

Benjamin Verdonck is an actor who is actively involved in the Flemish theatre world, participating in the projects and productions of others and cooperating with different theatre companies in a variety of ways. But he has also developed an independent activity, outside the normal theatre circuit. He divides his own projects or actions into a 'Public Domains cycle' ('an examination of the functions of theatricality outside its normal boundaries'), and a 'Richtkräfte cycle' ('an examination of the chances of survival of art — and of theatre in particular — in our society'). Verdonck is adamant that his 'actions' should be regarded as acting or as theatre. Yet with these actions he steps outside the usual practices of the theatre, which raises the inevitable question of how these projects relate to his actorship — and more generally — to theatre.

The achievements and projects which have brought Benjamin Verdonck fame — for example, *Bara\ke 2000* on Place Bara in Brussels and on Sint-Jansplein in Antwerp and *I like America and America likes me* — are theatrical in scope. They relate resolutely to, and differ from, the basic principles of theatre: the significance of time and place, the positions of the actor and the audience, the importance of the script, and so on.

The 'actions' take place on (or just off) the street, and are socio-political in nature. They do not set out to target the informed, critical theatre-going public, but address chance passers-by and in that way are directed at a wider, unselected public. These passers-by are suddenly and unexpectedly transformed into public. They are given a sample performance, whether they want it or not. What is unusual about the situation is that the passers-by first have to recognize the occurrence as 'theatre' and then accept the acting as such and go on looking, or dismiss it and walk past. But the acceptance or dismissal comes after the unexpected confrontation. In the auditorium, where people have consciously planned to enter, one is never 'confronted' with theatre in that way. The message of the action steals its way into the spectator while he is still 'misled and unprepared', before he realizes that what he is witnessing is a staged performance, and can classify (and neutralize) the events as 'theatre'. The show a passer-by stumbles upon unprepared, encroaches – or so it seems – more directly on life. The intention of these kinds of action is certainly more than to remove barriers and find a large public for a theatre performance. It also has to do with transforming the street and grabbing public attention.

But is this theatre? An action or an imposed situation is not the same as a performance. What is unique about an action is that one *does* it: one cannot 'act' an action. Benjamin Verdonck's actions are of course 'staged', but bringing them to the attention of the public is different from staging something in the theatre. An action is not enacted on stage, but takes place in the world. The dramatist makes a 'statement' by inserting a non-functional, and in some ways notable and inappropriate, enigmatic act – which can therefore be classified instantly, if not as 'mad', then as 'art' – as a 'fact' into the flood of everyday events. The action draws attention and is appealing, not so much because of the quality of the spectacle, but above all because of the relevance of its interfering character and/or the power of the image or of the gesture. When in the Christmas period Verdonck dresses up not as Santa Claus but as Santa's colleague St Nicholas and walks around on the Meir in Antwerp in the company of Black Peter for *I didn't know Santa came on Saturday*, the success of this action is relatively independent of his acting talent, but relies more on the extent to which his chance spectators can depart from their 'normal' pattern to ponder the situation.

The 'beginning' of what Benjamin Verdonck does, does not – as is the case in theatre – lie outside the performance, 'elsewhere': in a script, or a theme, or a director's idea, or the cast, etc. For his 'actions' Verdonck always takes his own confusion, disquiet or concern for the world as his starting point and he uses his talent and *métier* to make them public in a very direct way. For example, with his *Bara\ke* in Brussels and Antwerp, and with his as yet unperformed project *hirondel / dooi vogeltje / the great swallow*, he homes in on the problems of specific parts of cities. But the specificity and the long duration of the actions also trigger reactions that run parallel to the general social problems. The 'pillarist' and the local resident find themselves in very 'real' discussions about what living is – from 'Can you go to the WC there? Have you got water there? Can you wash? Is there drainage? Are there cooking facilities? Do you have something to eat?...' to 'What can I hear, what can I see, what can I smell and what do I feel? How far is it to the first tree and is that tree "tree enough" to make you want to build a hut or a nest there?' And frequently the 'situation' that Verdonck creates – quite apart from his character, his plot and the interaction – is visually powerful enough to survive as an 'installation'. The pillarist in the city is a strong image. And who wouldn't want to see that human-size swallow's nest somewhere high up on a Brussels office building?

Verdonck's actions differ from theatre acting not only because of the way they occupy public space and time. The status of the player differs too: the player is not an actor but a performer. The performer does not play a role, but *does* something. What he does is not incidental. In the performance he is not 'somebody else': what he does, is/becomes part of his own life. During *I like America and America likes me* Benjamin Verdonck did not play a man who spends three days talking to a pig about world conflicts. *He himself* lived and talked with a pig for three days, and those three days are a part of *his* life. The reason why the action was a success is not actor Benjamin Verdonck's marvellous performance – his actorship is incidental here.

The fact that the action is a deed and not a performance, can also be gathered from the way it aims to create an effect. It does not aim to move the spectators by means of the qualities of the performance, but first and foremost to make the visitor a witness, and to engage the collective attention and memory via the witness. A small exhibition accompanied the 'action', along with a discourse about the war and world problems. Verdonck may have talked to the pig about everything. But the effect of 'the man who lives (peacefully) with a pig in a cage' depends on the image itself, on a few words from the press

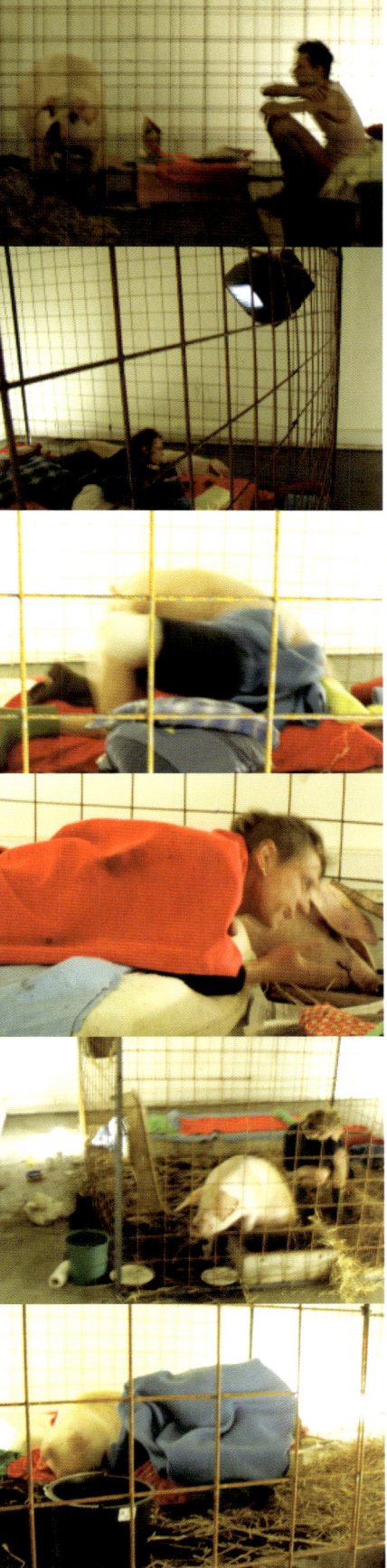

release, which, boosted by the media and CNN, goes down in world history as an artistic 'news item'. The action is not something to be known and remembered, so that it may serve as a 'reference' in a discussion about theatre, about the possibilities and borders of political theatre, but also about world politics, and about the potential place and the importance of the confusion and disquiet of one individual in world events.

In his projects Benjamin Verdonck thematizes in an artistic way and with theatrical means the framework within which theatre is performed. He does this in different ways, each of which goes beyond the prescribed elements of theatre: day-long performances, inaudible scripts, too much or too little distance from the audience, the reduction of theatricality to nothing. He magnifies the 'reflexivity' which the theatre has always known within acting itself. He wants to update and recharge the theatre. But at the same time the way he does this shows that what he wants to do takes him outside the realms of theatre. The gesture with which he points to the borders takes him 'somewhere else' too — into the colourful company of stylites, artists like Beuys, performers, street runners, jesters and Diogenes.

MARIANNE BUYCK

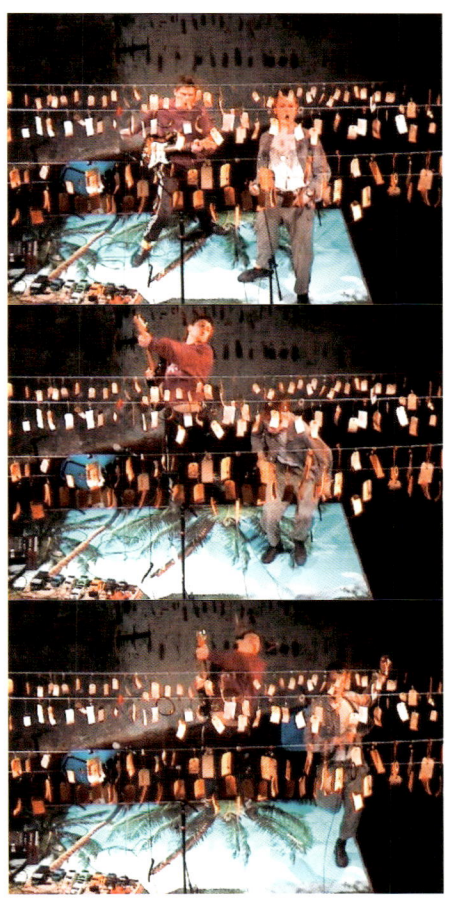

Benjamin Verdonck (1972) graduated from the Antwerp Conservatorium in 1992 and went on to work with De Tijd, Zuidelijk Toneel and Theatergroep Hollandia. As an actor he also regularly appeared in productions by Dood Paard, De Roovers, Walpurgis, BRONKS, etc. At the same time Verdonck worked on his own projects: sometimes under the wing of other theatre companies, sometimes outside the regular theatre circuit. Initially Verdonck made 'music theatre' with Muziekmakerij Think of One and Valentine Kempynck. There was the production *wat ik graag zou zijn als ik niet was wat ik ben hfst. 1, 2 en 2bis (1992–1995)* [What I would like to be if I were not who I am, chapters ...] after *Rayuela* by Julio Cortázar and *Hydra* (1998) by Heiner Müller. For Het muziek Lod they made the production *W/ ik denk vaak aan de hoeveelheid rundvlees die nodig zou zijn om bouillon te maken van het meer van Genève* [W/ I often think about the amount of beef it would take to make a broth of Lake Geneva] (2000). It was inspired by the book *W or the Memory of Childhood* by French writer Georges Perec and Verdonck's collection of more than four thousand metal rings bearing cards specifying in each case where he found it and what he was thinking about when he did. In 2002 Verdonck wrote and acted in a children's production based on Ovid's *Metamorphoses* with De Roovers, which was selected for the Theater Festival 2003. Together with Willy Thomas (Dito'Dito) he made *313*, based on 313 animal stories by Toon Tellegen. In the meantime Verdonck's theatre script *I'm Happy Men* was filmed in association with De Roovers and Alexis Destoop.

Verdonck set up the non-profit 'The POPsingers' breasts were not real' together with Valentine Kempynck. Within this structure he launched the 'public domains cycle': a study of the power and the functions of theatricality in the public space. The cycle comprises 'actions' such as *Bara\ke 2000*, a theatre production-cum-performance enacted on Place Bara in Brussels and on Sint-Jansplein in Antwerp. In both places he lived for two weeks in a hut on a seven-metre-high pile from where he conversed with passers-by. In May 2004 the play *hirondel / dooi vogeltje / the great swallow* will be performed from a self-built 'swallow's nest' on Place Brouckère in the heart of Brussels. *Shopping = Fun* is the name he gave to a number of 'actions' on the Meir in Antwerp.

As part of the 'Richtkräfte' cycle, Verdonck created (among other things) the performance *I like America and America likes me* (2002), for which he spent three days in an iron cage with a pig to express his confusion and concern about world conflicts, particularly the tensions between the USA and Iraq. This was a replay of the legendary performance by Joseph Beuys who lived in a gallery with a coyote in 1974.

As a visual artist and DIYer, Verdonck is a driving force behind the workers' collective Ateliers Makerij, which he founded with his brother Samuel Verdonck and with Tille Vos. With them he builds not only stage sets but also little houses, installations and constructions for his 'actions'. A small hut for the 1999 BRONKS Festival served as the basis for *Bara\ke*. For the 'Zomer van Antwerpen' Festival, they built the installation *hong kong woman disappeared*, while they also built a pavilion for the cultural department of the Flemish Community. YB

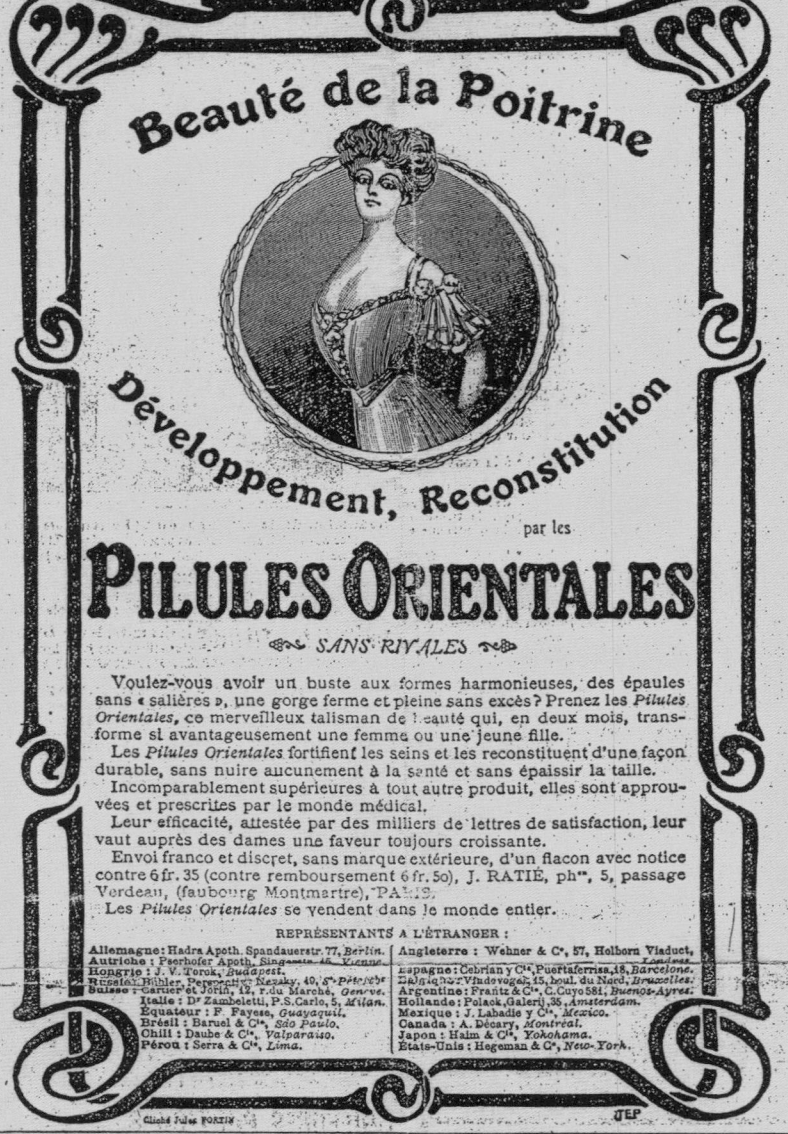

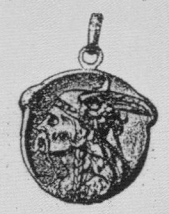

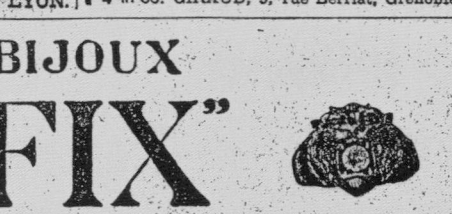

PAGNOLTRILOGIE

Norwegian fir, yellow pine and varnished iron. The untreated wood is abandoned to the natural elements. That is De Onderneming's stand and that is the experience *on* the seats during the five-hour production of *Marius, Fanny, César*. The five actors expose their audience to the natural elements as big questions about love and powerlessness file past before our eyes. Untreated, yes that too, in the sense of pure. Unadorned, without varnish, theatre is made and the actors hit home. All two hundred spectators laugh or sob gently in unison. Bravo for the sunglasses that are handed out to give the night-time scenes a dark perspective. Everything becomes misty, my plastic sunglasses are constantly steamed up by the vapour of tears.

Marcel Pagnol wrote his famous trilogy between 1929 and 1936. *Marius* was his second play. The public cried out for a sequel and *Fanny* appeared. The third part *César* is a film script in which Pagnol's favourite actor Raimu plays the lead role. It is essentially a pastiche of passion, family love and parochial morality centred on the boy Marius who has to choose between his love for Fanny and his longing for travel and adventure and the irresistible lure of the sea. Gradually young love turns to adult love, which also manifests itself marvellously in Fanny's and Marius' relationship with their parents.

Love is the simplest adventure for those who cannot go to the ends of the earth. I have seen the production twice: the first time during the Oerol Festival on the Dutch island of Terschelling and a year later on Antwerp's left bank. The 'leeward islands' nestling inside Marius' head become real through the presence of the sea, or the river Scheldt and, by the same token, they are put into perspective. On the Scheldt ships constantly sail past like living-rooms with a car on the roof and on the shallow sea windsurfers and other watersports enthusiasts skim across the picture. The distance is substantial and makes it clear that the horizon is in his head. In fact he knows that too: *'The Leeward Islands? I'd rather keep away from them, so that they stay as I have visualized them in my imagination.'* Desire for something different, fostering possibilities, the realization that choosing means losing — that is Marius. And the same might be said of half the audience.

How does the trilogy avoid becoming your average soap? Ultimately, it *is* about recognizable problems on a human scale; the ordinary triumphs. Why doesn't it become sentimental or nostalgic? The atmosphere is one of harmony, of a time that was still intact, when happiness was still quite normal.

We are indebted to Pagnol for that. His characters are unfinished, mysterious. Even if the use of words is crystal clear, nobody really speaks his mind. They are bubbling over with good and conflicting intentions. Everything is double. Neither they nor we are allowed to peruse their private domain. In contrast to today's 'emo'

Monsieur et madame Panisse vous annoncent avec joie
la naissance de leur fils
Marius-César

U wordt vriendelijk uitgenodigd op de koffietafel
die over een kwartier plaatsvindt in de hangar.
Gelieve de familie te volgen.
Bloemen noch kransen.

culture, which fosters that expression of emotions as the highest good, here we have a world in which feelings are not yet crystallized. It is as if Pagnol's lips are sealed; the words are on the tip of his tongue but he allows his characters to go their own inimitable way. In no way are they the puppets of his drama of ideas; indeed, they are sovereign.

The language – rich, vivid Flemish, but pared down and not remotely folkloric. Even if the language is intended for the open air, so more exclamatory than in an auditorium, the choice of words is never one-dimensional. On rereading the script, it was apparent once again how succinctly De Onderneming deals with the dialect. Every sentence is held up against the light and examined for its content. It never becomes pastoral, or 'retro' as it is now called. Never do they attempt to match 'the language of the ordinary man'.

De Onderneming's acting style also contributes to it being more a question of unravelling the documentary of that small Marseilles society than to cultivate everyday life (and preferably broadcast it in full) – which, since programmes like *Big Brother*, has become quite fashionable. The actors keep a distance from their characters by performing double roles, by overacting and by addressing the audience directly. There is next to no set – props are scanty and merely indexical. A bottle on a table is a café. The acting, too, is more allusive than demonstrative. The theatre-makers are in evidence, they stand alongside their roles and are the ever-attentive hosts, providing the audience with drink and soup.

The spectator becomes more of a fellow cast member by the hour, and even has his own props: a cup of vichyssoise soup, a raincoat, sunglasses, a local beer ('Pee Klak'), an obituary notice, sugared almonds and finally an invitation for cake and coffee at the funeral of Honoré Panisse. He increasingly becomes an accessory to the drama and to the alternative that De Onderneming propagates.

Alternative is perhaps a big word, but that is what it comes down to for Kris van Trier and Waas Gramser – the founding members of De Onderneming. Averse to the spirit of the age, they present an alternative. It is not a defence against something, but an assertion of their values and imagination.

The stand is the most explicit ingredient of this. The walls, the artificiality of the theatre, are taken down and city and community are allowed in. Van Trier and Gramser once said of it that most auditoriums have served a purpose for a certain sort of theatre. Now they simply exist. And it sometimes seems as if theatre companies only exist to fill those structures.

Another salient element is the original reinterpretation of the 'bread and circuses' concept. In between the acts a meal is cooked for the audience who can partake of it half-way through. The cuisine is of a high standard, and home-grown organic products are prepared. Concern for the world is great – sustainability, but also pleasure. They share with us what they regard as good and tasty and, dramaturgically speaking, they insert it very cleverly. In that sense De Onderneming is its own target group and its members hope that the public will follow their example.

The length of the performance is another indication of their 'alternative' approach. Putting on a five-hour production in today's breathless age has to be a political statement. The 'experience economy' now excels at events lasting a day or more, but those 'leisure centres' are directed at precisely defined, widely studied target groups, at a generalized 'other', while De Onderneming goes out of its way to establish a relationship with the audience by making the spectator a fellow actor, with props and all, and at the same time confronting him with a large measure of seriousness. The perfect, but hard stand is the well-chosen symbol of this: we are all still seated at the school desks of life and we are allowed to enjoy ourselves but we also have something to learn. Lesson 1: The personal is political.

ELLEN WALRAVEN

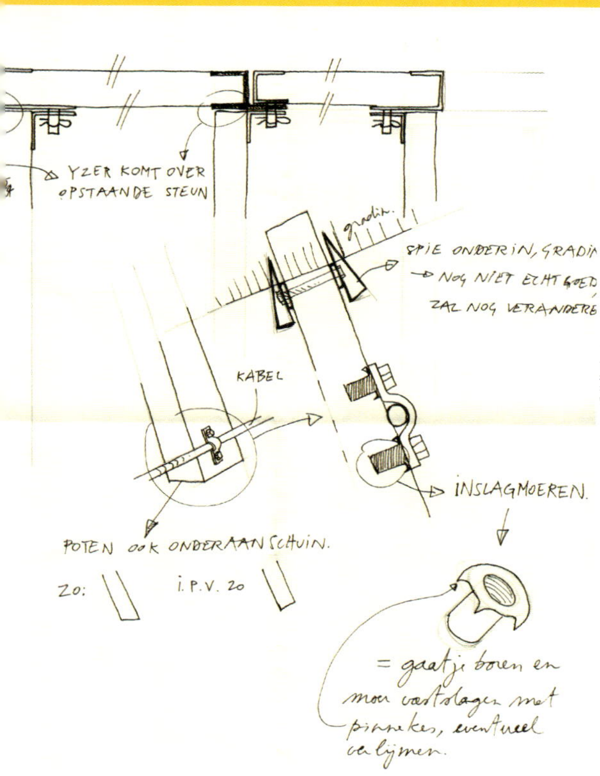

YZER KOMT OVER
OPSTAANDE STEUN
gradin
SPIE ONDERIN, GRADIN
NOG NIET ECHT GOED
ZAL NOG VERANDERE
KABEL
INSLAGMOEREN.
POTEN OOK ONDERAAN SCHUIN.
ZO:
I.P.V. ZO
= gaatje boren en
moer vastslagen met
pinnekes, eventueel
verlijmen.

de ONDERNEMING vzw
MOBIELE TRIBUNE 1e VERSIE
ZIJAANZICHT TRAP
SCHAAL 1/10
NOVEMBER 2001

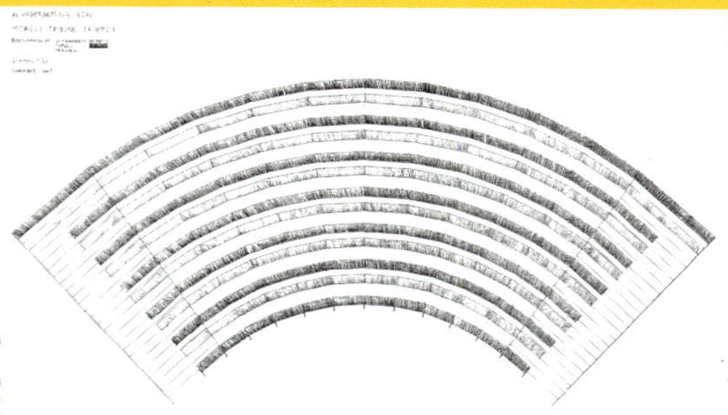

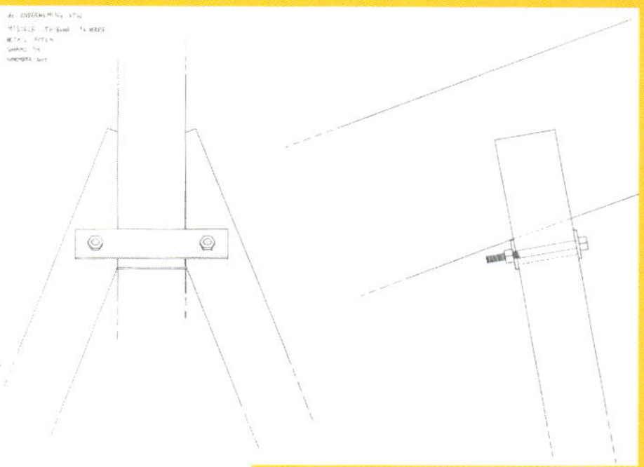

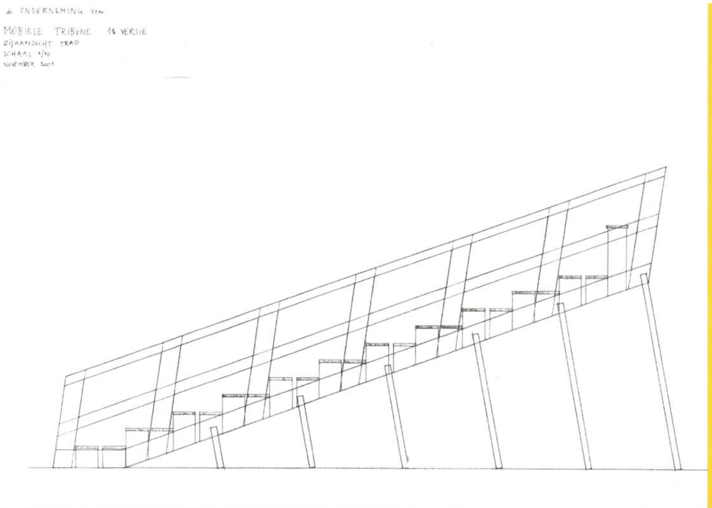

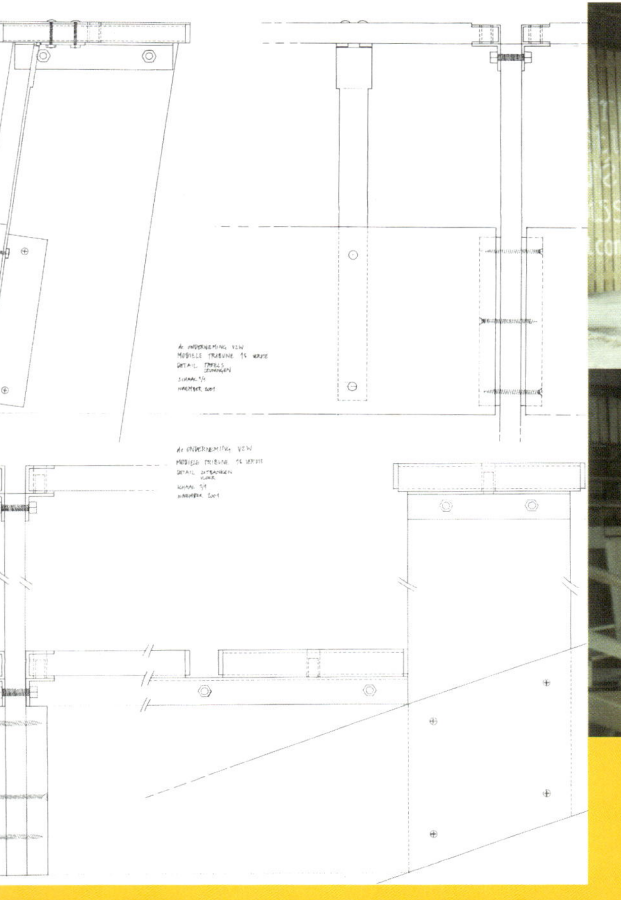

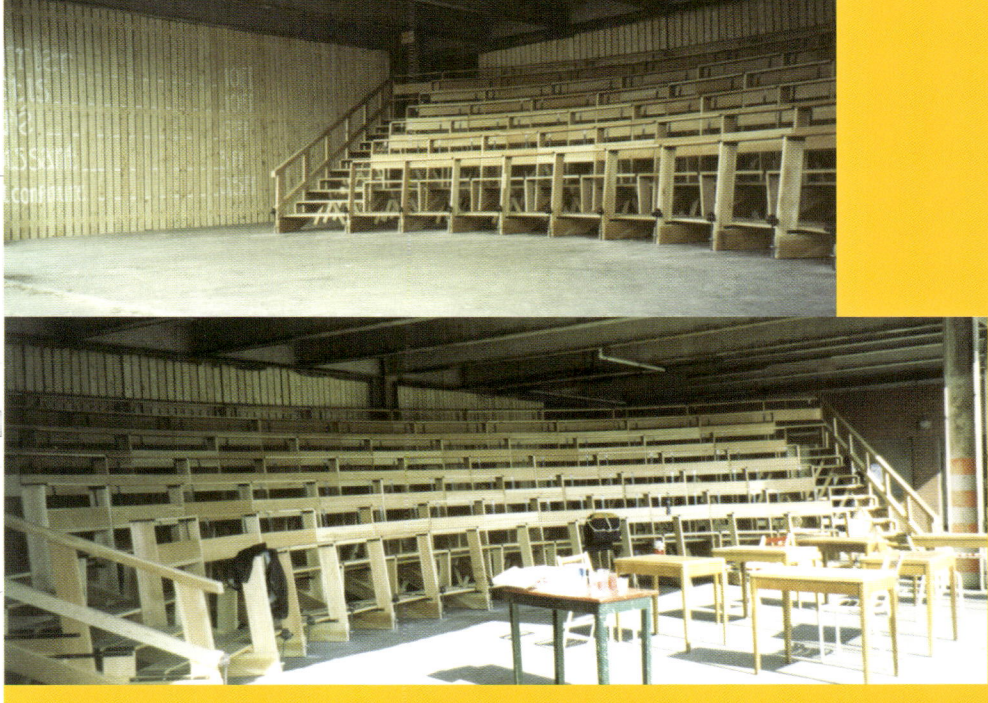

PAGNOL TRILOGY (DE ONDERNEMING)

Marius (1929) is the best-known stage play by the French author and director Marcel Pagnol (1895–1974). Set in a working-class bar in the port of Marseilles, it recounts the fortunes of a young man who has to choose between his love for a woman and the lure of the sea. At the special request of the public, Pagnol developed the story into a trilogy with *Fanny* (1931) and *César* (1936).

Pagnol's work had not been performed in Flanders since the 1950s, until in the spring of 1999 De Onderneming translated, adapted and staged *Marius*. Their version has continued to grow ever since. During the 'Zomer van Antwerpen' Festival 1999, *Marius* was performed in the open air on the banks of the river Scheldt. In 2000 *Fanny* and *César* were also integrated into a convivial marathon performance. The public drinks beer in César's café, sits at the wedding table, is given sugared almonds when a child is born and coffee by way of consolation when someone has died.

The Pagnol trilogy epitomizes the work of dramatists Waas Gramser and Kris van Trier with De Onderneming, a collective formed through a merger of other companies in 1998. The new collective retained a loose structure: it has no artistic director but is run by four core members — besides Gramser and Van Trier, also Ryszard Turbiasz and Günther Lesage — who take the initiative for new productions sometimes together and sometimes separately. These are created in alternating forms of cooperation with kindred spirits. The basis is often the script of a play or a novel, whereby a thorough reading, translation and rewriting accounts for a large part of the dramaturgical work.

De Onderneming draws no distinction between the artistic and organizational aspects of their activities. This is to ensure that they retain ethic and aesthetic control throughout the production process: from creation through communication and administration to the construction of their very own open-air stand. The collective also makes a strong commitment to people who otherwise have very little contact with theatre, by actively going in search of a new public, and by combining theatre with another important social activity: dining together.

This commitment led the collective to start mounting small-scale projects in the public space, in different locations in Antwerp (for example, outside the cathedral, in shopping streets, in schools and in the Zoo) and in front of the NATO building in Brussels. That was back in 1998. The commitment later acquired an international as well as a local dimension. In the year 2000 De Onderneming moved to a factory building in Hoboken, after which they invited local residents to performances — including *Nagras* (2000), another play by Pagnol, which was performed in a park in Hoboken.

Internationally De Onderneming tends to look southwards. *Marius* was given back to France, not with Pagnol's script, but in a new translation of their Dutch adaptation. In 2003 Waas Gramser and Kris van Trier were responsible for staging *La Nuit Unique*, a large-scale participation project for the arts centre Le Lieu Unique in Nantes. As well as artists and experts, a hundred representatives of the people of Nantes talked there about their relationship with art.   JJ

FIXEN VOOR BEGINNERS [1]

As kik na kick op de frictie tussen actie en fictie [2]
tis mor een fractie van de actie
de gratie van de spatie
gene fiffie gene sissie
fixen is een missie
gene piwi gene nikser
ik fix ne milkshake me ne mixer van dieë kiwi
da 'k ik gisteren in den Unic hem gepikt [3]

'k hem gene prit, mor da's niks, ik fix wel een elastiekske
me ne chik en wa spiksel. 'Ziet er nie zo fris uit, 's misschien wa primitief
fixen voor beginners, dat is mijn gerief.

as kik na kick oep as as kik na kick oep as kik na kick oep
fractie actie frictie fictie... Fixen voor beginners

oh shit, de fiets van mijn lief is gepikt en mijnen dikste vriend is just op mijnen bril
gaan zitten.
Mijn sis-kaart [4] die heb ik in den diepvries laten liggen en mijne kanarie is gestikt in
een pakske friet met pikkels

Maskesmachiiiiiiiiiine
Amaaaaaaaaaaaaaaaaaai

Ik werp mijnen blik gelijk ne frisbee in de wind
Ik zen op 1, 2, 3 op mijn destinatie
mijn energie mijn intuïtie, dat is mijn traditie
mijn oriëntatie... mijn organisatie
Ik zen nie vies van nen taxi naar de statie,
maar mijn fiets is mijnen trip, mijn grootste fixatie
een teletijdsmachine voor harmonisatie

As kik na kick oep as as kik na kick oep...
fixen voor beginners!

Op mini-trip naar Rimini verlies 'k ik mijnen bikini
'k hem wa schrik van cellulit in den G-string van men nicht
Op ne ligfiets naar de picknick [5] van ne punker me ne piercing in zijne... JESUS
drink ik ne sherry me ne fristi me ne tripel me nen gin tonic en wa pillen
-da's kei ying -
mor ik voel niks.
Misschien is er iet mis met uw bioritme, of moet' is naar uw perceptie laten zien.
-Gij ze nen hippie [6], jonge!

As as as as as, as kik na as kik na as kik as kik na
As as as as as, as kik na as kik na as kik as kik na kick oep de frictie tussen actie
en fixie ?

[0] In Morse code: -..-....-..-...—-..... etc. In contrast to the intrinsic humanism which this poem betrays (and which Het Maskesmachine [literally The Girls' Machine] shares with a knowing wink), the maskes – 'girls' in Antwerps, i.e. the Antwerp dialect – adopt the abstract and the formal as their working method. Thus the language is reduced by means of the Morse code to a rhythm which in its turn forms the basis for music, movement, light and image (see below).

[1] The texts printed here are the six songs the Maskesmachine recorded on their first CD. Fixen is Antwerps for 'fix' in the sense of 'arrange' or 'settle'. 'Fixing for beginners' was made as a manifesto for 'Fix Day' on 29 February, when the Antwerp squatters dubbed themselves fixers, because it sounds more positive and more active than krakers. In its early stages the Maskesmachine had links with this social youth movement, a 1990s offshoot of the non-profit organization Weik. The Antifare, an anti-fascist brass band, was also in the vicinity when volkskeukens were organized in Weik. These are in fact soup kitchens, producing cheap meals using the remains of biological vegetables, but dished up with alternative information. That environment also fed bicycle campaigns and other offshoots of the urban movement.

[2] 'askiknakik op de frictie tussen actie en fictie' ['so what if I get a kick out of the friction between action and fiction']. Kick, friction, action and fiction: the praxis of the Maskesmachine can be summed up in this series of words. The Maskesmachine is more an attitude to life than an organization, more a worldview ('Ik werp mijnen blik gelijk ne frisbee in de wind' [I cast my eyes like a frisbee in the wind]) than a clear structure: 'Reality is our playground, our beach and our pitch. Our habitat, from kitchen table to city, throws up a thousand and one impressions which are mixed and shaken. Flavoured with a full measure of maskes' violence and twaddle, those impressions are then given back in a changed and enriched form to the paving stones and the people who walk on them.' The changed – 'recycled' or 're-created' [see below] – forms in which the impressions are given back to the public, are first and foremost wilful performances involving singing and dancing, which recall the atmosphere of

HET MASKESMACHINE
THE FRICTION BETWEEN ACTION AND FICTION

BAARMOEDER [7]

baarmoederkoekenbakkesdichterbijelkaramellekboeretruttekopinkassavierwhiskey
(baarmoeder...)
baarmoederkoekebakkesdichterbijelk(a)arambaarmoederkoekenbakkesdichterbijel-
caraïbevaar (baarmoeder...)

vruchtwatersportistoftewelbet(h)aaldetnoggenoegaboltemdankuwelvaartsikkepit-
takippeveldslacompassie(vruchtwater...)
vruchtvruchtwatersportistoffelijkkoffieananasvruchtwatersportistoffelijkkoffiekoper-
afzuigkapster(vruchtwater)

zuigreflexibelwaardevollenbacardintercomandoreminirock&rollersk(ate)aidspatient-
housasterikzienaf(zuigrelex...)
zuigrefelxibelwaardevollenbacardis'tafzuigreflexibelwaardevollenbacardinter-
comteruit(zuigreflex)

baarmoederkoekenbakkesdicht baarmoederkoekenbakkesdicht
vruchtwatersportistoftewelkomkommer(vruchtwater...)[8]
zuigreflexibelwaardevollenbak
vruchtwatersportistoftewelkom!
DOUCHKEPAKKE

Douchkepakkedouchkepakkedouchkepakkedouchkepakke
Pakkedouchkepakkedouchkepakkedouchkepakkedouch
Kedouchkepakedouchkepakedouchkepakedouchkepa
Kapakkedouchkapakkedouchkapakkedouchkapakkedouch!

Mmmh jaja mmh ja ja
Mmh ja

Hallo, wij zijn een springkoord gaan kopen, want wij gaan naar Barcelona. De winkel is
niet open de sloten is verloren, ik voel me gebroken, ik gaan er ene smoren. Vroeger
rookten wij, stelduvoor...

Douchkepakke kepakkedouchke Douchekepakke kepakedouch
Wacht, wacht efkes wacht wacht wacht efkes wacht wacht wacht wacht
Douchkepakke kepakkedouchke Kepakkedouchke pakkedouchke

Nee ni nu, nu ni nee. Nie nog is, nie nog is

Roodborsje rood, op mijne schoot, kruimeltje brood, geval van nood.
Ga nog niet dood, we pakken den boot.
Barcelona is zo groot, we vinden wel een springkoord (2x)

circus, street theatre, acrobatics and vaudeville. Those performances rarely if ever take place on traditional concert or theatre stages (see below). Indeed, the Maskesmachine is not currently part of the
Flemish theatre and music landscape. There is certainly no structural subsidy and so far the only project subsidy has come from the SIF (Sociaal Impuls Fonds [Social incentive fund]). The absence of an
organizational, productional, technical and financial framework is increasingly seen by the *maskes* as
a disadvantage: 'Poor organization should not be allowed to hide behind the cloak of charm.' Consequently, the company has applied to the Flemish Community for a music theatre subsidy.

[3] *'den unic'* [the Unic]: widely known and legendary department store. The Maskesmachine
involves itself in city life: 'The Maskesmachine gives a new and cheerful view of the city.' Modern-day
city life creates new forms of nomadism. The French philosopher Jean-Luc Nancy describes this attitude to life as follows: 'Man lives as a passer-by: not as a traveller, embarked for another world, but as a

hurried or idling busy or unemployed passer-by, who passes by in the company of other passers-by
who are so close and yet so far away, who are so familiar and yet so strange, whose every stop is merely
temporary, amicst the racing traffic, of transport and routes, of doors that open and shut incessantly in
the secluded dwellings where the bustle of the street, the sounds and the dust nevertheless penetrate
from a world that passes by entirely.' Everyday life, full of everyday occurrences and movements, un-
folding in nondescript and often ignored places, is the Maskesmachine's most important source of inspiration. Its method consists in part of wandering round the city, observing people and places, on the
lookout for unusual locations for its performances: 'Drifting around is in our blood, the problem of mobility is one of our main preoccupations. We look for the city's sharp edges. Our fascination with filling-stations and other disposable spaces has to do with their general undervaluation. They are places that are
given low priority in the hierarchy of places and are perhaps best described as the whores of the road.
By performing our shows in such places, people take more time for them and are able to find
gratification in other ways than merely by satisfying their primary needs and those of their cars.'

VOOR MIJ ZEDDE GIJ SCHOON

172

Schoon   zo   schoon,   ongelooflijk
schoon
Schoon   zo   schoon,   ongelooflijk
schoon

Voor mij zedde gij schoon
Voor mij zedde gij schoon
Voor mij zedde gij ongelooflijk schoon

Gij ze zo schoon zo schoon, gij ze zo
ongelooflijk schoon
Gij   ze   zo   schoon   zo   schoon,   gij   ze
ongelooflijk schoon

Gij ze zo schoon
Gij ze zo schoon

[4] *'sis-kaart'*: official 'Medicard' in Belgium. Learning to live with these sort of everyday objects is one of the subjects of study of the Maskesmachine.

[5] *'ligfiets, picknick'* [reclining bicycle, picnic]. Work and re(-)creation are not enemies. Re(-)creation has even become a pivotal production technique for the Maskesmachine – the re-cre-ation of reality, which results in a new order that makes it easier to cope with reality. Re(-)creation is also part of the search for a pleasant working method, in which quality of life is part of the end product.

[6] *'hippie'*: the rest, peace and harmony the group aspires to and its search for the utopia of the *fixers'* ideal, underlie the humour, along with the over-self-confidence of the rap culture and the disturb-ing nature of the punk movement. Add to that the intense study and humility of Hildegard of Bingen...

[7] *'baarmoeder'*: uterus, the organ in women and female mammals in which the foetus devel-ops. As the name of the group suggests, the Maskesmachine consists of 'girls' aged from 9 to 99. That is not a coincidence, but it is not a dogma either. The production of a particular sort of 'femininity' is part of the intention of their work. At the same time the *maskes* readily admit that they cannot do without *gasten* [blokes] 'for what is a *maskesmachine* without a bloke, a book without a cover, a car without petrol?'

PLAKTANG [9]

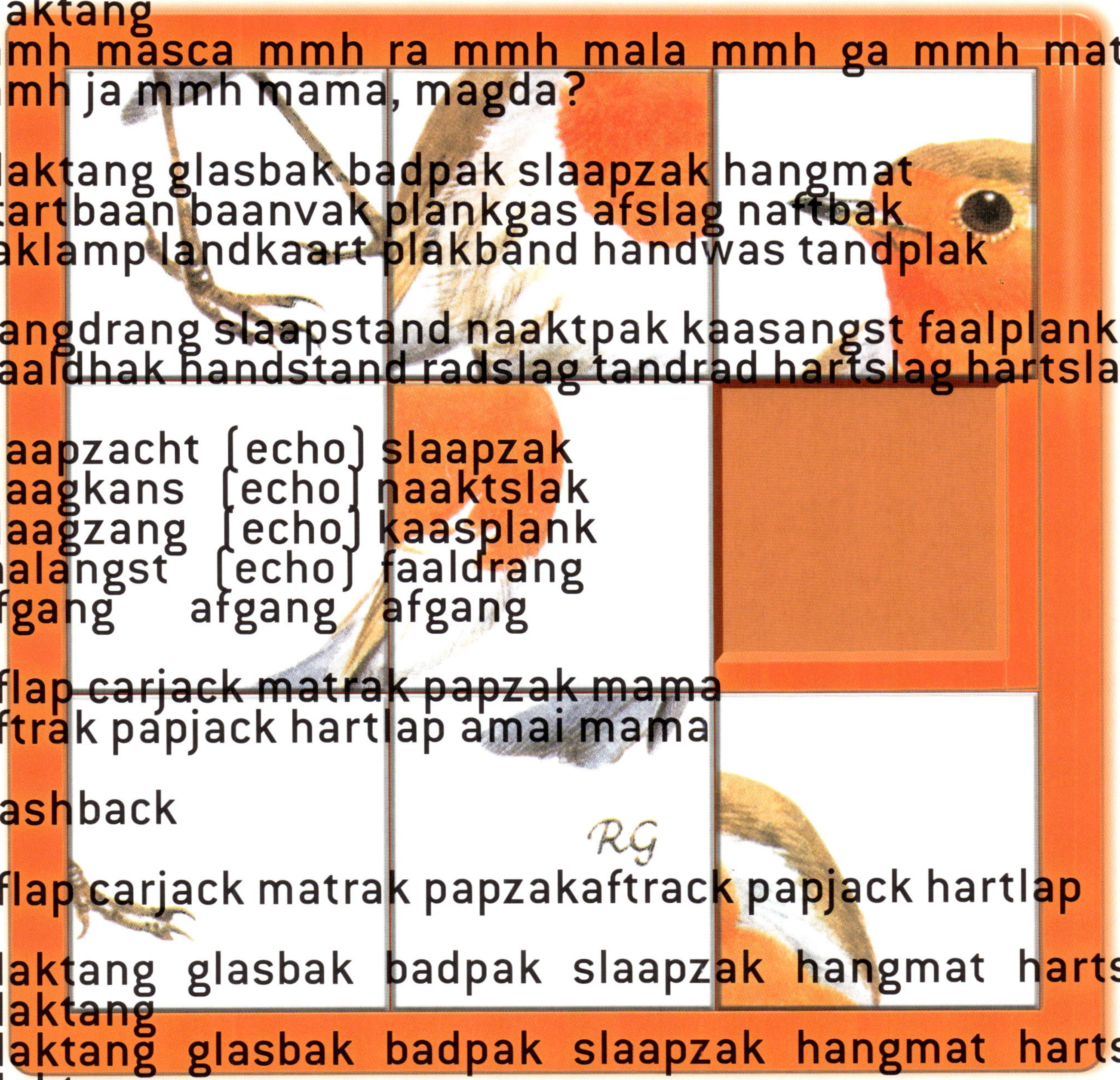

Plaktang glasbak badpak slaapzak hangmat hartslag plaktang
Platzak dampkap afwas ambras amai mama plaktang plaktang
mmh masca mmh ra mmh mala mmh ga mmh matras mmh ja mmh mama, magda?

Plaktang glasbak badpak slaapzak hangmat
Startbaan baanvak plankgas afslag naftbak
Zaklamp landkaart plakband handwas tandplak

Hangdrang slaapstand naaktpak kaasangst faalplank
Naaldhak handstand radslag tandrad hartslag hartslag

slaapzacht [echo] slaapzak
slaagkans [echo] naaktslak
klaagzang [echo] kaasplank
faalangst [echo] faaldrang
afgang   afgang   afgang

aflap carjack matrak papzak mama
aftrak papjack hartlap amai mama

flashback

aflap carjack matrak papzakaftrack papjack hartlap

plaktang glasbak badpak slaapzak hangmat hartslag plaktang
plaktang glasbak badpak slaapzak hangmat hartslag plaktang

[8] The Maskesmachine deals with language in an unusual way. Sound, rhythm, rhyme, alliteration, dialect, neologisms, associations, enumerations, absurdities, etc. are no less – if not more – important than the meaning of the words used. Linguistic theory draws a distinction between the 'signified' (*signifié*) and the 'signifier' (*signifiant*). Especially the linguistic work of the French psychoanalyst Julia Kristeva is relevant here. She draws a distinction between the symbolic and the semiotic. Kristeva associates the symbolic – the order of the meaning (the *signifié*), of the hierarchy, the law – with the father, and the semiotic with the mother. The semiotic has to do with the undifferentiated, with the *signifiant* – the shift in meaning, the way meanings flow over into each other, the absence of a hierarchy. The song '*Baarmoeder*' [Uterus], with its string of words spilling over into one another, illustrates this perfectly semiotically. Applied to the procedure of the Maskesmachine, one could say that they try to reveal the semiotic in the symbolic.

[9] '*Plaktang*'. Enumeration is an important principle of organization for the Maskesmachine. In fact, enumeration undermines the order. Enumeration prevents the creation of a hierarchy between important and unimportant, high and low, central and marginal, usable and unusable, functional and non-functional. It is this hierarchy which the Maskesmachine runs counter to. Enumeration, which is very much in evidence in a song like '*Plaktang*', is juxtaposition: everything has the same value and can therefore be combined. Sheer linguistic anarchy.

[10] Besides music, movement and language, the Maskesmachine also uses other forms of communication. There is a video project as well as the CD. Every field requires study: 'The Maskesmachine is not a disposable piece of apparatus. If it is used, it can still serve a purpose after that; if it doesn't work properly, it is oiled.'

ERWIN JANS

174

ALLES KOMT GOE

Goe goe goe goe
Alles komt goe(^{10}), alles goe, alles komt goe komt goe
Alles komt goe, alles komt goe, alles komt altijd goeoe (2x)

Ook al zedde soms is wa moe, alles komt altijd goe
Ook al weete soms nie goe hoe
Ook al zet uw lief ne supermottige tattoo
Alles komt altijd goe

but never lose heart and strive ever onwards

Het Maskesmachine – literally 'The Girls' machine' – is an Antwerp collective of young women who bring a mishmash musical repertoire in ever-changing formations and alliances, sometimes enriched with acrobatics, dance and video. Het Maskesmachine grew from a series of socio-artistic projects, squatters and marches, punk, politics and social criticism, urbanity and urban interventions. The Maskesmachine productions take place in 'conquered places' in the city of Antwerp [for example, the squat 'Villa Delphia' on the Scheldt quayside or a filling-station], in circus tents [whether or not erected by themselves] and in other public areas. The collective comprises *de zwevas*, Eves who specialize in acrobatics [Dutch *zweven* means 'floating' or 'flying']; *de reefteven* [rave bitches]; *de dansklare maskes* [always ready to dance] and *Belgat*, a designers' collective.

Het Maskesmachine was founded in 1999. Its members rehearse dances and songs in the street, alone, or together with the Antifare (antifascist underground brass band). There they collect extracts from daily life, which provide scores of ideas for them to work with. In the beginning they focused on children and the elderly, but gradually they began to cater for wider target groups.

Their interest in language led the *maskes* to Morse Code, a 'language' apt to become pure rhythm. The poem *Nooit de moed opgeven* [Never lose heart], which went round the world in numerous translations including Morse, is Het Maskesmachine's battle song in terms of subject matter and form.

In 2000 Het Maskesmachine took part in *Goesting* [Appetite], a narrative project in various parts of Antwerp. In the autumn of 2000 the collective staged their first show at a filling-station: *Plaktang*. In 2001 the girls put together *Vaert wel* [Fare thee well], a small festival in four endangered places in Antwerp. They gave a second show, *Vliegwiel* [Flywheel], on a caravan site at 'Petrol Zuid'. On the 'konijnenwei' [rabbits' meadow] kites were launched. Also in 2001 Het Maskesmachine gave a series of performances in the Cinema [alongside the river Scheldt, where the 'Zomer van Antwerpen' screens films in the open air], a show in a launderette as part of 'Hotel Ideal' [a meeting project in vacant shop premises mounted by Laika, Villanella and Cultural Centre Berchem], and street performances in Nantes for Le Lieu Unique arts centre.

In 2003 the collective recorded a CD. A radio programme regularly goes on air, and there are plans for a video and music theatre project. In the meantime the *maskes* have mounted school and community projects, for instance in old people's homes. The members also work together with music theatre collective Walpurgis, Muziekmakerij Think of One, etc.

Het Maskesmachine keeps out of the daily round. It is a chameleon with a thousand versions of the same acts and shows. However irregularly the members swing into action, the collective continues to plan ways of developing its unique style.   CVP

9 X 9

9

CHRISTINE DE SMEDT / 9 X 9

9 x 9 takes the general concept of the 'mass' to question a series of obvious facts regarding the concept of a 'dance performance'. In so doing the project becomes part of the recent tradition of conceptual and self-reflexive research, but then from an unexpected perspective. The first point of departure is 'the body as mass'. Traditionally, the reflection about dance departs from the individual body and its relationship with other individual bodies. Within and between those bodies, the hierarchies – which are based on physiological and social criteria such as gender, age and class – are taken up or explored. Postmodern dance has started to problematize these relationships from the perspective of difference, usually by means of microscopy and reduction. By contrast, *9 x 9* increases the volume, and investigates how relationships develop under the influence of multiplicity. After all, the singular is always embedded in the multiple, and it can never be entirely detached from it. The hierarchies do not dissolve into one unified collective body or a grey pool of anonymity, but start to drift, constantly creating new combinations in the midst of the dynamic diversity. Through the massive number of dancers, all the themes that imply orders of ranking are present concurrently and thus become unstable. The individual body never breaks through the moving mass to become entirely visible, and as a result it also loses its fixed anchorage and organization.

The second obvious fact concerns the choreographic strategies of masses in areas different from dance, such as physics, sports, urbanism, etc., which can throw new light on the choreographic process. Beyond the dominant twin concepts of choreography and improvisation (structure versus freedom and all their possible hybrids), new questions arise: about the sources and propagation of movement, about controllability, about the nature and quantity of information which a crowd and each individual within it need to arrive at a choreographic form. Fairly simple and reduced points of departure and formulae are able to generate complex forms. And these also require different methods for being acquired: a better understanding of the underlying structure, for example, and less imitation.

And finally the confines of the concept of 'choreography' itself come under discussion. A choreography is usually a more or less fixed pattern of movement, which allows more or less variation throughout the performances but always retains a fixed nucleus. *9 x 9* explores choreography as a way of thinking. In the course of the process a library of ideas was created which is permanently fed with new sources, contexts and interactions, always taking into account the specific properties of the location. This library of ideas is exactly the actual choreography. *9 x 9* is choreography as multiplicity: both a never-finished total project and a series of autonomous performances, both abstract and contextual, both theoretical and specific. Ordinary stage performances, festival happenings, living museum installations, lectures and workshops spring from the central idea. It is not so much about the absolute flexibility of a concept that can thrive disinterestedly in any other context, but about its productivity and ability to adapt.

In *9 x 9*, the radical nature of that self-reflexive medium research – not something that is guaranteed to attract a large audience – is complemented with a breadthwise gesture, that of working with groups of non-professional dancers. These performers, however, are not amateurs. That is, after all, a notion that is still suggestive of a lack of skill, which is often compensated by the emphasis on the value of the numerical or social representativeness of the amateur. That is a line of thinking inspired by an erroneous approach in the debate about the democratization of the arts. Rather it has to do with 'laymen' who could not care less about those sort of hierarchies; or dilettantes, who out of curiosity and mettle work on this gay science of the mass in movement. Representativity is at least never univocally articulated. *9 x 9* does not choose between individuality and multiplicity. The participants remain themselves but also fairly anonymous: no personal stories and no virtuoso solos. On the other hand, the differences are apparent in the crowd: no attempt is made at a perfect execution of complicated patterns, which pushes individuality out of the picture, but each individual does carry a responsibility in the whole thing. The difference is emphasized, but not named.

Also the group as a whole is barely identified or identified only indirectly: none of all those specific people represents a larger whole; they are just themselves, direct material in a choreography about, or rather of, their own movement.

There is not only a mass on the stage, a mass sits in front of it as well. The latter can feel more involved in the performance because of the affinity with the participants – fellow citizens and their often recognizable movements. Just as the choreography presupposes the continuity between the movement on and off the stage by taking often ordinary movements as the point of departure, so too can the individuals in the darkened auditorium feel that they are also always part of a mass, here and elsewhere. In addition, the simplicity also passes on the pleasure of moving: dancing is something of all times and for all people, in every possible guise. The individuality-in-multiplicity that the participants demonstrate is inviting and infectious.

9 x 9 does not speculate on the spectacular effect of masses, but tries to examine the working conditions and the construction process of such an effect. The seeming ordinariness of the events on stage serves another purpose as well: it shows the frame of the theatre. It is not the stunts, the light and sound effects or the display of virtuosity that ground the theatre. What is the frame of choreography and theatre? A body that establishes an interval of time. A body that moves. A moving body that defines the space. A curtain or, the reverse, no curtain. Wings or no wings. A lot of light or not much light. In *9 x 9* the experience of the theatre is constructed anew with simple building blocks. This applies not only to the performers, but also to the audience. The performers are close to the audience, share much of their everyday experience and show it as well. The position of the audience is moreover still regularly and explicitly thematized. All this makes the audience aware of its function in the theatre. This again links the experimental and social dimensions of the work.

9 x 9 uses the contrast and the interaction between mass and individuality mainly as a principle of form, and in so doing abstains from social comment or large-scale social ambitions. As a dance production it is inevitably a brief occurrence, as a creation it is a process that alights somewhere for several weeks before setting to work somewhere else. But it does leave its footprint, though without flaunting it, in the form of the experience of diversity, social contacts, groups of go-getters who continue working on their own, artistic pride and the necessary awareness of the diversity that is the heart of every mass. In this sense, too, the choreography multiplies itself: it creates new footprints, new relationships and new choreographies.

STEVEN DE BELDER

The *9 x 9* project is an initiative of choreographer and dancer Christine De Smedt. Her fascination with mass and masses all started during the SKITE project ('laboratoire de nouvelles formes chorégraphiques') in Lisbon in 1994. There, together with five choreographers, she mounted an eight-hour procession through the city. In the following years she went on to observe and record popular processions during a series of visits to Poland, Croatia, Bosnia-Herzegovina and tours of Belgium.

In 1998 she worked on *Escape Velocity*, a travel project and a series of installations in cooperation with Els Opsomer, Germaine Kruip and Vincent Malstaf. In Dubrovnik, Sofia, Budapest and Brussels they created installations and performances that focused on borders, identity and the indiscernible codes surrounding these concepts.

The idea for *9 x 9* came about during this experience, when De Smedt saw herself surrounded by the crowd and wondered how she could put this relationship between individual and mass across to the public. One solution might be by gathering together a group of performers on stage, she came to realize. In April 2000 she began to develop a basic structure in association with nine choreographers and performers. Taking as their starting point the link between choreography, mass and multiplicity, they set out to probe the artistic possibilities of forms of mass choreography that often occur well outside the context of art: from the spontaneous movement of the mass through the city, through such semi-organized forms as demonstrations, to the strict organization of masses in mathematics, popular and mass culture.

Where possible, 72 performers with no specific dance experience are recruited in each location. The description of the desired group varies: the last fourteen performances involved choir singers, arts centre employees, babies with their parents, people aged over fifty, young people, or simply representatives of a neighbourhood or town. Under the direction of the artistic team the show is created from scratch in each location and further developed during a fairly short but intensive rehearsal process.

Since 1990 Christine De Smedt (1963), who studied criminology, has been part of the Ghent choreographers' collective Les Ballets C de la B. She danced in Alain Platel's *Mussen* [Sparrows] and helped create Hans Van den Broeck's *How to Approach a Dog*. In 1993 she put on her first solo production, *La force fait l'union fait la force*. In 1994, when she was artist-in-residence with Klapstuk in Leuven, she also became active internationally. In that same year, for example, she took part in the interdisciplinary SKITE projects in Paris and Lisbon. Between 1995 and 1999 she danced in productions by Meg Stuart, for whom, moreover, she has acted as artistic assistant since 1997.

In 1997 she also launched *Crash Landing* with Meg Stuart and David Hernandez: a multidisciplinary improvisation project in which dancers, visual artists and musicians tried to inject new life into the concept of 'improvisation'. Two years later, in 1999, she worked with visual artist Christelle Fillod on *Project on a Freighter*, a travel project on a cargo ship to Norway. In 2002 she created *Solo with Mathilde Erlbacher* for Milli Bitterli, as part of Tanzquartier Wien's solo project *In Bester Gesellschaft*.

MU

181

The photographs on this page and the following, with the exception of one or two, were taken by 'the public'. They are snapshots taken by the people of the adventurous journey of 'The Giant and the African Caravan' during the 'Zomer van Antwerpen' festival back in August 1998. It is a small selection from a large number and they evidence one of the most extraordinary productions the Royal de Luxe company has shown in Antwerp to date.

The people of Antwerp have a soft spot for giants. According to the Brabo legend, the seaport was subjugated by the giant Druon Antigoon, while at the Steen, Lange Wapper towers above a couple of drunkards. Every year the *reuzekens*, as the giants are called in Antwerp, still dance in the *Ommegang* (historical procession), at civic guards festivities and fairs. And together with large numbers of children in the nursery school, I learnt the song about the giant that could dance well with his thick legs of 'chewed paper' or *geknauwd papier*, which is *Antwerps* for papier mâché. A metropolis such as Antwerp does not concern itself with the small fry of fairytales.

During the four hot days in August 1998 the people embraced the two Royal de Luxe giants. At that time the fourth edition of the 'Zomer van Antwerpen' – which was restricted to the month of August – did not enjoy the fame it does today and the journey of the giants marked the festival's real breakthrough among the public at large.

The small giant appeared out of nowhere to win over the hearts of the people. Indeed, the project had been announced without fanfare, and visual

material for the press had been placed under an embargo. And then in the café in the evening you would suddenly hear: 'Hey, have you seen the giant? Well you should then.' You know that it has to be something magical when people who are not regular consumers of culture can talk of nothing else but a production. That certainly applied to the giants and the rumour spread as quick as lightning through the city. It became a spontaneous hype of the positive sort. Those who had not seen the giants were simply left out of the conversation. I remember a bus ride past a square just when the small black giant was settling into his hammock after his tiring journey among the little white folk. At the first glimpse you heard 'oohs' and 'aahs' and – though there was scarcely any traffic – the bus automatically slowed down as if the spectacle was included in the ticket.

Why it was Royal de Luxe that struck a chord among the general public – also with their other productions – is food for science. Was it the spectacle of the large giant wandering round in a cathedral of rope and seeming to greet every individual personally with his enormous eyes and whose wisp of a smile suggested that he himself was surprised at all the attention? Was it the sheer physical display of the manpower required to make the giants walk? Admiration for the technique? The humanness of a giant that needs a footbath after a walk? The hilarity of the bizarre music installations which followed the giants? Was it something to do with the endearing tale of the father giant that roamed the world in search of his son? The wonderful weather? Perhaps it was, as it often is, a combination of all these things.

Lots of stories are going round about the giants. There is the son who recounts how every day his mother went to look at the giant, 'just as someone with a season ticket for the zoo goes to look at "her" elephant'. There is the anecdote of the woman who took the little giant breakfast every morning. There is the statement of the spectator who claimed that 'there had not been so much atmosphere in the city since the "Rubens Year" [1977]'. And Alderman for Culture Eric Antonis agreed. If it had been election day in Antwerp after the giants' party, then the political cards would certainly have been stacked against discontent and antipolitics.

Antwerp has not yet forgotten the giants. 'Are the giants coming back?' someone asked hopefully when I mentioned this article. It is a question the independent arts organization Antwerpen Open, organizer of the 'Zomer van Antwerpen' festival among other things, is still asked with great regularity. That is not just the appreciation of a grateful public as after an enjoyable evening at the theatre; it is the warm-heartedness the people of Antwerp showed for 'their' giants. It culminated in an exuberant evening party on Grote Markt and a gigantic procession through the city the next day. And eventually in these photographs and children's drawings which were submitted at the request of Antwerpen Open. The photographs were placed in two giant albums and presented to Royal de Luxe. However, they thought that memory should remain in the city itself. And so it should.

WILFRIED EETEZONNE

A sense of dissatisfaction with the existing theatre tradition in France drove Jean-Luc Courcoult together with several friends to found Royal de Luxe in the Aix-en-Provence area in 1979. With this company he puts on shows in places that are freely accessible to everyone, drawing inspiration from medieval pageant-plays, from *commedia dell'arte* and from large-scale Asian processions.

Courcoult wants to move the spectator with stories. So as to address as many people as possible with his performances, he attunes these stories to the imagination of children. By giving his productions several layers of meaning, he avoids too much simplicity, of which people tend to tire very quickly.

Characterized as they are by unexpected and powerful images, Royal de Luxe's shows have a performance-like feel. The company once installed a gigantic metal fork in a car and then proceeded to drive round the city in that impaled vehicle. Then at night they sawed another car in two and welded the two parts together with a tree in the middle. Passers-by wondered the next day if the tree had actually grown through the car. This border area between fantasy and reality is reminiscent of Luis Buñuel. Such productions make people dream. And that is exactly what Courcoult wants, because he is convinced that people who cannot dream, become suspicious and intolerant.

Courcoult is fascinated by machines which he regards as living creatures. Like his actors, they represent viewpoints. As sculptures they represent a different reality, while at the same time providing a humorous touch. But the comical in Royal de Luxe touches on the sorrow and tragedy of life.

In 1984 the company left Aix-en-Provence and headed for Toulouse. Nantes has since become Royal de Luxe's base. The company travels the world and has been to Antwerp on several occasions. The first time was in 1993 when the troupe was invited as part of 'Antwerpen 93'. Subsequently Antwerpen Open/Zomer van Antwerpen acted as Royal de Luxe's coproducer in the port on the Scheldt. In 1999 and 2002 they successively staged *Petits contes nègres* and *Petits contes chinois, revus et corrigés par les nègres*, magnificently acted by people and puppets with the help of stunning technical tours de force. The meadow where the performances take place, is always taken by storm, which is hardly surprising, for when these master magicians of the street theatre allowed their Giant ('De Reus') to roam the streets of Antwerp in 1998, the people of Antwerp fell head over heels in love with Royal de Luxe.   VK

(ENVOI)

FOR THE GENERATION OF THE NINETIES

MICHEL UYTTERHOEVEN

I. Impressionistic historiography

In order to get a better understanding of what this book is about, an outline of the historical context in which the generation of the Nineties operates is apposite, if not necessary. So we will go on an excursion to four cities and four moments in the recent history of the world: Brussels, Expo 1958; Paris, May 1968; Berlin, November 1989; and New York, September 2001. I shall take giant strides and will not worry about getting my feet dirty in the process.

1958. For years Brussels has been an enormous building site to accommodate the millions of visitors to the world exhibition: bridges, tunnels, new stations and hotels, a larger airport. The exhibition grounds are filled with futuristic architecture, crowned by the Atomium, symbol of the belief in the omnipotence of nuclear physics. Expo 58 is the culmination of ten years of reconstruction after the Second World War, the starting point of technological revolutions (the early years of television in Belgium and the first experiments with space travel) and the welfare state, the affluent society, when large sectors of the population buy their first fridge, car, telephone.

Artists pick up the thread of prewar Modernism – the paintings of Picasso and Malevich; the provocations of Duchamp and Dada; the architecture of Le Corbusier; the innovative Bauhaus design; the dance of Martha Graham and Kurt Jooss; the novels of Joyce, Mann, Proust; the music of Berg, Bartók, Stravinsky.

In the literature of the Low Countries, the *Vijftigers* [generation of the 1950s] tries to come to intellectual and artistic terms with the unspeakable excesses of the war, epitomized by those two chilling names: Auschwitz and Hiroshima. In the visual arts the postwar years produce figures such as Sam Francis and Willem de Kooning, Yves Klein and Francis Bacon, the Cobra group; Flemish and Dutch poets like Hugo Claus and Lucebert; architects like Mies van der Rohe, Oscar Niemeyer and nearer to home Renaat Braem; composers such as Messiaen, Xenakis, Shostakovich.

The first avant-garde theatre in Flanders emerged in the chamber theatre movement. Those chamber theatres of the 1950s and 1960s (Nederlands Kamertoneel, Arca, Antigone, De Korre, Brussels Kamertoneel, Mechels Miniatuurtheater, etc.) were an open protest against the insipid conservatism of the big repertory theatres, both in the choice of the works themselves and in the form in which they were presented, as though no Second World War had intervened. The chamber theatres played Beckett, Ionesco, Sartre, Pinter (Theatre of the Absurd), and showed an interest in a new Flemish dramaturgy by programming the first texts for theatre by Hugo Claus, Tone Brulin and Piet Sterckx.

May 1968. Protest is the order of the day, first in Paris and soon afterwards in the rest of the Western world. No to capitalism (from a Marxist or even Maoist critique of society), no to the compulsion of the consumer economy (the hippies), no to the war in Vietnam (the songs of Bob Dylan and Joan Baez), no to discrimination (against women, gays and blacks), no to whatever was felt to be condescending, constricting and oppressive, for the imagination must hold sway again. A counterculture was to unmask the authoritarian bourgeois values as alienating and inhuman, and cause the whole of society to shake on its foundations for a moment.

In the arts painting burst out of its frame and became performance, sculpture got down from its pedestal to become installation or environment, artists from a variety of disciplines worked together in happenings, musicians laid the score aside and played together as equals in jam sessions, improvised music, free jazz. Emblematic names and trends include Fluxus, John Cage and his experiments with sound and randomness, Yoko Ono's actions (sometimes together with John Lennon), the rituals of Hermann Nitsch, the video installations of Nam June Paik, the life and works of Andy Warhol. Or closer to home, the first performances by Panamarenko or the occupation of the Brussels Palais des Beaux-Arts ('a bastion of self-complacent smugness in the service of mainly well-to-do consumers of culture') by Marcel Broodthaers and his companions in 1968. Joseph Beuys' maxim – 'everyone is an artist' – translated the spirit of democratization to the artistic sector.

Of course, the performing arts did not miss out on the wave of protest of May 1968 either: in the US the Bread and Puppet Theater, the Performance Group of Richard Schechner (precursors of the Wooster Group) and Teatro Campesino sprang up; in France there was Ariane Mnouchkine and her Théâtre du Soleil; the UK had its fringe theatre, while in Italy Dario Fo continued in his theatrical work the tradition of the commedia dell'arte; and in Germany there was agitprop theatre in the spirit of Brecht and Piscator. In spite of their very different forms and backgrounds, all these performing artists were dedicated to 'political theatre'.

The Netherlands followed spectacularly with 'Actie Tomaat' [Tomato action], with Flanders hesitatingly following its lead in a more modest way. In September 1968 a few dramatists set up the Werkgemeenschap van de Beursschouwburg, a cooperative followed in the 1970s by such companies as Het Trojaanse Paard, Mannen van den Dam, and Vuile Mong en zijn Vieze Gasten. They wanted to turn their back on the élitist mentality and on stardom, and proposed working collectively as an alternative. They looked for a new, younger audience and presented works that were close to the everyday reality of (working) people. The undisputed climax was the legendary production of *Mistero Buffo* (1972) by Arturo Corso and the Internationale Nieuwe Scène, an adaptation of the Passion by Dario Fo. *Mistero Buffo* toured the country and abroad for years. The eventual impact of the consciousness-raising variety of political theatre in Flanders may be dubious in artistic terms, but it has certainly not run out of steam yet. We shall return to this later.

In 1968 Carlos Tindemans published the manifesto 'T 68 or the future of the theatre in the Southern Netherlands', which he co-authored with Hugo Claus and Alex Van Royen, an impassioned and visionary call for a national theatre in the spirit of the legacy of Herman Teirlinck. One sentence: 'We put an end to the theatre of the good old days, bourgeois gratification, amusement you bolt down, theatre like an easy chair that offers the sublimation of all dreams.' T 68 remained a dead letter.

As a result of the oil crisis and the first encounters with the limits of growth, the 1970s were marked by the ideals that the idealists of May 1968 still aimed for, on the one hand, and by the realists, on the other hand, who drew attention to the stagnating economy and announced a light at the end of the tunnel as long as a policy of austerity was implemented. But the whiff of gunpowder of the revolution was gone for good. 'No Future,' the punks screamed.

And yet, and yet: on 9 November 1989 somebody levered a block of concrete loose which caused a whole geopolitical system to tremble and fall. Through the breaches in the Berlin Wall, the inability of totalitarian Communism to construct a decent standard of living for its population emerged before the cameras of the whole world. East Europeans wanted newspapers, cars, television, telephones and computers like ours, as well as what all this implies in the way of information, mobility, relaxation, communication and comfort. Democracy had made it, the 'free market' was victorious, capitalism triumphed and could continue unhindered its globalizing campaign of conquest. The moloch of the USSR shrank to become Mother Russia, and the former satellite states opted unanimously for a political and economic alliance with the European Union. Flows of migrants from the East entered Europe on top of the migrants from Africa and Turkey. This reinforced the success of the far right and the extreme nationalism of the idea of *Eigen volk eerst* [putting one's own people first].

In the 1980s Postmodernism found its way into several artistic disciplines in Flanders. In other countries it had already seeped into the discourse of art history at an earlier stage, depending on the genre. Postmodern architecture and literature, music and video art, fine art. Besides architecture, it is above all in dance that the rift can be seen, when Merce Cunningham allowed himself to be acclaimed the godfather of postmodern dance by dance critic Sally Banes. His oeuvre and that of later generations of choreographers in New York (Judson Church and Grand Union) certainly is visibly different from the modern dance of Martha Graham or from Maurice Béjart here. In theatre too, the work of, say, Bob Wilson, the Wooster Group, Jan Fabre and Jan Decorte marked a sharp break with the theatre that preceded it.

Postmodernism is precisely what many (older) audiences have difficulty in accepting. It shows the relativity of images and words, gives short shrift to the grand narratives of the Enlightenment and Progress, cites shamelessly from the whole of art history, drops the distinction between high and low culture, distances itself even more radically from the (Expressionist) idea that the work of art 'must express something' (for example, emotions), adopts an ironical stance and sets out to alienate, and definitively abandons the social aspirations of Modernism. In short, while Modernism still propagated a programme that strongly believed that society can be moulded, Postmodernism is more excited by fashionable effects and with an ironic gesture dismisses giving meaning to people and society. Although Postmodernism sets out to radicalize Modernism, the confusion of ideas is considerable and the discourses of the different artistic disciplines move in so many directions that the term has become a catch-all phrase that promises to be able to open too many locks.

The performing arts of the 1980s were dominated by the 'Flemish wave'. Elsewhere in this volume Rudi Laermans presents an accurate picture of that mythical generation of the Eighties: Radeis and its offshoots, Rosas, Needcompany, Ivo Van Hove, Guy Cassiers, Luk Perceval, Wim Vandekeybus, Lucas Vandervost, Jan Fabre, Guy Joosten, Alain Platel. In a Flanders that was demanding increased cultural autonomy, their work moved within a period of twenty years from the margin to occupy the centre in the institutional landscape of the performing arts and their creativity became canonical, even for artists far outside the region. We briefly recall the emergence of contemporary dance, the arts centres, festivals, the revolt in the National Opera under Gerard Mortier.

That cluster of artistic energies has led to a more businesslike approach, internationalization, mediatization; to new, striking buildings; and in the end, though much slower, to recognition and decent funding by the Flemish Community and other government bodies.

A few clicks on my laptop mouse bring me entire encyclopaedias, historical libraries, newspapers and magazines from all over the world, databases and image banks (thanks to www), but I still hesitate to put the world of the Nineties down in a few lines on paper. Would it be reticence with regard to the paradox of the dehumanizing information overkill concerning the human condition?

The wars in the Balkans alarmed Europe (logo: Sarajevo), the United Nations looked on helplessly (logo: Srebrenica), the US military stepped in to sort it out. Large parts of the world lived in a state of permanent warfare: the Near East, Africa, the former Soviet Union republics in Central Asia. Shortage, overpopulation and epidemics (AIDS, Ebola) set even more streams of refugees on the march, often in inhuman conditions. While capitalism continued to globalize and moved to where labour was cheapest, the power and authority of the traditional nation state were eroded. Europe tried to build a multicultural society by trial and error, but could find no answer to the growing sense of insecurity on the part of its ageing native population.

The year 2001 – the first of the third millennium – will go down in history for the events of 11 September in New York. The images of the Twin Towers collapsing were efficiently branded on to the collective world memory by the media like a tattoo. President Bush declared war on terrorism and, without a UN mandate but with Blair as his ally, went on the warpath against Iraq for the second time. While I am writing these words, Osama Bin Laden and Saddam Hussein have still not been found, let alone the weapons of mass destruction.

The question was briefly raised of whether art was still possible after the Twin Towers disaster and the sublime images of the extremely theatrical terrorist attack, but only a few days later the architectural design with the 'towers with holes' appeared on the internet and the circus went on as before. For by now art has become big business, high tech and industry: every town or village today has its arts centre, its summer festival or exhibition and everything that entails in terms of organization (management), communication (hype) and logistics (technology). The commercial theatre sector concentrates on musicals, cabaret and comedies; the music sector is engaged in a movement of concentration on a global scale and with the same interests (Belgian concert and festival organizers sold their businesses to a US mega-concern). The media hang on every word of the art pundits and viewer rating fetishists. Everything has to be fun, not too difficult, entertaining, cheerful, optimistic.

Kees Vuyk: 'For a long time the leading circles in society – politicians, managers, artists and intellectuals – shared a vision of the place of art in society. Art was regarded as avant-garde, a laboratory, a place for research and experiment. That is why they accepted that art was élitist, not comprehensible and accessible for everyone. At the same time, there was a widely shared conviction that these élitist airs and graces of art were appreciated by everyone. After all, it was supposed that one day this avant-garde – at least, elements of it – would become mainstream and would then automatically penetrate to the experience of the masses. The image of art as avant-garde went hand in hand with a vision of society as a system in progress, on its way towards a better future for all. Art is in the forefront, according to this view, but it is not out of line. It points the way to the future. This view of the relation of art and society has been shattered during the last few decades on the basis of actual events and on the basis of new – postmodern – theories. The breakdown of our cultural traditions, the growth of information about what is going on in other parts of the world, linked to large-scale migration flows partly stimulated by that increase of information, make it no longer possible to think about society as a monoculture. Today's post-modern network society is a whirling system in which there is no longer any clear distinction between progressive and conservative, ideal and tradition, élite and mass, or – and this is important for art – between high and low culture. This changed vision has far-reaching consequences for the position not only of politics and policy but also of art in society. They have both been cast adrift and find it difficult to set a course. Where is it heading? Is it heading anywhere at all?'

That is the climate in which artists graduated from academies and conservatories in the 1990s.

II. In defence of the generation of the Nineties: a critique of Laermans

The following is a critical commentary on the essay by Rudi Laermans elsewhere in this book on the differences between the generations of the Eighties and the Nineties in the performing arts. It cannot but sharpen the discussion and invite the reader to advance new considerations and refinements.

Let me immediately make it clear that I am in thorough agreement with large portions of Laermans' 'miniature cultural sociology': his pastoral evocation of the Flemish performing arts landscape with little friction between those on the throne and the pretenders to that throne, the organizational institutionalization versus the artistic 'anti-institutionalism', the overpampering of young talent, his account of how the generation of the Eighties has come to form the canonical centre of performing arts in Flanders.

But I tend to disagree when he deliberately limits his focus: in the case of the generation of the Eighties, because some of the names I listed above do not fit in with his argument; and in the case of the Nineties, because he admits that he includes in his survey only those artists whom he has seen at work on stage.

Our focus is thus considerably wider for both generations. Admittedly, there are transitional figures in PIG-MENT too: the Beursschouwburg is mutton dressed as lamb, Eric De Volder is a late-blooming Radeis, Royal de Luxe and Enrique Vargas have roots in the 1980s and earlier, but only become relevant to us after their much talked about first performances in Antwerp 93 (Royal de Luxe) and Klapstuk 99 (Vargas).

Perhaps Laermans' limited panorama also obstructs a more accurate historical appraisal: he could not have written so intricately about the generation of the Eighties in 1993, and he will think differently about the generation of the Nineties in 2013. Perhaps the length of the period under review determines the appreciation in terms of artistic 'oeuvre'. The artists and companies that we have grouped under the category of 'Nom donné par l'auteur' can be seen to be building up a highly personal and consistent oeuvre. But even figures like Meg Stuart, Circus Ronaldo, Benjamin Verdonck, Waas Gramser and Kris van Trier can be regarded without difficulty as authors of robust and deliberate production lines that 'thematically and stylistically bear the hallmark of the maker'. But, once again: perhaps we should take more time and distance to evaluate and to decide to whom we should confer the 'oeuvre' label.

Laermans: 'For the preceding generation there is still a canon, both a historical one and a professional one; the generation of the Nineties, on the other hand, set themselves against it in the first place with their momentaneous "self".' He takes this to mean that for the generation of the Eighties, 'practically every one of their performances shows a strong awareness of theatre or dance, opera or "the performing arts in general" as specific media', while the generation of the Nineties lacks 'the strong awareness of tradition' and fails to recognize 'the medium-specific identity of theatre or dance'.

Again I disagree. Without a doubt the art-historical context is more present than ever in the curricula of our academies (as Laermans is aware as a teacher at PARTS), and while there is room for improvement in some aspects of artistry, I would be surprised if the generation of the Eighties was so much better in that respect. But to dismiss the generation of the Nineties as a bunch of other-worldly ignoramuses is going too far. To take a few examples: Art Basics for Children (in its configuration at HETPALEIS, Antwerp) is actually an unusually ingenious course in art history, minus the deadly dull academic connotations, but experience orientated and holistic, almost anthroposophical in design. Ben Benaouisse enters into dialogues in his work with Ilya Kabakov, Marcel Broodthaers, Jan van Eyck's *Ghent Altarpiece*, Georges Perec and George Steiner. Benjamin Verdonck does the same with Joseph Beuys and Gordon Matta-Clark. Inne Goris cites Marlene Dumas, Louise Bourgeois and Cindy Sherman as sources of inspiration. Christine De Smedt's *9 x 9* goes further on the basis of an in-depth understanding of the video installations of (and her collaboration with) Gary Hill. Eric De Volder does the same with Tadeusz Kantor and Jerzy Grotowski. Circus Ronaldo alludes to decades of (family) history and the tradition of the circus and juggling.

I do agree with Laermans that the generation of the Nineties does not pay much attention to the definition of how all that archaeological digging is eventually expressed in a public performance, but to derive from that a 'manifest indifference' or a 'remarkable lack of concern for the history of art' is simply incorrect. I think that they could not care less about the discussions and terminological confusion connected with terms and definitions (see above, for example Modernism versus Postmodernism, the visual arts entering the field of the performing arts without being asked). Laermans has two sentences to say about that, with which I am heartily and sincerely in agreement: 'The generation of the Nineties is a generation of makers and doers', and above all: the performing artists of the Nineties 'do not argue, they infiltrate the body'. That is a very accurate definition of the 'hybrids' to whom we devote a separate chapter in PIGMENT.

III. Political theatre revisited

There is no revolution in the air. There are no dominant ideologies that divide the world, states or cities (everyone crowds into the centre). We consume till we burst and impetuously drain the natural resources of our planet dry. Only a power cut, an earthquake, a terrorist attack, a mass murderer, a crash on the stock exchange, a church full of Afghan refugees, a stranded oil tanker or a heat wave disturb our daily routine for a moment. All is quiet and even Brussels has its beach (albeit *sur les pavés*).

Still, almost every page of PIGMENT is alive with concern, disquiet, commitment. About incest (*Achter 't eten*), about the background and future of migrants in this white country (*Invasif II*), about the atrophy of our senses (*Sprookjesbordeel*), about survival strategies in the metropolis (Maskesmachine), about what is dubious (De Zweep), about our highly personal odyssey (Vargas), about the impact of images (Filmfabriek), about people and theatre and amusement (Circus Ronaldo), about the responsibility of wanting to be an artist in this madly rushing day and age (PARTS). Sometimes it lies in small words or letters: Lampe (Kant's servant), Damaged Goods (Meg Stuart's dancers in the age of AIDS), *Vrouwenvouwen* or Les Bains::Connective.

No big words, no little red books, let alone analyses of society or carefully thought out alternatives or *contre-*

projets. When Benjamin Verdonck goes into retreat and spends three days in a cage with a pig, it is 'because of confusion' about an imminent US attack on Iraq. A few photocopies on the wall of a side room refer to *Coyote* by Joseph Beuys. (But the attention of the all-American CNN guarantees worldwide coverage of his hyperindividual action.) That is already a significant difference from Flemish political theatre of the 1970s: the Big Truth and the unshakeable certainty with which it was announced have gradually gone the same way as the Big Story of the Communist utopia and lost all credibility. Wim Van Gansbeke: 'The medium is the message. After *Mistero Buffo* the politico-social consciousness-raising theatre made the mistake of reversing that slogan: the message is the medium. Priority was given to the message, but it hardly ever managed to become embedded in an *artistic* project with significant new dramaturgy, design, expression, or style of narrating and acting.' The generation of the Nineties leave the messages up to the politicians, the media and the publicity machine. At most they raise questions, pinpoint trouble spots, note the paradoxes of our by no means easy living together. And fortunately they can draw as they wish for their artistic projects from the arsenal of new possibilities that was established by their prececessors/mentors, the generation of the Eighties, and tested in terms of dramaturgy (Jan Decorte among others), design (Jan Versweyfeld), expression (the new dance), narrative style (Lucas Vandervost) and style of acting (Discordia and followers).

The generation of the Nineties seems closer to the slogan of the militant women's movement: 'The personal is political.' That also explains the concern of its members to engage with one another democratically in their working relations, to take their relation with the neighbourhood where they work seriously, and to go out to the public space instead of hiding away in the gloom of the theatre.

That exploration of the public domain, away from the codes that lie like a dead weight on the conventional stage, even if it is a black box with a flat floor, creates a horizon of new opportunities for experiment. No invited and paying viewers, subscribers and connoisseurs, but an unprepared, disorderly 'found' audience, including 'the man in the street'. Isn't it better, then, to have a lot of flexibility, talent for improvization and technique (in short: artistry) at your fingertips to turn in a split second what is at first recognized as a strange event in the everyday life of the street or square into a situation which the passer-by is prepared to pay attention to for a longer time and to experience as theatre?

The fact that the work of the generation of the Nineties is orientated towards the public should be regarded – for the time being – as a blessing, especially now that the commercial sector is also starting to produce comedies as well as cabaret and musicals and has announced that it will presently be tackling the main repertoire. It is likely that the free market forces will win a resounding victory over the repertory theatres and that large sectors of the public will turn their backs on the municipal theatres – in spite of the exorbitant price of tickets, a new stardom of soap actors and a highly questionable quality.

The circle is complete: from the chamber theatres' critique of the insipid conservatism of the repertory theatres and the dissatisfaction with the bourgeois values of political theatre, back to daddy's theatre. Someone is complaining that 'We've allowed recuperation to happen again!', but her voice is too feeble and no one hears it. The big theatres in Flanders are faced with the challenge of a thorough self-critique. I wish you luck, Jan Goossens, Guy Cassiers and Johan Simons.

That is why today we should welcome the concern of the present generation of the Nineties to make theatre open and get-at-able, affordable, recognizable and easily accessible. It is a strong statement in the discussion of the social relevance of the performing arts, not because a minister asks for it in an exceptionally provocative speech (Anciaux at Vooruit, Ghent, September 2000), but because, on the basis of the dynamism in their work and reflection on it, so many of our best artists had already put this burning, complex and long-term question on the agenda before that speech was made.

The pendulum will swing the other way in time, but for the time being it is the start of a line of defence against the powerful promotion machines that the free market sector, flanked by the populist discourse of intellectuals like Walter Van den Broeck and Gust De Meyer, cultural managers, media magnates and politicians will deploy against the arts. We had better be ready for them.

LITERATURE
• E. De Kuyper, *Grand Hotel Solitude*, Nijmegen: Sun, 1991.
• M. van Kerkhoven, *Van het kijken en van het schrijven: teksten over theater*, Leuven: Van Halewyck, 2002.
• W. van Gansbeke, 'Herinneringen van een oude krokodil', in Van Kerkhoven, *op. cit.*
• R. Erenstein, *Een theatergeschiedenis der Nederlanden: tien eeuwen drama en theater in Nederland en Vlaanderen*, Amsterdam: Amsterdam University Press, 1996.
• R. Goldberg, *Performance. Live art since the 60s*, London: Thames and Hudson, 1998.
• L. Van den Dries (ed.), *Bij open doek. Liber Amicorum Carlos Tindemans*, Kapellen: Pelckmans, 1995.
• S. Banes, *Terpsichore in sneakers*, Middletown, CT: Weslexan University Press, 1987.
• D. Van Bedaer-Hellemans, L. Van den Dries and M. Van Kerkhoven (eds), *Het politieke theater heeft je hart nodig. Het theater tussen emotionele werking en politieke werkelijkheid*, Antwerp, 1982.
• W. Van den Broeck, *Op gelijke voet: brief aan cultureel Vlaanderen*, Leuven: Van Halewyck, 2003.
• G. De Meyer, *Manifest van een cultuurpopulist*, Leuven: Acco, 2003.
• M. Uytterhoeven, 'Een archipel van gedeelde cultuur. Kunst op zoek naar gemeenschap, mensen op zoek naar de vormgeving van hun versplinterde identiteit', in *Alledaags is niet gewoon. Reflecties over volkscultuur en samenleven*, Brussels: Koning Boudewijnstichting, 2002, pp. 233–244.
• K. Vuyk, 'Na de omkering', *TM* 7 no. 5 (June 2003), pp. 38–40.

BIBLIOGRAPHY

Jean-Marc Adolphe, 'Cosmopolitisme et hybridation: le succès du théâtre flamand en France', *Septentrion, Revue de culture néerlandaise* no. 1 (2003), pp. 22–29.

Alledaags is niet gewoon: Reflecties over volkscultuur en samenleven, Brussels: Koning Boudewijnstichting / Fondation Roi Baudouin, 2002.

F. R. Ankersmit, *De macht van representatie*, Kampen: Kok Agora; Kapellen: Pelckmans, 1996.

Peter Anthonissen, 'Anvers sur scène: théâtre sous pression = Antwerp on Stage: Theatre under Pressure', *Ubu-Scènes d'Europe* no. 20/21 (2001), pp. 3–7.

Philip Auslander, *Liveness: performance in a mediatized culture*, London & New York: Routledge, 1999.

—— *Performance: critical concepts in literary and cultural studies*, London & New York: Routledge, 2003.

Robert Ayers, 'Meg Stuart: Not Really Dance at All', *Dance Theatre Journal* 15, no. 1 (1999), pp. 8–11.

Barbara Baert, 'Woord, huid, sluier', *Etcetera* 20, no. 81 (2002), pp. 1–12.

Els Baeten, *Theater buitengaats: Buitenlands beleid, cultuurbeleid en de internationale praktijk van de podiumkunsten in Vlaanderen*, Brussels: Vlaams Theater Instituut, 1999.

Els Baeten, Geert Opsomer & Ann Olaerts, *Naar een ontwikkelingsbeleid voor de podiumkunsten: De noden van de niet structureel gesubsidieerde initiatieven*, Brussels: Vlaams Theater Instituut, 1996.

Marleen Baeten, 'De bezem van de tovenaar', *Etcetera* 15, no. 59 (1997), pp. 43–47.

—— 'De spannende concentratie van meerstemmigheid', *Etcetera* 18, no. 72 (2000), pp. 88–89.

—— 'Meisjes in de hoofdrol', *Etcetera* 20, no. 80 (2002), pp. 31–33.

—— 'You're innocent when you dream (Tom Waits): Assepoester en Blauwbaard', *Etcetera* 21, no. 85 (2003), pp. 65–66.

Sally Banes, *Writing dancing in the age of postmodernism*, Hanover (NH): Wesleyan University Press, 1994.

Mohamed 'Ben' Benaouisse, 'Alimentation générale', *Etcetera* 20, no. 81 (2002), pp. 29–31.

—— *Invasif*, Amsterdam: De Brakke Grond, 2002.

—— *Invasif II*, Ghent: Victoria, 2002.

Susan Bennett, *Theatre audiences: a theory of production and reception*, 2nd edn. London & New York: Routledge, 1997.

Herbert Blau, *The dubious spectacle: extremities of theater, 1976–2000*, Minneapolis: University of Minnesota Press, 2002.

Edith Boxberger, 'World in Pieces. "Video Art": Meg Stuart and Gary Hill Explore the One-dimensionality of a Relationship', *Ballet International – Tanz Aktuell* no. 7/8 (1997), pp. 26–27.

Michael Bridger, *Hybridity, Performing arts international; v. 1, pt. 1*, Amsterdam: Harwood Academic, 1996.

Sue Ellen Case & Janelle Reinelt, *The performance of power: theatrical discourse and politics*, Iowa City (IO): University of Iowa Press, 1991.

Guy Cassiers, Kris Defoort & Roddy Doyle, *The woman who walked into doors*, 2001.

Selma Jeanne Cohen, George Dorris, Thomas F. Kelly & Dance perspectives foundation, *International encyclopedia of dance*, Oxford: Oxford University Press, 1998.

Eric Corijn, Walter De Lannoy & Wim De Pauw, *Crossing Brussels: De kwaliteit van het verschil = Crossing Brussels: La qualité de la différence*, Brussels: VUB Press, 2000.

Katrien Darras & Dries Moreels, *Etcetera 84: twintig jaar berichten over theater, dans et cetera*, Leuven: Van Halewyck, 2002.

Steven De Belder, 'Het laboratorium nodigt ten dans. Wetenschap als metafoor voor de danspraktijk', *Etcetera* 19, no. 79 (2001), pp. 38–42.

—— 'Verloren gelopen in een tunnel', *Etcetera* 18, no. 74 (2000), pp. 81–82.

Peter De Bie. 'Peep & Eat', *Performance Research* 4, no. 1 (1999), pp. 42–43.

Peter De Bie & Kristel Marcoen, *Laika tafelt*, Antwerp: Laika; Amsterdam: De Brakke Grond, 2002.

Pieter De Buysser, *De maten van het mogelijke. Werkbank voor een anti-tragedie*, s.l., s.a.

—— 'Een kleine doortocht buiten verdenking', *Etcetera* 19, no. 75 (2001), pp. 32–38.

—— 'Het theater van de ongrond', *Dietsche Warande & Belfort* no. 5 (2001), pp. 599–609.

Peter De Jonge, Rudi Laermans & Myriam Van Imschoot, *Tunnel Paris September 2000, Highway 101 / The Journal #2*, Damaged Goods, 2000.

Marc De Kesel, Bart Meuleman & Bart Verschaffel, 'Professional / Dilettant', *De Witte Raaf* 5, no. 90 (2001).

Jef De Roeck, 'Denkende dansers in werkhuizen P.A.R.T.S.: A. T. de Keersmaeker opent school in Brussel', *Ons Erfdeel* 39, no. 2 (1996), pp. 288–290.

Eric De Volder & Dick van der Harst, *Diep in het bos = Au fond du bois*, Ghent, 2003.

—— *Vadria*, 2000.

Hildegard De Vuyst, 'Wat vroeger was is nu voorbij', *Etcetera* 12, no. 46 (1994), pp. 58–60.

Hildegard De Vuyst, Johan Wambacq & Kristel Marcoen, *Alles is rustig: het verhaal van de kunstencentra*, Brussels: Vlaams Theater Instituut, 1999.

Tuur Devens, 'Van Volkstheater Vandenberghe tot Circus Ronaldo', *Etcetera* 17, no. 67 (1999), pp. 51–54.

Luc Dhooghe, 'De verbouwing van de Beursschouwburg te Brussel. Verbouwing op het ritme van de stad', *Proscenium* 2, no. 9 (1998), pp. 14–18.

Thomas Dreher, *Performance Art nach 1945: Aktionstheater und Intermedia, Das Problempotential der Nachkriegsavantgarden; Bd. 3*, Munich: Wilhelm Fink Verlag, 2001.

R. L. Erenstein, *Een theatergeschiedenis der Nederlanden: tien eeuwen drama en theater in Nederland en Vlaanderen*, Amsterdam: Amsterdam University Press, 1996.

Mark Franko, *Dance as text: ideologies of the baroque body*, Cambridge: Cambridge University Press, 1993.

Coco Fusco, *Corpus delecti: performance art of the Americas*, London & New York: Routledge, 2000.

Pascal Gielen, 'Bruxelles, Brussels, Brussel', *Ballet International – Tanz Aktuell* no. 1 (2000), pp. 30–31.

—— 'Dans om de macht. Positionering van de hedendaagse dans in Vlaanderen', *Boekmancahier* 10, no. 36 (1998), pp. 126–141.

Jean Giono, Waas Gramser & Kris van Trier, *Nagras*, Antwerp: De Onderneming, 2000.

RoseLee Goldberg, *Performance: Live art since the 60s*, London: Thames and Hudson, 1998.

Waas Gramser & Kris van Trier, *Marius / Fanny / César*, 2002.

—— *Marius / Fanny / César*. Translated by Monique Nagielkopf, 2002.

Marc Hooghe, 'Waarover we het hebben als we over tolerantie praten', *Etcetera* 20, no. 81 (2002), pp. 5–9.

Joost Houtman & Luk Perceval, *Wie slaapt vangt geen vis: Luk Perceval over theater en leven*, Leuven: Van Halewyck, 2001.

Herwig Ilegems, Bart Meuleman & Mark Verstraete, *Er hangt zwart in de lucht*, 1999.

Thomas Irmer, 'Schwarze Wasser. "Aars" von Peter Verhelst und Luk Perceval', *Theater der Zeit* 55, no. 9 (2000), p. 55.

Erwin Jans, 'Geven is een mooi, kwetsbaar en subversief gebaar: de acties van Benjamin Verdonck', *Etcetera* 21, no. 87 (2003), pp. 32–33.

Irmela Kästner, 'Meg Stuart. Is dat nog dans?', *Notes* 10, no. 9 (1995), pp. 18–19.

Susan Kattwinkel, *Audience participation: essays on inclusion in performance*, Westport (CT): Praeger, 2003.

Nick Kaye, *Art into theatre: performance interviews and documents*, Amsterdam: Harwood Academic, 1996.

Dennis Kennedy, *The Oxford encyclopedia of theatre and performance*, Oxford: Oxford University Press, 2003.

Baz Kershaw, *The politics of performance: radical theatre as cultural intervention*, London: Routledge, 1992.

Yves Knockaert, 'Kameropera en muziektheater in Vlaanderen', *Ons Erfdeel* 43, no. 1 (2000), pp. 131–133.

Rudi Laermans, 'De denkbeeldige lichamen van Meg Stuart', *Etcetera* 15, no. 60 (1997), pp. 29–33.

—— 'Het lichaam als medium. Notities rond de Weense stop van Highway 101 van Meg Stuart / Damaged Goods', *Etcetera* 18, no. 73 (2000), pp. 66–72.

—— 'Het onzichtbare podiumlichaam', *Etcetera* 19, no. 77 (2001), pp. 56–58.

—— *Schimmenspel. Essays over de hedendaagse onwerkelijkheid*, Leuven: Van Halewyck, 1997.

Rudi Laermans, Hans-Ulrich Obrist & Myriam Van Imschoot, *Dynamic memory Zürich February 2001*, *Highway 101 / The Journal #5*, Damaged Goods, 2001.

Rudi Laermans, Jeroen Peeters, Jan Ritsema & Tine Van Aerschot, *A-Prior: Meg Stuart*, Brussels, 2001.

Rudi Laermans & Myriam Van Imschoot, *Ghost Brussels December 2000*, *Highway 101 / The Journal #3*, Damaged Goods, 2000.

Rudi Laermans, Myriam Van Imschoot & Peter Westenberg, *Stedelijke onregelmatigheden / Urban Anomalies Rotterdam January 2001*, *Highway 101 / The Journal #4*, Damaged Goods, 2001.

An-Marie Lambrechts, Marianne van Kerkhoven, Katie Verstockt & Herman Asselberghs, *Dans in Vlaanderen*, Bruges: Stichting Kunstboek, 1996.

An-Marie Lambrechts, Peter Missotten & Anne Quirynen, *The Mind Machine of Dr. Forsythe*. Antwerp, 1993.

André Lepecki, 'Dans les replis de l'air', *Mouvement* no. 3 (1998), pp. 54–56.

Miche Loulergue & Odile Quirot, *Royal de Luxe 1993–2001*, Arles & Paris: Actes sud, 2001.

Bonnie Marranca & Gautam Dasgupta, *Conversations on art and performance*, Baltimore: Johns Hopkins University Press, 1999.

John Martin, *Intercultural performance handbook*, London: Routledge, 2003.

Simone Meier, 'Schwere Alibi-erpressung und andere emotionale Straftaten. Meg Stuart und Damaged Goods verüben "Alibi" und ein Attentat auf Frank Sinatra in Zürich', *Theater Heute* no. 1 (2002), pp. 32–33.

Kurt Melens, 'Bericht aan Bart Meuleman: "Cut the crap, act now!"', *Vlaamse Gids* 82, no. 4 (1998), pp. 48–50.

Bart Meuleman, 'Bericht aan de dramaturg: opkrassen!', *De Witte Raaf* 12, no. 75 (1998), p. 15.

—— 'H. Claus – groothandel sinds 1952. Wat blijft er overeind?', *Etcetera* 13, no. 50 (1995), pp. 55–58.

—— *Hyperventilatie*, Leuven: Stuc, 1994.

—— 'Mind your own business', *De Witte Raaf* 8, no. 47 (1994), pp. 6–7.

—— 'Over de bittere noodzaak om voor lege zalen te spelen', *Etcetera* 15, no. 60 (1997), pp. 57–58.

—— *Voetstuk / Piédestal*, Brussels: Dito'Dito, 1998.

Dirk Meyhöfer, *Mobile Bühnen = Mobile stages*, Stuttgart: Avedition, 1999.

Jane Milling & Graham Ley, *Modern theories of performance: from Stanislavski to Boal*, Hampshire & New York: Palgrave, 2001.

Roberta Mock, *Performing processes*, Bristol & Portland (OR): Intellect, 2000.

Ivan Nagel, *Streitschriften: Politik, Kulturpolitik, Theaterpolitik 1957–2001*, Berlin: Siedler, 2001.

Hans-Ulrich Obrist, 'Highway 101 Revisited: an Interview with Meg Stuart, Stefan Pucher and Jorge Leon', *Janus* 3, no. 8 (2001), pp. 32–38.

Beth Osnes & Sam Gill, *Acting: an International encyclopedia*, Santa Barbara (CA) & Denver (CO): Abc-Clio, 2001.

Patrice Pavis, *Analyzing performance: theater, dance, and film*, Ann Arbor: University of Michigan Press, 2003.

Luk Perceval & Peter Verhelst, *Aars! (An anatomical study of the Oresteia)*. Translated by Barbara Fasting, 2000.

—— *Aars! (Anatomische studie der Orestie)*. Translated by Rainer Kersten, 2000.

—— *Aars! (Anatomische studie van de Oresteia)*, 2000.

—— *Aars! (étude anatomique de l'Orestie)*. Translated by Monique Nagielkopf, 2000.

Peggy Phelan, *Unmarked: the politics of performance*, London & New York: Routledge, 1993.

Pascale Platel, *Connaissez-vous votre géographie?*, 2000.

—— *De koning van de paprikachips*, 1998.

—— *Ola Pola Potloodgat*, Brussels, 2001.

Helmut Ploebst, 'Beweging in een spookhuis', *Etcetera* 18, no. 72 (2000), pp. 86–88.

Helmut Ploebst, 'Confetti in the Sound Desert', *Ballet International – Tanz Aktuell* no. 11 (1998), pp. 49–50.

—— 'Damaged Goods on Highway 101. The new Meg Stuart Project premieres in Brussels and will be continued in Vienna', *Ballet International – Tanz Aktuell* no. 5 (2000), pp. 44–45.

—— 'De kleren van de keizer', *Etcetera* 21, no. 85 (2003), pp. 37–39.

—— 'The Flesh is Stronger than the Word: Meg Stuart', *Ballet International – Tanz Aktuell* no. 2 (1999), pp. 20–23.

—— *No wind no word. Neue Choreographie in der Gesellschaft des Spektakels. = New Choreography in the society of the spectacle*, Munich: K. Kieser, 2001.

—— *Swamp Vienna July 2000, Highway 101 / The Journal #1*, Damaged Goods, 2000.

—— 'Work on the Future of Dance. "Crash Landing" – Meg Stuart's Perilous Improvisation Project in Leuven', *Ballet International – Tanz Aktuell* no. 12 (1996), pp. 38–39.

Ana Márcia Prati Goulart, *Meg Stuart. Untersuchungen zur Dramaturgie des zeitgenössisches Tanztheaters*, Munich, 1997.

Freddie Rokem, *Performing history: theatrical representations of the past in contemporary theatre*, Iowa City (IO): University of Iowa Press, 2000.

Mariellen R. Sandford, *Happenings and other acts, Worlds of performance*, London & New York: Routledge, 1995.

Richard Schechner, *Performance studies: an introduction*, London & New York: Routledge, 2002.

Richard Schechner, Willa Appel & Victor Witter Turner, *By means of performance: intercultural studies of theatre and ritual*, Cambridge & New York: Cambridge University Press, 1990.

Richard Shusterman, *Performing live: aesthetic alternatives for the ends of art*, Ithaca (NY) & London: Cornell University Press, 2000.

Gerald Siegmund, 'Das Gespenst Wirklichkeit', *Theater Heute* no. 6 (2003), pp. 8–9.

—— 'From America to Europe: Meg Stuart', *Ballet International – Tanz Aktuell* no. 4 (1999), pp. 38–39.

—— 'Het geheugen van ballet. De verdwijntrucs van William Forsythe', *Etcetera* 18, no. 73 (2000), pp. 60–65.

Jan Stofferis, 'De ontbrekende schakel: Circus Ronaldo tussen traditioneel circus en theatercircus', *Mores* 2, no. 2 (2001), pp. 18–24.

Meg Stuart, 'Ich bin aus ganz klarem, leerem Glas', *Ballet Tanz* no. 1 (2002), p. 44.

—— 'Paroles d'artistes: Meg Stuart', *Mouvement* no. 10 (2000), p. 18.

Christine Tinlot, 'P.A.R.T.S., trois ans déjà', *Scènes* 1, no. 1 (1998), pp. 126–129.

Pieter T'Jonck, 'Een onbeschrijflijke toestand', *Etcetera* 20, no. 80 (2002), pp. 59–61.

—— 'An Experiment with Large Numbers. Mass Choreography by Christine De Smedt in Ghent', *Ballet International – Tanz Aktuell* no. 1 (2001), p. 49.

—— 'Hoe vertaal je ALIBI?', *Etcetera* 21, no. 86 (2003), pp. 28–30.

John Tulloch, *Performing culture: stories of expertise and the everyday*, London & Thousand Oaks (CA): Sage Publications, 1999.

Wim Vandekeybus & Peter Verhelst, *Scratching the Inner Fields*, Brussels: Ultima Vez, 2001.

Clara van den Broek, 'Een Waaslandwolf in Toneelland', *Etcetera* 19, no. 75 (2001), pp. 24–31.

Luk Van den Dries, *Omtrent de opvoering: Heiner Müller en drie decennia theater in Vlaanderen*, Ghent: Koninklijke Academie voor Nederlandse Taal- en Letterkunde, 2001.

Rud Vanden Nest, 'Gouden plak', *Etcetera* 20, no. 82 (2002), pp. 68–69.

Frank Vande Veire, 'Tegen de nieuwe heidenen', *Etcetera* 20, no. 81 (2002), pp. 9–11.

Marianne van Kerkhoven, *Van het kijken en van het schrijven: teksten over theater*, Leuven: Van Halewyck, 2002.

—— 'Wat denkt een vrouw die beneveld voor zich uit zit te staren?' *Etcetera* 20, no. 80 (2002), pp. 50–54.

Marianne van Kerkhoven, Patrice Pavis, Hans Thies Lehmann & Geert Opsomer, *Van Brecht tot Bernadetje: wat maakt theater en dramaturgie politiek in onze tijd?*, Brussels: Vlaams Theater Instituut, 1998.

Katleen Van Langendonck, 'De extase van de toeschouwer', *Etcetera* 20, no. 83 (2002), pp. 27–31.

Peter Verhelst, *Maria Salomé*, Borgerhout: Bebuquin, 1997.

—— *Maria Salomé*. Translated by Monique Nagielkopf, 2001.

—— 'A Minuscule Tongue-shaped Dream about Divine Theatre = Minuscule tongvormige droom over goddelijk theater = Winziger zungenförmiger Traum vom göttlichen Theater', *Theaterschrift* no. 13 (1998), pp. 162–169.

—— *Mondschilderingen*, Amsterdam, 2002.

—— *Red Rubber Balls*. Translated by Hans Theys. Amsterdam: International Theatre & Film Books, 1999.

—— *Red Rubber Balls (studie van een hangend lichaam)*, Borgerhout: Bebuquin, 1999.

——, *Romeo en Julia*, Amsterdam: International Theatre & Film Books, 1998.

Joke Verlinden, *Meg Stuart in dialoog met Hedendaags Danstheater*, 2001.

Geert Verschraegen, 'De wereldmedia en de grenzen van het lichaam', *Etcetera* 20, no. 82 (2002), pp. 13–15.

Bart Vervaeck, 'Belachelijk, niet te snappen, en toch ernstig', *Ons Erfdeel* 40, no. 5 (1997), pp. 735–743.

—— 'Dans le ventre du boa: l'œuvre de Peter Verhelst', *Septentrion, Revue de culture néerlandaise* no. 3 (2001), pp. 13–17.

Ian Watson, *Negotiating cultures: Eugenio Barba and the intercultural debate. Theatre: theory, practice, performance*, Manchester: Manchester University Press, 2002.

Christophe Wavelet, 'Chorégraphier le public', *Mouvement* no. 10 (2000), pp. 48–49.

—— 'Un parcours cathartique', *Mouvement* no. 10 (2000), pp. 42–47.

Lilo Weber, 'Visitors Only', *Ballet Tanz* no. 6 (2003), pp. 8–11.

Arnd Wesemann, 'Always Come Back', *Ballet International – Tanz Aktuell* no. 4 (1999), p. 59.

ART BASICS FOR CHILDREN
A. Dansaertstraat 98
B 1000 Brussels Belgium
T+32 2 5020027 F+32 2 5020027
mail@abc-web.be www.abc-web.be

BART MEULEMAN
c/o De Zweep
Lammekensstraat 76
B 2140 Antwerp Belgium
T+32 3 2720005 F+32 3 2720005

MOHAMED 'BEN' BENAOUISSE
c/o Invasif vzw
Peperstraat 15
B 9000 Ghent Belgium
invasifben@yahoo.fr marika.ingels@pandora.be

BENJAMIN VERDONCK
c/o the pop singers' breasts were not real
Leopoldlei 24
B 2660 Antwerp Belgium
benjaminverdonck@pandora.be

BEURSSCHOUWBURG
A. Ortsstraat 20
B 1000 Brussels Belgium
T+32 2 5500350 F+32 2 5500340
info@beursschouwburg.be www.beursschouwburg.be

CHARLOTTE VANDEN EYNDE
c/o dixit vzw/Ilse Vandesande
Gasstraat 90
B 2060 Antwerp Belgium
T+32 3 2251066 F+ 32 3 2252135
ilse.dixit@wpzimmer.be

CHRISTINE DE SMEDT / 9 X 9
c/o Les Ballets C de la B
Citadellaan 40
B 9000 Ghent Belgium
T+32 9 2217501 F+ 32 9 2218172
info@lesballetscdela.be www.lesballetscdela.be

CIRCUS RONALDO
c/o Frans Brood Productions
Land Van Waaslaan 84
B 9040 Ghent Belgium
T+32 9 2341212 F+32 9 2659650
info@fransbrood.com www.circusronaldo.be

CONCERTGEBOUW BRUGES
't Zand 34
B 8000 Bruges Belgium
T+32 50 476999 F+32 50 476979
info@concertgebouw.be www.concertgebouw.be

DE FILMFABRIEK
Hoogstraat 33
B 3360 Bierbeek Belgium
T+32 16 460100 F+32 16 461276
areyouvital@filmfabriek.com www.filmfabriek.com

DE ONDERNEMING
Maria Henriëttalei 65
B 2660 Hoboken Belgium
T+32 3 8279181 F+32 3 8278245
info@deonderneming.be www.deonderneming.be

ENRIQUE VARGAS
c/o Teatro de los Sentidos
C/ La Perla 29, Bajos
ES 08012 Barcelona Spain
T+34 93 2171770 F+34 93 4151794
etvargas@telcom.es www.teatrodelossentidos.com

HET MASKESMACHINE
Tavernierkaai 9
B 2000 Antwerp Belgium

HET MUZIEK LOD
Pelikaanstraat 25
B 9000 Ghent Belgium
T+32 9 2661133 F+32 9 2661130
info@hetmuzieklod.be www.hetmuzieklod.be

INNE GORIS
c/o vzw Zeven/Inne Goris
Steensstraat 44
B 1060 Brussels Belgium
T+32 2 5394288
innegoris@pi.be

LES BAINS::CONNECTIVE
Berthelotstraat 34
B 1190 Brussels Belgium
T+32 2 5344855 F+32 2 5344855
info@bains.be www.bains.be

MEG STUART / DAMAGED GOODS
Onze-Lieve-Vrouw van Vaakstraat 83
B 1000 Brussels Belgium
T+32 2 5132540 F+32 2 5132248
info@damagedgoods.be www.damagedgoods.be

MUZIEKFORUM GENT
Onderstraat 22
B 9000 Ghent Belgium
T+32 9 2665790 F+32 9 2665795
info@dekrook.be www.gent.be/forum

OLYMPIQUE DRAMATIQUE
c/o Thassos vzw
A. Rodenbachstraat 19b
B 2140 Borgerhout Belgium
T+32 3 2350490 F+32 3 2351105
thassos@pi.be

P.A.R.T.S.
Van Volxemlaan 164
B 1190 Brussels Belgium
T+32 2 3445598 F+32 2 3435352
mail@parts.be www.parts.be

PASCALE PLATEL
F. Lousbergkaai 104/2
B 9000 Ghent Belgium
T+32 9 2220191 F+32 9 2220191

PETER VERHELST
c/o Het Toneelhuis
Jodenstraat 3
B 2000 Antwerp Belgium
T+32 3 2248800 F+32 3 2248801
info@toneelhuis.be www.toneelhuis.be

PETER DE BIE
c/o Laika
Boomgaardstraat 215
B 2018 Antwerp Belgium
T+32 3 2308191 F+ 32 3 2309570
info@laika.be www.laika.be

PIETER DE BUYSSER
c/o Lampe vzw
Ieperlaan 62
B 1000 Brussels Belgium
T+32 2 2176606 F+32 2 2176606
pieter@lampesite.be www.lampesite.be

ROYAL DE LUXE
c/o Antwerpen Open
Wapper 2
B 2000 Antwerp Belgium
T+32 3 2248500 F+32 3 2248501
info@antwerpenopen.be
www.multimania.com/royaldeluxe/

T H E   A U T H O R S

Lydia Asbestaris was a secondary school teacher and worked in the Nieuwpoorttheater, was coordinator of Canon, assisted with the 'Klimaat' projects of HETPALEIS, and worked with Anno 02. She is coordinator of communication, education and public relations for the Flemish Theatre Institute.

Els Baeten studied sociology at the University of Leuven. She was attached as a research assistant to Leuven University's department of sociology and has been working with the Flemish Theatre Institute since 1987. She researches and publishes regularly on art, culture and policy.

Steven De Belder studied philosophy, history and dramaturgy. He was connected with the dramaturgy department of Antwerp University from 1999 to 2003. He publishes on theatre and dance and has co-edited several collections. As from November 2003 he is interim training coordinator at P.A.R.T.S.

Paul Boudens is a graphic designer. He works for various fashion designers (including Walter Van Beirendonck, Olivier Theyskens, Dries Van Noten, Wim Neels, Yohji Yamamoto) and for MoMu (ModeMuseum Antwerp) and Rosas. In 2001 he was art director of the fashion project 'MODE2001 LANDED-GELAND' in Antwerp. Ludion published his first retrospective, *Paul Boudens Works Volume 1*, in 2003.

Yasmina Boudia studied history at Ghent University, followed by a postgraduate course in archival studies and contemporary documentation at Brussels University (VUB). She is an archivist for the Flemish Theatre Institute.

Clara van den Broek studied Romance languages and dramaturgy. She is currently a freelance actress and a member of the SkaGeN collective. She also works for *Etcetera* and was dance critic for the newspaper *De Morgen*.

Marianne Buyck is an intercultural manager. She is associated with Steunpunt Mensen zonder Papieren and works for refugee and immigrant organizations. She is a freelance writer on dance and theatre for *Etcetera* and other magazines.

Edwin Carels is permanent programmer of the Rotterdam Film Festival and curator of various other film festivals, in which he focuses on the relation between visual art, film, video and photography. He is a writer and also teaches film history and theory at the Sint-Lukas Hogeschool in Brussels.

Manu Claeys studied Germanic philology, anthropology and English studies (Universities of Leuven and Minnesota). He was an editor for the publishing houses Kritak and Van Halewyck from 1989 to 1996. He has published in various papers and periodicals on cultural policy, populism and political ecologism. He is the author of *Het Vlaams Blok in elk van ons*, on the extreme right in Flanders.

Stany Crets is an actor, director and dramatist. He began his career with the Blauwe Maandag Compagnie, and subsequently worked with the theatre companies Koninklijke Vlaamse Schouwburg, Mechels Miniatuur Theater (later 't Arsenaal), Publiekstheater and the commercial television channel VTM. He appears regularly in films and television series.

Bernard Van Eeghem studied architecture in Ghent and art history in Brussels, but has sold his soul to theatre. He is currently working on a production with DAStheater and on *Nil Nisi Bene*, with Catherine Graindorge (Théâtre de la Balsamine, May 2004).

Wilfried Eetezonne is a journalist for *De Morgen*.

Myriam Van Imschoot was dance critic for *De Morgen*. She is currently attached to the Institute of Cultural Studies of Leuven University, where she is writing a dissertation. She founded Sarma, a platform for dance criticism.

Erwin Jans was dramaturgist for the Koninklijke Vlaamse Schouwburg (Brussels) from 1993 to 1999. He is currently dramaturgist with the Rotterdam ro theater. He teaches theatre and drama in the department of cultural studies at the University of Leuven and dramaturgy in the theatre department of Hogeschool Antwerpen and Antwerp University. He regularly publishes essays in *De Tijd* and *Etcetera*.

Joris Janssens has worked as a literary historian in Dutch Studies at Leuven University and the University of Vienna. He has been a dramaturgist with the Flemish Theatre Institute since November 2001.

Patrick Jordens worked for some time as a theatre teacher and dramaturgist for BRONKS young people's theatre. He is currently coordinator and communications officer for Art Basics for Children (ABC). He has done freelance reviews for Radio 3 and *De Morgen*.

Marianne Van Kerkhoven is a dramaturgist with the Kaaitheater in Brussels, and since 2001 with Het Net in Bruges as well. She was editor-in-chief of the four-language theatre periodical *Theaterschrift*. She regularly publishes on theatre and dance in *Etcetera* and elsewhere. Her essays on theatre have been collected under the title *Van het kijken en van het schrijven* (2002).

Veerle Keuppens worked between 1987 and 1999 for the public broadcasting companies, including TV1, Studio Brussel and Radio 3 ('De Kunstberg'), where she was theatre critic. She went on to work as main dramaturgist for HETPALEIS in Antwerp. Since April 2003 she has been coordinator of research and development at the Flemish Theatre Institute.

Rudi Laermans is a full professor in the department of sociology at the University of Leuven, where he is also director of the Centre for the Sociology of Culture. His teaching and research activities are concentrated in the fields of theoretical sociology, contemporary cultural theory and the sociology of art. He is also a guest lecturer at P.A.R.T.S. and is an active essayist and critic.

Anna Luyten studied philosophy, applied literary theory and dramaturgy at the University of Ghent. She works as a journalist for *De Standaard* and teaches philosophy in the department of dramatic art of Hogeschool Antwerpen.

An Mertens studied Romance languages, specializing in Spanish language and culture. She has been following the performing arts for years. She recently spent six months travelling through Central and South America and held talks with theatre directors, choreographers, critics and programmers for IETM (Informal European Theatre Meetings).

Dries Moreels is coordinator of collections for the Flemish Theatre Institute and active on the editorial board of *Etcetera*. After studying Germanic languages, he has concentrated more and more on theatre. He was also associated with RITS in Brussels for three years.

Kris Motmans studied modern history at Ghent University. He published *Dam – Den Oude Dijck Daer Men Comt Van Dambrugge* (City of Antwerpen and Koning Boudewijnstichting, 2002), an inquiry in book form into the 'memory' of the Dam district in Antwerp. He is coordinator of VOBK (Vereenigde Organisatievormen Beeldende Kunst).

Josse De Pauw was one of the founders of Radeis (1976–84) and Kaaitheater. He is a dramatist, and as actor and director he is active with, among others, Kaaitheater, Victoria, and Het Net. He has featured in some thirty films. From 2000 to 2004 he is artistic director of Het Net in Bruges. In 2000 he published *Werk*, a collection of notes, plays and stories from the period 1990–2000.

Dirk Pauwels was a mime artist with Radeis between 1976 and 1984. Afterwards he was associated, among others, with Theater van de Niets Parisiana/KIM. He was co-founder and artistic director of the Ghent arts centre Nieuwpoorttheater. At the moment he is artistic director of Victoria in Ghent.

Jeroen Peeters is a freelance dramaturgist, critic and curator. In 2001 he was dramaturgist with Tanzquartier Wien. He writes on contemporary dance in various journals and is a dance critic for *De Morgen*. He is one of the founding members and editor of Sarma, a platform for dance criticism.

Koen Peeters is author and editor of *Dietsche Warande en Belfort*. He has written six novels: *Conversaties met K.* (1988), *Bezoek onze kelders* (1991), *De postbode* (1993), *Het is niet ernstig, mon amour* (1996), *Bellevue/Schoonzicht* (1997, with Kamiel Vanhole) and *Acacialaan* (2001).

Caroline Van Peteghem studied Germanic philology at the University of Ghent and took an additional course in cultural management. In this connection she carried out research on the position of dramatists in Flanders. She is communications officer at the Flemish Theatre Institute.

Maarten De Pourcq studied classical languages and literary theory at Leuven University. Since 2002 he has been a research assistant in the department of Greek philology. He is writing a dissertation on Greek tragedy in the intellectual climate after Heidegger. He contributes to various journals, including *Janus*.

David Van Reybrouck studied archaeology and philosophy at the universities of Leuven, Cambridge and Leiden. He is currently working at Leuven University, where he is carrying out research on the history and architecture of the zoos of Western Europe. His *De Plaag. Het stille knagen van schrijvers, termieten en Zuid-Afrika* was published in October 2001. He also writes poetry and is a freelance contributor to *De Morgen*.

Ilse Thienpont studied cultural management (Antwerp, 2001) and history of art (Ghent, 2002). She took part in a research project on the socio-economic impact of the European and international institutions in Brussels before she became assistant to the business director of the Flemish Theatre Institute in February 2002.

Pieter T'Jonck is a building engineer and architect. He has his own architectural practice, worked at the University of Ghent as a research assistant, and teaches scenography at Antwerp Academy. He publishes on dance, theatre, architecture and urban design in several newspapers, magazines and books (including *De Standaard, De Tijd* and *Etcetera*).

Hendrik Tratsaert trained as a translator at the Provinciaal Instituut voor Hoger Onderwijs in Ghent and studied dramaturgy at Leuven University. He has been editor-in-chief of the interdisciplinary arts magazine *Janus* since 1999.

Michel Uytterhoeven studied social pedagogy, theatre studies and architectural science. He was the first artistic director of Klapstuk, the Leuven dance festival. He subsequently worked for the Flemish Opera, Antwerp 93, Meg Stuart / Damaged Goods, and the City of Antwerp. He is currently director of the Flemish Theatre Institute.

Paul Vermeulen is a building engineer and architect. He shares a practice with Henk De Smet. He is a writer, was editor of the architectural periodical *Archis* from 1994 to 2000, and teaches architectural criticism at Leuven University.

Roel Verniers studied theatre production, dramaturgy and international politics. He was theatre critic for the newspaper *De Standaard* and for three years coordinated the Flemish edition of the Theatre Festival. Since 2003 he has been working for Tweetakt, an arts festival for children and young people, and for the Antwerp arts centre Villanella.

Ellen Walraven studied theatre, film and television studies at the University of Utrecht. She was dramaturgist for theatre company De Tijd. Since 1990 she has been a member of 't Barre Land (Utrecht), a collective of artists and dramaturgists.

Nikol Wellers studied musicology at Leuven University before becoming business manager of Stuc, Antwerp 93, Walpurgis, Theater Stap successively and head of project management for Brussels 2000. She is now business director of the Flemish Theatre Institute.

PHOTOGRAPHIC CREDITS

The publishers owe a great debt of gratitude to the photographers who kindly made available their images.

CHARLOTTE VANDEN EYNDE
page 8, top row – photo a: © Raphael Zubler – *Vrouwenvouwen* (Sharon Zuckerman and Charlotte Vanden Eynde); b: © Herman Sorgeloos – *Vrouwenvouwen* (Charlotte Vanden Eynde); c: © Herman Sorgeloos – *Vrouwenvouwen* (Ewelina Guzik).
p. 8, middle row – a–e: © Guillaume Bennaval – *Ligging* (a–c, e: Charlotte Vanden Eynde; d: Constance Neuenschwander); f: © Anne Marie Rijsman – *Stand*.
p. 8, bottom row – a–b and d–f: © Johan Dehaes – *Lijfstof*; c: © Kurt Vandendriessche – *Lijfstof*.
p. 9, top and 2nd rows: © Herman Sorgeloos – *Zij Ogen* (Sharon Zuckerman and Charlotte Vanden Eynde).
p. 9, 3rd and bottom rows: © Herman Sorgeloos – *Benenbreken* (Charlotte Vanden Eynde).
p. 10, top and middle rows: © Herman Sorgeloos – *Vrouwenvouwen* (Ewelina Guzik, Constance Neuenschwander, Sharon Zuckerman and Charlotte Vanden Eynde).
p. 10, bottom row: © Raymond Mallentjer – *Stand* (Constance Neuenschwander, Ewelina Guzik, Varinia Canto Vila and Charlotte Vanden Eynde).
p. 11: © Johan Dehaes – *Lijfstof* (Ugo Dehaes and Charlotte Vanden Eynde).
p. 12, top row: video stills – Jan Decorte / Het Toneelhuis, *Amlett* (Charlotte Vanden Eynde).
p. 12, bottom row: video stills – Jan Decorte / Het Toneelhuis, *Amlett* (Jan Decorte and Charlotte Vanden Eynde).
p. 13, top row: video stills – Jan Decorte / Het Toneelhuis, *Cirque Danton* (Lisa Man, Kurt Vandendriessche, Pieter Ampe, Yves De Pauw, Johan De Smet, Houwari Moumen, Stefaan Van Brabandt, Iris Van Cauwenberghe, Isabelle Van Waes and Maya Wilssens).
p. 13, bottom row: video stills – Jan Decorte / Het Toneelhuis, *Cannibali!* (a: Lisa Man; b: Inge Paulussen and Lisa Man; c–d: Sigrid Vinks and Charlotte Vanden Eynde).

PASCALE PLATEL
p. 14: © Phile Deprez – BRONKS, *Connaissez-vous votre géographie?*
pp. 17–18: © Katleen Exelmans – BRONKS, *Ola Pola Potloodgat*.
p. 19: © Vincent Tillieux – BRONKS, *De koning van de paprikachips*.

PIETER DE BUYSSER
p. 20: Gautier d'Agoty, *Anatomy* (from G. Bataille, *Les larmes d'Éros*).
p. 22: video still – Lise Solar and Alice Chauchat (in *Solar,* film by Pieter De Buysser).
p. 23: video still – 'Oh the sun, the sun, there she is again and again!' (from *Solar*).
p. 25: Lepri, *La bouche de la vérité* (from G. Bataille, *Les larmes d'Éros*).

HET MUZIEK LOD
pp. 26–27: © Peter Dewindt – Het muziek Lod and Toneelgroep Ceremonia, *Zwarte vogels in de bomen*.
pp. 28, 31: © Peter Dewindt – Het muziek Lod, *Diep in het bos*.

BART MEULEMAN
pp. 38, 41–42: © Koen Broos – De Zweep and Het Gevolg, *Show*.

OLYMPIQUE DRAMATIQUE
pp. 32, 34, 36–37: © Patrick De Spiegelaere – Olympique Dramatique, *De krippel*.

MOHAMED 'BEN' BENAOUISSE
pp. 44–49: From Ben Benaouisse, *Invasif III* (De Brakke Grond, Amsterdam, 8 November– 8 December 2002).

HET SPROOKJESBORDEEL
pp. 56, 60–61: © Phile Deprez – Het Toneelhuis, *Het Sprookjesbordeel*.

PETER DE BIE / LAIKA
p. 62 – a: © Phile Deprez – Laika, *Undeuxdouce*.
p. 62 – b: © Phile Deprez – Laika, *COUPe ROYALe*.
pp. 63, 65: © Phile Deprez – Laika, *Undeuxdouce*.
pp. 66–67: © Phile Deprez – Laika, *Patatboem*.

MEG STUART / DAMAGED GOODS
pp. 68–69, 72–73: © Armin Linke – Meg Stuart / Damaged Goods, *Visitors Only*.

DE FILMFABRIEK
p. 74: © Kurt d'Haeseleer, De Filmfabriek – Material from *S*CKMYP* (a lounge video installation), 2003.
p. 75 – top: © Kurt d'Haeseleer, De Filmfabriek.
p. 75 – bottom: © Wies Hermans, De Filmfabriek – Demo CD-ROM *S*CKMYP*, 2003.
p. 76: © Kurt d'Haeseleer, De Filmfabriek – material from *S*CKMYP*, 2003.
p. 77 – top: Video scenery: © Kurt d'Haeseleer and Peter Missotten, De Filmfabriek – stage view from *Paysage Sous Surveillance* (by George Asperghis – Ictus Ensemble), 2002.
p. 77 – bottom: © Kurt d'Haeseleer, De Filmfabriek – Material from *S*CKMYP*, 2003.
p. 78 – a: © Kurt d'Haeseleer, De Filmfabriek.
p. 78 – b: © Peter Missotten, De Filmfabriek – from *Tintagiles – De dood van een prinsje* (by Peter Missotten), 2003.
p. 78 – c: © Kurt d'Haeseleer, De Filmfabriek.
p. 78 – d: Video scenery: © Kurt d'Haeseleer and Peter Missotten, De Filmfabriek – Stage view from *Paysage Sous Surveillance*, 2002.
p. 79: © Kurt d'Haeseleer, De Filmfabriek.

INNE GORIS
pp. 80–81: © Koen Broos – BRONKS, *Zeven*.
pp. 83, 85: © Koen Broos – Het Toneelhuis and Tweetakt, *Pride and Prejudice* (youth workshop).

ART BASICS FOR CHILDREN
p. 86, top and 2nd rows – a: © ABC archive – Mobile studio at HETPALEIS, Antwerp.
p. 86, 2nd row – b and c: © ABC archive – Kamishibai in Antwerp.
p. 86, 3rd row: © ABC archive – Kamishibai at 'Klein Kasteeltje', Brussels.
p. 86, 4th and 5th rows: © ABC archive – Mobile studio in Antwerp, Tielt, Bruges and St Petersburg.
p. 87, top: © Olivier Rouxhet – *ABC of Dance* ('Rosas XX', Paleis voor Schone Kunsten, Brussels).
p. 87, 2nd row: © Thierry Lewyllie – *ABC of Dance*.
p. 87, 3rd row: © ABC archive – Mobile studio in Bruges.
p. 90, top row: © ABC archive – Mobile studio in Bruges.
p. 90, 2nd row: © ABC archive – Garden at 'Klein Kasteeltje', Brussels.
p. 90, 3rd row – a–b and 4th row – a–b: © Thierry Lewyllie – Exhibition 'Wie zoet is krijgt lekkers', Stadsbibliotheek, Antwerp.
p. 90, 3rd row – c and 4th row – c: © Thierry Lewyllie – *Droomparcours* at De Munt / La Monnaie, Brussels.
p. 91: © ABC archive – Kamishibai tent.

LES BAINS::CONNECTIVE

pp. 114–115: © Les Bains::Connective –
The building's condition in 1997.
p. 115: Ceiling slab from the 'Tomb of the Diver'
(Paestum, 475 BC).
p. 116: © Marie-Hélène Elleboudt – Les
Bains::Connective and Brussels 2000 [C²].
p. 117: © Marie-Hélène Elleboudt – Musiclab:
Bl!ndman Quartet.
p. 118: © Lawrence Malstaf – Les
Bains::Connective and Brussels 2000 [C²].
p. 119: © Kassim Ahmed – Connective Dinner.

BSB(BIS)

pp. 120–122: © Hans Roels – BSBbis.
p. 124: © Jan Kempenaers – Entrance hall
of the renovated Beursschouwburg.

P.A.R.T.S.

pp. 126–127: © Pascal Lemaître – P.A.R.T.S.
p. 128, top: © Nathalie Willems – Claire Croizé
and Igor Chichko, Donne-Moi (final project,
June 2000).
p. 128, centre: © Herman Sorgeloos – Fernand
Schirren.
p. 128, bottom: © Herman Sorgeloos – Damiaan
De Schrijver and Isabelle De Keyzer (first-year
theatre workshop, 1996–97).
pp. 130–131: © Nathalie Willems – Elizabeth
Farr (Classical Dance class, 2000–01).

CONCERTGEBOUW BRUGES

pp. 132–133: © Jan Termont – View of
Concertgebouw and the city of Bruges.
pp. 136–137: © Paul Robbrecht – Sketch of
the Concertgebouw.
p. 138: © Patrick De Spiegelaere – Opening
night of the Concertgebouw and of Bruges
Cultural Capital 2002.
p. 139 – a: © Kristien Daem – Exterior.
p. 139 – b: © Kristien Daem – Chamber
Music Hall.

MUZIEKFORUM GENT

p. 140: Land registry map of the Krook (source:
Forum voor Muziek, Dans en Beeldcultuur).
p. 141 – a: rear side Brabantdam;
b–d: Waterhoek – Grote Huidevettershoek;
e: Woodrow Wilsonplein (source: Ghent, Dienst
Stedenbouw en Ruimtelijke Ordening).
p. 142: Gerard Mortier (source: Forum
voor Muziek, Dans en Beeldcultuur).
p. 145 – a: Cross-section Muziekforum (source:
Forum voor Muziek, Dans en Beeldcultuur);
b: Aerial view of the Krook (source: Forum voor
Muziek, Dans en Beeldcultuur).

CIRCUS RONALDO

pp. 152–157: © David Van Reybrouck –
Circus Ronaldo in Lille, December 2002.

BENJAMIN VERDONCK

p. 158: © Benjamin Verdonck / David Bovée –
From Benjamin Verdonck, 'Janus is ...', Janus 13
(spring 2003) Animal & Man: p. 72.
p. 159: © Nico Ampe – Benjamin Verdonck / City
Min[e]d, Bara\ke 2000.
p. 161: © Ilknur Cengiz – the pop singers'
breasts were not real vzw / Nieuwpoorttheater,
I like America and America likes me.
p. 162, top row: © Guido Jan Bral / Luc Polfliet –
Villanella / Zomer van Antwerpen, hong kong
woman disappeared.
p. 162, 2nd row: © Benjamin Verdonck / Iwan
Van Vlierberghe – the pop singers' breasts were
not real vzw, Shopping is Fun.
p. 162, 3rd and 4th rows: © Benjamin
Verdonck / Mark Rietveld – the pop singers'
breasts were not real vzw, I didn't know Santa
came on Saturday.
p. 163: © Nico Ampe – Het muziek Lod, W/ ik
denk vaak aan de hoeveelheid rundvlees die
nodig zou zijn om bouillon te maken van het
meer van Genève.

PAGNOL TRILOGY

pp. 164–165 and 169: Props used in the Pagnol
trilogy.
p. 167: © Koen Schetske – Drawings and plans
of the stand.
p. 168, top row: © Kris van Trier – The stand
at Martigues, Le Havre, Hasselt and Gap.
p. 168, 2nd row: © Kris van Trier – Oerol Festival
(a, c–d) and Paris (b).
p. 168, 3rd and 4th rows: © Kris van Trier –
Oerol Festival.

CHRISTINE DE SMEDT / 9 X 9

p. 176, top and 2nd rows: video stills – 9 x 9
with choir singers during 'Julidans', Vondelpark,
Amsterdam (7 July 2001).
p. 176, 3rd and 4th rows: video stills – 9 x 9 with
employees of Centre Pompidou, Paris.
p. 177: video stills – 9 x 9 with islanders at
the Oerol Festival, Terschelling.
pp. 178–179, top row: video stills – 9 x 9 with
babies and their parents at the Rotterdamse
Schouwburg.
p. 178, 2nd and 3rd rows: video stills – 9 x 9
with people from Turnhout at CC de Warande
(Turnhout).
p. 178, 4th and 5th rows: video stills – 9 x 9
with senior citizens at Teatro do Campo Alegre
(Porto 2001).
pp. 180–181: © Jean-Pierre Stoop – 9 x 9,
first series with people from Ghent at the
Minardschouwburg (Ghent).

ROYAL DE LUXE

p. 182: © Jerry Koninckx – The small giant
in Antwerp, August 1998.
p. 183: © Elly Vanhoomissen – The small giant.
p. 184: © Christine Verdyck – The big giant.
pp. 186–187: © Jerry Koninckx – The big giant.

This publication was made possible by the generous support of
the Ministry of the Flemish Community, Administration of the Arts.

Edited by
Michel Uytterhoeven

Assistant editor and coordination
Joris Janssens

Editorial board Flemish Theatre Institute
Lydia Asbestaris (LA), **Els Baeten** (EB), **Yasmina Boudia** (YB),
Joris Janssens (JJ), **Veerle Keuppens** (VK), **Dries Moreels** (DM),
Ilse Thienpont (IT), **Michel Uytterhoeven** (MU), **Caroline Van
Peteghem** (CVP), **Nikol Wellens** (NW)

Authors of the essays
Manu Claeys, Joris Janssens, Veerle Keuppens, Rudi Laermans,
Michel Uytterhoeven

Authors of the 'stories'
Marianne Buyck, Edwin Carels, Stany Crets, Steven De Belder,
Josse De Pauw, Maarten De Pourcq, Wilfried Eetezonne, Erwin
Jans, Patrick Jordens, Anna Luyten, An Mertens, Kris Motmans,
Dirk Pauwels, Jeroen Peeters, Koen Peeters, Pieter T'Jonck,
Hendrik Tratsaert, Clara van den Broek, Bernard Van Eeghem,
Myriam Van Imschoot, Marianne van Kerkhoven, David Van
Reybrouck, Paul Vermeulen, Roel Verniers, Ellen Walraven

Designed by
Paul Boudens
(pp. 74–79: De Filmfabriek)

Translated by
Peter Mason and **Alison Mouthaan-Gwillim**

Copy-editing by
Anagram, Ghent, with **Patricia De Laet**

Printed by
Die Keure, Bruges

Copyright © 2003 Ludion Ghent–Amsterdam;
Flemish Theatre Institute, Brussels; the authors

www.ludion.be
ISBN 90-5544-498-7
D/2003/6328/42

Printed in Belgium

EDITORIAL NOTE
In most cases, no official English equivalents of titles of pieces,
productions, etc. are available. In order to improve readability,
however, literal translations are provided in brackets in roman
type and lower case throughout.
No attempt has been made to translate the rap lyrics in Erwin
Jans' contribution on Het Maskesmachine (pp. 170–175).
Their juicy Antwerp dialect, laced with puns and other word play,
can safely be regarded as untranslatable.